The Israeli Path to Neoliberalism

In recent years, Israel has deeply and quickly transformed itself from a self-perceived social-democratic regime into a privatized and liberalized "Start-Up Nation" and a highly divided society. This transition to neoliberalism has been coupled with the adoption of a hawkish and isolationist foreign policy. How can such a deep change be explained? How can a state presumably founded on the basis of socialist ideas, turn within a few decades into a country characterized by a level of inequality comparable to that of the United States?

By presenting a comprehensive and detailed analysis of the evolution of the Israeli economy from the 1930s to the 1990s, *The Israeli Path to Neoliberalism* seeks to explain the Israeli path to neoliberalism. It debunks the "from-socialism-to-liberalization" narrative, arguing that the evolution of Israeli capitalism cannot be described or explained as a simple transplantation of imported economic models from advanced liberal democracies. Rather, it asserts that the Israeli variant of capitalism is the product of the encounter between imported Western institutional models and policy ideas, on the one hand, and domestic economic, social and security policy problems on the other. This mechanism of change enables us to understand the factors that gave rise to Israel's unique combination of liberalization and strong national sentiments.

Providing an in-depth analysis of Israel's transformation to neoliberalism, the book is a valuable resource for those studying the economic history of Israel, or the political economy of late-developing countries.

Arie Krampf is a Senior Lecturer in International Relations at the School of Government and Society, at the Academic College of Tel Aviv Yaffo, Israel. His research focuses on the political economy of Israel, International Political Economy, European monetary integration and Economic History.

Routledge Studies in Middle Eastern Economies

This series provides up-to-date overviews and analysis of the region's economies. The approaches taken are not confined to a particular approach and include analysis of growth and future development, individual country studies, oil, multinational enterprises, government policy, financial markets and the region's role in the world economy.

For a full list of titles in the series: www.routledge.com/middleeaststudies/series/SE0852

Economic Co-Operation in the Gulf
Issues in the Economies of the Arab Gulf Co-Operation Council States
Badr El Din A. Ibrahim

Turkish Accession to the EU
Satisfying the Copenhagen Criteria
Eric Faucompret and Joep Konings

Turkey and the Global Economy
Neo-Liberal Restructuring and Integration in the Post-Crisis Era
Edited by Ziya Öniş and Fikret Şenses

Industrialization in the Gulf
A Socioeconomic Revolution
Edited by Jean-François Seznec and Mimi Kirk

The Israeli Central Bank
Political Economy, Global Logistics and Local Actors
Daniel Maman and Zeev Rosenhek

Human Development in Iraq
1950–1990
Bassam Yousif

State Reform and Development in the Middle East
Turkey and Egypt in the Post-Liberalization Era
Amr Adly

Political Economy of the Gulf Sovereign Wealth Funds
A Case Study of Iran, Kuwait, Saudi Arabia and the UAE
Sara Bazoobandi

The Economic Development Process in the Middle East and North Africa
Alessandro Romagnoli and Luisa Mengoni

The Israeli Path to Neoliberalism
The State, Continuity and Change
Arie Krampf

The Israeli Path to Neoliberalism

The State, Continuity and Change

Arie Krampf

LONDON AND NEW YORK

First published 2018 by Routledge

2 Park Square, Milton Park, Abingdon, Oxfordshire OX14 4RN
52 Vanderbilt Avenue, New York, NY 10017

Routledge is an imprint of the Taylor & Francis Group, an informa business

First issued in paperback 2020

British Library Cataloguing in Publication Data
A catalogue record for this book is available from the British Library

Library of Congress Cataloging in Publication Data
Names: Krampf, Arie, author.
Title: The Israeli path to neoliberalism : the state, continuity and change / Arie Krampf.
Description: Milton Park, Abingdon, Oxon ; New York, NY : Routledge, 2018. | Series: Routledge studies in Middle Eastern economies
Identifiers: LCCN 2017046196| ISBN 9781138721869 (hbk) | ISBN 9781315193922 (ebk)
Subjects: LCSH: Neoliberalism–Israel–History–20th century. | Capitalism–Israel–History–20th century. | Israel–Economic policy. | Israel–Economic conditions–20th century.
Classification: LCC HC415.25 .K73 2018 | DDC 330.95694–dc23
LC record available at https://lccn.loc.gov/2017046196

ISBN: 978-1-138-72186-9 (hbk)
ISBN: 978-0-367-59333-9 (pbk)

Typeset in Times New Roman
by Wearset Ltd, Boldon, Tyne and Wear

The book is dedicated to the anonymous technocrat who does her job properly.

Contents

Illustrations

Figures

Tables

Preface

This book is the product of over a decade's worth of intermittent research and writing. During this period I have been affiliated with different institutions, interacted with numerous scholars and shared my thoughts with many colleagues. As a result, this book is comprised of several layers, with each reflecting a somewhat different level of analysis.

The text itself was written in two "spurts." The spark for the first was my PhD dissertation, which provided the basis for period from the 1930s to the 1960s, which was also published in my book in Hebrew by Magnes Press in 2015. The English translation of the dissertation was carried out with the financial assistance of the Skirball Department of Hebrew and Judaic Studies at New York University after I received the Adler Dissertation Award for an outstanding dissertation in Israel Studies. I would like to thank the selection committee and, in particular, Ronald Zweig in this regard.

For the current publication I have adjusted the theoretical chapters, and extended the research period covered by the book, to include the transition to the neoliberal period. The intellectual challenge in extending the text of this book was to present a conceptual framework able to explain both the continuities and the transformations of Israeli capitalism from the 1930s to the 2000s.

Acknowledgments

Numerous sources—colleagues, friends and institutions—have provided me with invaluable insights which have had both a direct and an indirect impact on the final product presented in this publication. I wish to thank Rivka Feldhay and Yuval Yonay, who provided constructive and positive supervision of my PhD, on which the empirical foundation for this book was laid. Jürgen Renn of the Max Planck Institute for the History of Science, where I had the opportunity to work on Globalization of Knowledge as a postdoctoral fellow; Tanja Börzel and Thomas Risse of the KFG: the Transformative Power of Europe, at the Free University of Berlin, for their guidance in honing my methodological and theoretical skills. Special thanks also to the Young Researchers Forum at the Chaim Weizmann Institute for the Study of Israel and Zionism at Tel Aviv University, led by Anita Shapira and Orit Rozin, it proved a unique and lively forum which brings together young and senior scholars in Israel. Furthermore, I would like to thank Dani Gutwein, Avi Bareli, Uri Cohen and Gili Gofer for their insightful comments and intriguing conversation. I would also to like to thank Alex Cukierman, Perry Mehrling, Peter Hall and David Levi-Faur for fruitful discussions on topics and issues discussed in the book. Additionally, I conducted many interviews over the course of writing this book, not all of which are specifically referred to in the text, hence for their time as well as the fruitful and informative discussions, I would like to thank Stanley Fischer, Assaf Razin, Rafi Melnik and Amnon Neubach.

Thanks go also to my colleagues and friends who read the various incarnations of the text and contributed precious insights to its development: Oleg Komlik, Yair Barak, Ricky Shiv, Doris Wydra, Melanie Garson and Anna Padoa.

I would also like to thank my friends and colleagues at the Academic College at Tel Aviv Yafo, my academic home in recent years. Particularly, Naomi Chazan and Assaf Meydani, the past and present deans of the School of Government and Society, have my appreciation for granting me the time and resources to bring this project to completion.

Finally, special thanks to Ian Silver, who edited the manuscript and assisted me in shaping its structure and fluency, as well as Emma Tyce, who made the whole process of going from manuscript to book a smooth and pleasant experience.

Introduction

Market nationalism and Israeli capitalism

In response to the social protest that broke out in the summer of 2011, Yuval Steinitz, then the minister of finance and a member of the right-wing Likud Party, one of the ardent advocates of the liberalization policy in Israel, explained why he opposed the demands of the protestors:

> We are in the midst of an economic world war ... every state is fighting for its own national economy and for employment for its own citizens. It is impossible to manage the state as if we are on an island and without understanding our main mission: a defensive battle over the Israel economy for the benefit of the state of Israel.[1]

In recent decades, the Israeli political economy has gone through two seemingly contradictory processes. On the one hand, Israel went through a rapid and intensive period of liberalization: it embraced the liberal creed and adopted market-oriented policy practices of liberalization, deregulation and globalization. On the other hand, the foreign policy of Israel became much more isolationist and the national identity more nationalistic and anti-liberal.

An observer who is acquainted with the economic history of Western countries would be surprised at the correlation between liberalization and nationalization in the Israeli case. The economic history of Europe in the twentieth century demonstrates that liberalization, economic integration and globalization have been associated with a cosmopolitan identity building, as opposed to a hawkish and isolationist national identity.

The coupling of liberalization and nationalization in the case of Israel is related to a historical puzzle, concerning Israel's economic history: how could a state that was presumably founded on the basis of socialist or social democratic ideas, turn within two or three decades into a country characterized by a level of inequality comparable to that of the United States? Indeed, Israel was not the only country to go through deep structural changes with the advent of globalization, but in the Israeli case the change was more extreme than in others.

The underlying aim of this book is to understand these two puzzles, concerning the evolution of Israel's economic regimes. The book will argue that whereas the Israeli economy—and the Jewish economy during the British

Mandate—went through several deep transformations, the economic strategy throughout this period was shaped primarily by state preferences. The state shaped the economy and changed it, in accordance with changing material conditions, and within epistemic and institutional constraints. But in the last analysis, state preferences were the single most essential element that shaped the economic strategy and structure.

From socialism to capitalism?

The economic history of Israel is often told as a story of transformation from socialism to capitalism: a change from an era in which the state—or the national institutions in the pre-state era—intervened in the economy to achieve socialist goals, to an era in which the economy was managed by market forces and rational economic principles. The narrative of *from-socialism-to-capitalism* is appealing: it is simple, it conforms to well-established ideologies in Western advanced economies, and it fits well with human tendencies to think about the past in nostalgic terms. The narrative of from-socialism-to-capitalism has been embraced by liberal economists as well as by social-democratic activists: the former describe the change as a "maturing" of the Israeli economy (Aharoni, 1991; Ben-Basaṭ, 2002; Ben-Porath, 1986), whereas the latter condemn it as an unfortunate ideological shift.

The narrative of from-socialism-to-capitalism, however, leaves some questions unanswered. First, there is evidence that in fact, during the so-called socialist era policy-makers did use socialist rhetoric but at the same time the policies cannot be portrayed as either socialist or social-democratic. Rather, the interventionist policies during the Mandatory Palestine and early years of statehood consisted of an aggregation of policy instruments used to achieve national objectives associated with statehood and nation-building (Levi-Faur, 1998, 2001; Maman and Rosenhek, 2012; Rosenhek, 2002; Shalev, 1992, 1998; Sternhell, 1998).

Second, the narrative of from-socialism-to-capitalism employs terms too broad to be defining concepts: when viewed globally, it is plain that *capitalism is not one*.[2] The US economy, the Swedish economy and the Chinese economy are all capitalistic economies. However, each of these has different institutional features. In other words, each has its own institutional path. In that sense, the historical narrative of from-socialism-to-capitalism used as a catchphrase misses the point that in fact Israel was transformed from one type of capitalism to another type of capitalism (Ben-Porat, 1993; Gozansky, 1986). The key question is how to describe these types of capitalism and whether there were also continuities.

To understand how the transformations and continuities characterized Israeli capitalism, it is necessary, therefore, to suspend our taken-for-granted perceptions about the economic history of Israel. Moreover, one should not rush to embrace traditional Western-originated concepts such as socialism, social-democracy, capitalism, liberalism or neoliberalism to portray economic regimes on the world periphery. It could well be the case that economies on the periphery have developed their own models of capitalism, which do not fall neatly into the categories defined by the Global North.

This book will argue that the Israeli variant of capitalism cannot be described or explained as an imported economic model from a Western style—be it European or North American—country. Rather, it will be argued here, the Israeli variant of capitalism was the product of an encounter between imported Western institutional models and policy ideas, on the one hand, and domestic political, economic and social policy problems that prevailed in the region on the other hand.

The Israeli variant of capitalism

The question of how Israeli capitalism can best be characterized has haunted historians, political economists, economists and sociologists for years. There were several "waves" or "generations" of writings on this topic. The first wave of political-economic studies about Israel and Zionism was written by authors, who embraced the perceptions and ideologies of the political elite and the founders of the state. They described the socio-economic Jewish regime in Palestine as *constructive socialism*. The term was coined by the Jewish settlers themselves during the pre-state period, and it became a key element in the Zionist national identity through which political leaders justified deviations from the broadly socialist agenda (Gorni, 1996). In later years the term was employed by historians as an analytic term to explain the behavior of the political elite and the Israeli government during the first and second decades following statehood (Gorni and Greenberg, 1997). The historical framework of constructive socialism assumes that, whereas policy-makers adhered to socialist values and ideals of social equality and solidarity, they encountered a harsh geopolitical reality in Mandatory Palestine and Israel that compelled them to be "pragmatic."

The constructive socialism approach was dismissed by the next wave of historians. In his (1998) book, *The Founding Myths of Israel*, Zeev Sternhell rejects the constructive socialism thesis and argues that the Jewish Labor Movement, whose leaders became also the leaders of the Zionist movement, prioritized the national cause over the social cause. The Labor Movement was more interested in building a state than building a just society and it employed socialist discourse only to legitimize its policies and to secure political support. Rather than constructive socialism, Sternhell portrayed the regime as *national socialism*. He explains:

> [The Zionist variant of] socialism always sought to correct social distortions in order to ensure the unity and stability of the nation. It believed that there was an inseparable connection between national problems and social problems, and that the solution to social questions depended on a solution to the national question.

Sternhell adds that "national socialism did not reject market practices and never proposed an alternative to it" (ibid., p. 116).

Sternhell's thesis is supported by the work of Derek Penslar. According to Penslar (2001), the economic strategy of the World Zionist Organization (WZO) during the 1920s is best portrayed as *non-capitalistic constructivism*: the Jewish settlements in Mandatory Palestine were not managed on the basis of economic efficiency and market forces, but this fact does not made them necessarily socialists. The non-capitalistic constructivism regime was based on collaboration between a national organization, the World Zionist Organization, and a civil-political organization, the Labor Movement.

In the 1980s and the 1990s, social scientists entered the fray and used new theories of political economy in order to reframe the economic history of Israel. Scholars debunked the constructive socialism argument by exposing the path followed by Mapai, the dominant Labor Party, which prioritized national causes as well as its own political survival over socialist and social-democratic policy objectives (Grinberg, 1991; Rosenhek, 2002; Shalev, 1992; Shapira, 1975).

Whereas the sociologists attempted to explain why Israel did not evolve toward a European-style social democracy, liberal economists were puzzled by the fact that Israel did not embrace liberal market practices (Aharoni, 1991; Ben-Basaț, 2002; Ben-Porath, 1986; Plessner, 1994). Interestingly enough, economists explained the deviation of Israel from the liberal market economy regime on the basis of its alleged socialist heritage—a heritage, which the sociologists argued did not exist. Yoram Ben-Porath writes:

> The preferences of collective action rested on the Zionist version of socialism that evolved in Palestine from eastern and central European ideologies of the late nineteenth and early twentieth centuries. Throughout the Mandate period and its first twenty-nine years of statehood, Israel was led by the labor movement, which laid down the norms and the organizational modes for running the economy and society.... The socialist ideology included a distrust of the market, a view of profits as mere rewards to parasitism and (paradoxically) a view of services as unproductive.
>
> (1986, p. 14)

Despite their fundamentally different perspectives, sociologists and economists share the assumption that the economic model of Israel does not fall neatly into the conventional European concepts of social-democracy, socialism or liberal-market economy. Moreover, both sociologists and economists share the view that the economic regime in Israel was distorted by the short-term interests of power groups.

Yakov Metzer and Nahum Gross, in their long list of publications about the Israeli economy before and after the establishment of the state, argue that the Israeli economic model deviated from the liberal market model because the state (or the national organizations in the pre-state era) had to intervene in the market in order achieve certain national goals. Nation-building, they argue, is a kind of public good that justified state intervention.[3] Along similar lines, David Levi-Faur employs Nordlinger's state-centric theory in order to analyze the developmental policy of the government during the first decade of statehood (Levi-Faur, 2001). Levi-Faur later expands on this perspective by arguing that the Israeli model can best be captured by the concept of the *developmental state* (Levi-Faur, 1998). The developmental state is a model of economic governance, introduced by scholars of East Asian economies, to explain the divergences of these economies from the liberal market model, on the one hand, and from planned socialism, on the other (Woo-Cumings, 1999). This perspective was further elaborated on by Maman and Rosenhek (2011).

The transition to neoliberalism

The transition experienced by the Israeli economy during the 1980s raises new questions regarding the underlying forces that shape the Israeli political economy. For mainstream market-oriented economists, the transition to neoliberalism poses no puzzle: the transformation of the Israeli economy into a more liberalized economic regime was bound to happen due to market forces. The so-called neoliberal regime is in essence a set of efficient policies which any government would have embraced unless exposed to significant short-term pressure from domestic interest groups. The transition to neoliberalism from a liberal perspective may be viewed as the acceptance of the "reality principle" by Israeli policy-makers.

However, sociologists and political economists show that in fact the Israeli economy did not fully follow the Western liberal model. Michael Shalev argues that "the traditional exceptionalism of the political economy in Israel is disappearing before our eyes," but at the same time Israeli capitalism has retained some of its distinctive features. Primarily in this regard, "despite a dramatic reduction in the role of the state … the legacy of Zionist collectivism persists in many of the practices—and even more, the discourses—that surround the political economy" (Shalev, 1998, p. 143).

Maman and Rosenhek pose a very similar question: how did Israel, as a developmental state, respond to globalization? They argue that the transformation of the state was driven by the state's attempt

> [to] reinstate the pivotal positioning of the Ministry of Finance within the state configuration and to restore its power vis-à-vis other state agencies, mainly by "tying its own hands" through various institutional arrangements that were meant to lock in fiscal restraint and other anti-inflationary policies.
>
> (Maman and Rosenhek, 2012, p. 350)

This book contributes to existing literature by showing how changing economic ideas played a role in shaping the preferences of the state over a period from the 1930s to the 1990s. The book offers an answer to the question "what does the state want?" and show how the answer to the question changes over time in response to changing material and political circumstances, and within domestic political

political constraints. Such an analysis will have to account not only for issues of power relations between the state and societal actors, but also for the epistemic foundations, on the basis of which policy-makers shape their perception of the "public good." Moreover, such an analysis will also have to account for the response of policy-makers to global and geopolitical changes over which they have no control.

This book, therefore, seeks to explain the Israeli path to neoliberalism as a policy response of the policy-makers to new domestic, international and geopolitical conditions within the prevailing institutional, political, economic and epistemic constraints.

Notes

1 "Steinitz against the social protest." Available at: *Ynet*. www.ynet.co.il/articles/0,7340, L-4241310,00.html
2 In reference to Luce Irigaray's famous dictum about the feminine sex, *This Sex Which Is Not One* (1985).
3 Metzer and Gross rely on the work of Harry G. Jonson. See Gross and Metzer, 1999) and Metzer (1979). See also Johnson (1967).

References

Aharoni, Y., 1991. *The Israeli Economy: Dreams and Realities*. Routledge, London.

Ben-Basaț, A. (Ed.), 2002. *The Israeli Economy, 1985–1998: From Government Intervention to Market Economics*. MIT Press, Cambridge, MA:

Ben-Porat, A., 1993. *The State and Capitalism in Israel*. Greenwood Press, Westport, CT.

Ben-Porath, Y. (Ed.), 1986. *The Israeli Economy: Maturing Through Crises*. Harvard University Press, Cambridge, MA.

Gorni, Y., 1996. The Historical Reality of Constructive Socialism. *Israel Studies* 1, 295–305. doi:10.1353/is.2005.0032.

Gorni, Y. and Greenberg, Y., 1997. *The Israeli Labor Movement*. Open University Press, Tel Aviv (in Hebrew).

Gozansky, T., 1986. *Development of Capitalism in Palestine*. Haifa University Publishing Company, Haifa.

Grinberg, L.L., 1991. *Split Corporatism in Israel*. State University of New York Press, Albany, NY.

Gross, N.T. and Metzer, J., 1999. Palestine During the Second World War, In: Gross, N.T. (Ed.), *Not by Spirit Alone: Studies in the Economic History of Modern Palestine and Israel*. The Hebrew University Magnes Press and Yad Izhak Ben-Zvi Press, Jerusalem, pp. 324–300 (in Hebrew).

Irigaray, L., 1985. *This Sex Which Is Not One*. Cornell University Press, Ithaca, NY.

Johnson, H.G., 1967. A Theoretical Model of Economic Nationalism in New and Developing States. In: Johnson, H.G., *Economic Nationalism in Old and New States*. University of Chicago Press, Chicago, pp. 1–16.

Levi-Faur, D., 1998. The Developmental State: Israel, South Korea, and Taiwan compared. *Studies in Comparative International Development (SCID)* 33, 65–93. doi:10.1007/BF02788195.

Levi-Faur, D., 2001. *The Visible Hand: State-Directed Industrialization in Israel.* Yad Ben-Zvi Press, Jerusalem (in Hebrew).

Maman, D. and Rosenhek, Z., 2011. *The Israeli Central Bank: Political Economy, Global Logics and Local Actors.* Taylor & Francis, London.

Maman, D. and Rosenhek, Z., 2012. The Institutional Dynamics of a Developmental State: Change and Continuity in State–Economy Relations in Israel. *Studies in Comparative International Development* 47, 342–363. doi:10.1007/s12116-012-9098-3.

Metzer, J., 1979. *National Capital to National Home, 1919–1921.* Yad Itzhak Ben-Zvi, Jerusalem (in Hebrew).

Parliament. Various years. *Divrei Ha'knesset* [Minutes of Parliamentary Sessions] (in Hebrew).

Plessner, Y., 1994. *The Political Economy of Israel: From Ideology to Stagnation.* State University of New York Press, Albany, NY.

Penslar, D.J., 2001. *Planning the Zionist Utopia.* Yad Ben-Zvi Press, Jerusalem (in Hebrew).

Rosenhek, Z., 2002. Social Policy and Nation-Building: The Dynamics of the Israeli Welfare State. *Journal of Societal & Social Policy* 1, 15–31.

Shalev, M., 1992. *Labour and the Political Economy in Israel.* Oxford University Press, Oxford.

Shalev, M., 1998. Have Globalization and Liberalization "Normalized" Israel's Political Economy? *Israel Affairs* 5, 121–155. doi:10.1080/13537129908719515.

Shapira, J., 1975. *Historical Ahdut ha-Avoda.* Am Oved, Tel Aviv (in Hebrew).

Sternhell, Z., 1998. *The Founding Myths of Israel: Nationalism, Socialism, and the Making of the Jewish State.* Princeton University Press, Princeton, NJ.

Woo-Cumings, M. (Ed.), 1999. *The Developmental State.* Cornell University Press, Ithaca, NY.

1 States and markets in late-developing economies

Liberal values such as individualism, property rights, economic freedom and the rule of law, are part and parcel of the institutional infrastructure that makes market economies what they are. These liberal values are embedded in the institutional structures of liberal market economies: the judicial system, the legislative system based on representation and an autonomous monetary authority. In liberal-democratic societies, so the argument goes, these institutions were established to protect market and societal actors from the capricious actions of the sovereign (North and Weingast, 1989). Therefore, these institutions are considered by liberal thinkers as a precondition for a well-functioning market economy.

The liberal model of economic governance provides a sufficient approximation of actual institutional structures in liberal-democratic market economies. In such economies sovereigns restrict their intervention in the economy by laws, regulations and institutions, which protect economic freedom and private property rights. In exchange sovereigns expect higher returns in terms of growth, taxes, exports and the lowering of the costs of financing the national debt. The history of the formation of liberal-democratic states is quite consistent with this simple portrayal: market actors demanded and received more rights, and sovereigns received higher returns.

To what extent is this narrative consistent with the economic history of late-developing countries? The very short answer is that it is not very consistent. If the evolution of Western liberal democracies is described as a *bottom-up* and *inside-out* process, in the sense that domestic market actors played an active role as drivers of change, the evolution of late-developing market economies can be described as a *top-down* and *outside-in* process in which domestic governing institutions and external actors played a decisive role in shaping the economies. In late-developing countries, formal state institutions were created *prior to* the maturation of domestic markets and sophisticated societal actors. Market actors were economically weak and politically unorganized. Therefore, the market economy was not built by private forces, but by the sovereign, that is, by the state.

Therefore, the path of late-developing economies to a mature market economy assigns a different role to state institutions than their role in liberal market economies. Whereas in the advanced liberal market economies, institutions were designed to protect market and societal actors from the sovereign, in late-developing economies, these institutions were used to enhance the capacity of the sovereign to realize its preferences, which included, among other things, industrialization, job creation and promoting exports. Attaining these objectives required capacities to confront market and societal actors or mobilize them rather than protecting them. In that sense, the market-building in late-developing economies included the use of illiberal policy instruments, which made it a contradictory process: quasi-liberal institutions were built by illiberal means.

Therefore, the market-building process in late-developing countries was contradictory. On the one hand, this process was shaped and inspired by the liberal values, ideas and institutions of the advanced economies. On the other hand, to build markets, governments had to employ illiberal measures, which included discrimination, breaching private property rights and restricting economic freedom. Moreover, the goal of building a market economy was perceived as one of the state interests, and in that sense it was driven not only by the prioritization of individual rights and free entrepreneurship, but mainly by state preferences. This duality is fundamental and it must be accommodated by any political economic theory of late-developing countries.

Historicity and geography of economic rationality

Tracing the political economy of a late-development country must acknowledge what is termed here the *historicity* and *geography* of economic ideas. Any social scientist or historian who is interested in explaining the evolution of socio-economic regimes—namely, the types of structures, policies and ideas used—sooner or later faces the theoretical—perhaps philosophical—dilemma: should the behavior and policy decisions of the historical protagonists be interpreted on the basis of knowledge and information available to them then, or on the basis of knowledge and information available to us today?

For economists who believe in the immutability of economic laws, the answer is clear and simple: there is only one set of economic laws, which are not affected by prevailing institutions, and therefore the behavior of policy-makers—as well as of all other economic actors—should be evaluated on the basis of the most up-to-date mainstream economic theories. However, what this approach gains in theoretical rigor, it loses in realism: it would not capture how policy-makers *really* reach decisions, but rather how abstract policy-makers *should* have reached their decisions. In order to trace how policy-makers actually made policy choices, it is necessary to acknowledge that economic rationality has a history of its own and that this history—the history of economic ideas—must be an essential part of any economic history.

Economic history provides us with ample examples that demonstrate the historicity of economic rationality. A century ago, the idea that governments should increase taxes and spending during a recession was ludicrous; yet by the 1960s this view was the standard of most governments. Another example to consider is that in the 1950s the trade-off between employment and inflation was taken as a fact that justified anti-cyclical policies; today this causal link is questionable. These examples demonstrate that "what actors believe is rational in a given context and … what constitutes 'rationality' shifts over time" (Epstein, 2008, pp. 10–11).

Economic rationality not only has a history, but also a geography whereby policy-makers make choices in a particular geopolitical and geographical context, which is taken into account in the policy-making process. Take, for example, the Keynesian paradigm, which was born in the context of the Great Depression in the United States, and was embraced later by Britain as well as by many other advanced economies. However, Germany did not adopt a Keynesian approach (Hall, 1989), which does not imply that German policy-makers failed to learn good lessons from the United States or Britain. It means that economic rationality depends largely on the specific economic and institutional environment. Albert Hirschman was very aware of the geography of economic rationality and he pointed out that economic practices in peripheral countries may seem "odd, irrational, or reprehensible social behavior" to a Western observer (1984, p. 91). Developing countries are characterized, argues Hirschman, by "hidden rationalities" that cannot be identified by Western liberal observers.

To capture both the historicity and the geography of economic rationality it is useful to take Peter Hall's concept of *policy paradigm* as a starting point. Peter Hall defines the concept of policy paradigm as an assemblage of conceptual, normative and symbolic elements that frames economic reality, defines urgent policy problems while simultaneously offering types of legitimate policy solutions. A policy paradigm is a "framework of ideas and standards that specifies not only the goals of policy and the kind of instruments that can be used to attain them but also the very nature of the problems they are meant to be addressing" (Hall, 1993, p. 279).

By tracing ideational and discursive changes, scholars can identify institutional changes *before* they are manifested in material or institutional variables, because the actors' costs of talking about a needed change are much lower than taking the risks of making the actual change. In other words, actors are likely to talk and write about the need for a change before they take action. Therefore, tracing the emergence of a new paradigm can provide us with a glimpse into the expectations and the plans of policy-makers and other actors.

Another advantage of tracing paradigm changes in economic history is that it provides researchers with more information in order to capture actors' preferences. Whereas some scholars assume that state preferences can be deduced from theory and behavior, tracing discourse and ideas provides another empirical source to reconstruct a broader picture of the environment in which actors take decisions.[1]

Ideas also change their meaning across the geographical space. Policy ideas have a practical meaning only within a well-defined institutional, political and economic context: Keynesianism means a very different thing in a closed economy such as the United States as opposed to an open peripheral economy, such as Israel, for example. Margaret Weir and Theda Skocpol (1985) show that Keynesian ideas were received differently in different countries on the basis of the local actors' interests. Similar processes have been identified by International Relations scholars, who have studied the diffusion of ideas, norms and policies (Acharya, 2004; Checkel, 2007; Risse-Kappen, 1994), and by comparative political economists, who focus on the national origin of economic ideas (Campbell and Pedersen, 2014). The local dimension of policy paradigms is especially essential in the context of the division between the Global North and the Global South. A certain set of ideas may prove to be welfare-maximizing in the Global North, while causing damage if implemented as-is in late-developing economy in the Global South. Developmental economists are particularly aware of this problem. The implication of this analysis is that economic historians must distinguish between the nominal meaning of economic policy ideas and their practical meaning. Whereas in many cases the ideas remain constant nominally, their practical meaning changes significantly in different institutional and political contexts. This fact obviously poses a challenge for comparative political economists: if notions such as liberal economics, Keynesianism and social democracy gain different practical meanings in different institutional contexts, a comparison of economic regime becomes a much more challenging task.

This book, therefore, rather than trying to characterize the Israeli economic regime by using "universal" tokens, which originated in the advanced economies, instead identifies local policy paradigms. These paradigms were inspired and affected by economic policy ideas imported from European and American policy discourses, but they are in no way a replication of these ideas. Through the period from the 1930s to the 1990s four local policy paradigm are identified: (1) the agrarian paradigm; (2) the paradigm of rapid development; (3) the paradigm of economic independence; and (4) the neoliberal paradigm. Each paradigm is characterized by a particular economic rationality, a national ethos, a prioritization of goals and a particular pattern of state-society and state-market linkages.

State preferences

The claim that ideas play a role in shaping policy strategies and economic structures tacitly assumes the existence of a discursive space in which actors make rational choices in the face of policy problems. This space may be minimal, constrained, restricted, bound and even transient. But such discursive space must exist if ideas have an impact on outcomes. The existence of such a discursive space presupposes "that elements within the state, acting, presumably, in pursuit of the national interest, decide what to do without serious opposition from external actors, thereby confirming a central tenet of state theory" (Sacks, quoted in Hall, 1993, p. 276). If such a space does not exist, then policy paradigms are reduced to nothing more than ideologies that legitimize the power of the powerful. The existence of such a space can be guaranteed by the autonomy of the state. Therefore, in our analysis, the concept of state autonomy plays a key role.

The notion of state autonomy must be elaborated on before continuing further. The term "state autonomy" is used in the literature in two different ways. In some cases the state is a concept that refers to the set of institutions, rules and constitutions that restrict the sovereign and that protect the civil society from the sovereign. Rational choice institutionalists highlight this aspect of the state. Margaret Levi argues that the "rulers rule," but they do that "within the constraints of the political constitution" (1989, p. 2). Why would the rulers restrict their coercion practices? Revenue, suggests Levi. Given the bargaining power of the rulers, the transaction costs and the discount rate, the rulers have an incentive to bind their hands in exchange for revenue. A similar argument is made by Douglas North and Barry Weingast, who show how the establishment of the judicial system, the parliament and the central bank in seventeenth-century England institutionalized the differentiation between the market and the sovereign, in the sense that markets were protected from the sovereign's whims by state institutions (North and Weingast, 1989).

Hence, rational choice institutionalists distinguish not only between states and markets, but also between the *state-as-a-sovereign* (the "rulers" or the government) and the *state-as-institutions* (the rules and procedures that restrict the state-as-a-sovereign) that protects markets and societal actors from the sovereign. In the sense, the rational choice modeling of the state acknowledges that modern states fulfill two contradictory functions. This duality is echoed in Weingast's views regarding the "fundamental political dilemma of an economic system":

> A government strong enough to protect property rights and enforce contracts is also strong enough to confiscate the wealth of its citizens. Thriving markets require not only the appropriate system of property rights and a law of contracts, but a secure political foundation that limits the ability of the state to confiscate wealth.
>
> (Weingast, 1995, p. 1)

Realists and state-centric scholars use the term "state" in a different way: for them, the state is the sovereign. In the past, the sovereign was the monarch, and in modern societies the sovereign is manifested in a more complex group of "policy-makers." Eric Nordlinger, writing within this tradition, argues that state preferences are nothing more or less than a "resource-weighted parallelogram" of public officials' preferences (1981, p. 15). However, even realist and state-centric scholars acknowledge that rational policy-makers may delegate powers to gain revenue.

The contradictory nature of the state is particularly essential to analysing the political economy of market building in late-developing countries. Whereas in advanced liberal democracies, the state-as-institution is much more developed, in late-developing economies the dual function of the state is more pronounced and observable. These states confront (certain) market actors and thereby they discriminate against certain other actors, they breach private property rights and they restrict the economic freedom of certain actors, and at the same time they protect (certain) market actors, they guarantee the private property rights of (certain) actors and their economic freedom.

The dualistic and contradictory statehood in late-developing countries raises a problem of legitimacy: how do policy-makers justify their choice of discriminating actors, while at the same time building liberal market-oriented institutions? This question brings us to the interaction between the ideologies of liberalism and nationalism.

Economics and nationalism

The literature on the economic history of the West often makes a distinction between economic liberalism and economic nationalism. Whereas economic liberalism is associated with free markets—domestically and internationally—economic nationalism is associated with state intervention in the economy either to favor certain powerful actors or to realize certain state objectives such as building military capacity or promoting exports (Pickel, 2005). The association of liberal values with market practices and national ideologies with state intervention is largely shaped by the European experience in the interwar period, which was characterized by a wave of nationalist movements that dictated a retreat from free trade and the implementation of economic protectionism. The dichotomous perception of the liberal market versus nationally driven interventionist policies was only deepened after World War II when the European integration process started and was legitimized on the premise that it would protect Europe from slipping once again into economic nationalism and war (Eichengreen, 1992, 1996).

However, the experience of late-developing countries and their attempts at market-building processes undermine the traditional dichotomy between economic liberalism and economic nationalism. In late-developing economies, the processes of market-building and the liberalization policies are just as "national" as any other type of state intervention. In late-developing economies, states build markets to further their interests and in most cases these endeavors are legitimized by nationalistic narratives, values and identities. Therefore, building a market economy can be framed as a "national project" just like any other national project. In practice, Abdelal argues, the effects of economic nationalism "are much more variable and context-specific, and less destructive of international economic order, than economists have usually appreciated" (2001, p. 34). Along similar lines Andreas Pickel argues that nationalism is a process of a historical construction of an imagined political-cultural-economic national space and therefore does not have essentialist features. Based on this, he rejects "the standard view that economic nationalism is dysfunctional and neoliberalism is functional" (Pickel, 2003, p. 120). Moreover, in fact, free trade can also be framed as a form of economic nationalism (Trentmann, 1998). Therefore, Eric Helleiner suggests that economic nationalism "is most properly defined by its nationalist content rather than as variant of realism or as an ideology of protectionism" and, as such, it "can be associated with a wide range of policy projects, including the endorsement of liberal economic policies" (2002, p. 307). More generally, as Joan Robinson put it, "[T]he very nature of economics is rooted in nationalism" (1962, p. 124).

In order to trace the historical path of late-developing economies, it is necessary to absolve ourselves from the Western/liberal perspective of economic history, which assumes that the building of markets economies is accompanied by embracing liberal values, and that intervention in the economies is driven by inefficient practices based on national sentiments. To trace the evolution of economic regimes in late-developing countries, one must discover how certain national ideologies and certain economic rationalities are combined to form policy paradigms that shape policy, strategy and structure.

Professionals and politicians

Local policy paradigms are formed based on economic ideas and actors' interests. Due to the very different ontology of ideas and interests, there is no simple theory that conceptualizes the interaction between ideas and interests. This book adopt an actors-oriented approach, which assumes that policy paradigms are formed mainly by economic experts—economists—and by politicians, who represent interests.

Economists began to play a significant role in shaping policy making in the 1930s when, following the Great Depression, governments started to use macroeconomic policies as a stabilizing instrument (Barber, 1990). Macroeconomic policy-making required a new type of skill that politicians did not possess, and the demand for professional economists in governments dramatically increased. Political scientists have devoted much attention to the role of economic experts in policy-making and policy execution.

The views of the role of economic experts in policy-making range along a continuum stretched between two diametrically opposed positions. Public choice theorists assign economic experts an overall positive role in economic policy-making (Buchanan *et al.*, 1980). Politicians, they argue, are motivated primarily by their short-term survival interests and are prone to follow populist policies. Therefore, to protect the public interest, public choice scholars recommend the delegation of powers to independent agencies, that is, to non-majoritarian institutions, in which policy choices are made by professionals and experts rather than by elected politicians (Thatcher and Sweet, 2002). This approach perceives economic expertise as kind of public good which is necessary to overcome the collective action problems associated with policy-making in democratic societies.

At the other end of the axis, sociologists and critical political economists are skeptical regarding the contribution of economic experts to social welfare (Nowotny, 2003). Sociologists and constructivists reject the positivist ontology, according to which economic experts possess superior knowledge or skills (Abdelal *et al.*, 2010). From a sociological perspective, politicians assign positive value to economic knowledge not because it represents the economic reality better than other discourses, but because they gain social and symbolic capital as experts (Blyth, 2012). The constructivist ontology implies that economic ideas are merely an ideology that legitimizes the interests of the elite. The delegation of power to such experts does not maximize welfare but rather leads to a democratic deficit that decreases or even eliminates the citizenry's capacity to shape its destiny.

This book argues that in the process of policy-making, ideas are not chosen because they are believed to be truthful. The issue is not "persuading agents in positions of institutional authority of the correctness of one particular diagnosis … among competing models" (Blyth, 2007, p. 762). Rather, the question is the extent to which ideas can be used to frame and address policy problems effectively. Therefore, without adopting a positivistic anthology, one may assume that experts possess better capacity than politicians to address policy problems. As Fritz Scharpf put it, experts or technocrats, unlike politicians, draw their legitimacy from their "degree of effectiveness in achieving the goals, and avoiding the dangers, that citizens collectively care about" (1997, p. 19). Along similar lines, John Campbell argues that experts provide "road maps out of troublesome or uncertain policy situations" (2002, p. 29).

Experts, therefore, have an asset that politicians would like to have: an enhanced capacity to address problems. Having said that, however, politicians possess the necessary power and prestige which can be used to mobilize experts. On the premise of these assumptions, we can build a simple but realistic model of the interaction between politicians and experts.

Economic experts are good at solving policy problems due to their experience and know-how. The problem-solving capacity of economic experts is derived not only from their academic education as economists, but also from the fact that they have spent most of their careers dealing with such problems within a certain policy area; in contrast to this, the average politician moves from one policy area to another throughout his or her career. Therefore, when politicians face an urgent or complex problem, they are likely to ask the advice of an expert.

Additionally, experts possess social capital—prestige and reputation—that can be used by the politician to legitimize the implementation of desired policies that are not popular with the public. The social capital of experts may be linked to their actual capacity to address policy problems, but it may also be the product of their public image only. Politicians similarly possess assets that economic experts would like to have access to: financial resources, power and influence. When an economic expert is invited to provide policy recommendations to politicians, he or she is offered material remuneration as well as a reputational boost and an opportunity to influence policies.

The political economic exchange between politicians and experts creates an incentive to cooperate and to construct a local policy paradigm. Cooperation implies not only that politicians learn from experts, but also that experts learn from politicians. Economic experts, who are more informed about prevailing global trends in economic policy-making, provide standardized intellectual road maps; politicians, who are more susceptible to local policy problems and to political and institutional constraints bring their input regarding the framing of problems and the feasibility of responses. Together, they come up with an understanding of what the most urgent problems are, what the national priority is, and how to realize this priority.

This model has its limits. First, we do not have simple criteria to define a politician and an expert. Both social positions are socially constructed and context-dependent. Therefore, this book will define politicians as actors who perceive themselves as such and whom others perceive as such. Similarly, experts are actors who perceive themselves as experts and who are recognized by other actors as such.

Linkages between the state and market actors

The policy-making process is shaped by policy paradigms, but it is constrained by the state's capacities. If the policy paradigm determines *what the state wants*, capacities determine *what the state can do.* Realist and state-centered political economic theories assume that state capacities depend on the state's coercive power—its sovereignty—which enables it to confiscate (nationalize) private property. Confiscation and nationalization are essential elements in the governing of markets, which is manifested in taxation and spending.

Traditionally, states govern markets by using two types of policy instruments: *regulation* and *intervention.* Governing through regulation is carried out by dictating transparent rules, which are imposed on all market actors homogeneously and are not changed frequently (Braithwaite, 2008; Levi-Faur and Jordana, 2005). The OECD defines regulation as the "imposition of rules by government, backed by the use of penalties that are intended specifically to modify the economic behavior of individuals and firms in the private sector."[2] Regulatory institutions provide rules for market actors but they also protect market actors from the sovereign. Governing through regulation is consistent with the liberal values of the rule of law, economic freedom and private property rights. States also govern markets through intervention, policy instruments that involve breaching of private property rights. Fiscal policy—taxing and spending—as well as of transfer payments fall within the category of intervention. The intervention of governments in markets is legitimized by the approval of the parliament, which are supposed to represent the public interests.

Governing through regulation and intervention proved ineffective in late-developing countries for several reasons. One of those reasons is that effective regulation and intervention require a highly skilled and autonomous bureaucracy, which late-developing countries lacked. Another reason is that rapid industrialization required more intrusive policy instruments, to affect the allocation of resources. In late-developing countries, states played a role in mobilizing capital, redistributing it and in spreading and reducing risk associated with industrial investment (Gerschenkron, 1962). The active role of the state is required due to the absence of a developed private sector, so that the state has to function as a "surrogate entrepreneur" that replaces the private sector (Hobson, 1997, p. 72). Albert Hirschman argues that, in under-developed economies, economic development depends not so much on finding optimal combinations for given resources and factors of production as on calling forth and enlisting for development purposes the resources and abilities that are hidden, scattered or badly utilized (1958, p. 5).

In principle, late-developing countries could have nationalized private property, in order to tighten their control over the allocation of resources. However, nationalization, as pointed out above, eliminates markets and it involves high domestic and international political and economic costs. Therefore, many late-developing countries governed markets by creating state-market linkages.

Peter Evans explains that effective statehood in late-developing countries requires "a concrete set of social ties that binds the state to society and provides institutionalized channels for continual negotiation and renegotiation of goals and policies" (1995, p. 12). Whereas Evans emphasizes the negotiation that takes place between the state and societal actors, Linda Weiss underlines the interdependence between states and market actors: "Economic projects are advanced by public-private cooperation, but their adoption and implementation are disciplined and monitored by the state." This regime leads to *interdependence* between the state and market actors (Weiss, 1995, p. 45).

From a liberal perspective, links between the state and market or societal actors are not a sign of the state's strength but a sign of its weakness. When the state cannot dictate rules and impose them, it has to negotiate with market and the societal actors by making threats ("if you do not change your behavior, your property will be confiscated") or by offering privileges ("if you change your behavior, you will get subsidies, tax relief or other concessions"). The result of this process is a blurring of the boundaries of the state, as the market and societal actors become part of the state. The actors who are linked to the state do not give up their penchant for profit, but they take into account the impact of their behavior on the state preferences.

Developmental economists highlight the contribution of state-market linkages to the public interest. This political economic structure enables the state to control the allocation of resources more effectively, and to realize its preferences. In poor countries, the state can boost the intensification of farming, for example; in small under-developed economies, the government can encourage industrialization and export industries. Linkages indeed "distort" the price mechanism, but they may do so in a way that contributes to social welfare. Governments that have strong preferences for state-building projects and expanding domestic production capacities will tend to create linkages with workers and labor organizations.[3] On the other hand, governments that are interested in promoting exports would tend to create alliances with employers and particularly with exporters.[4] In under-developed countries where the provision of food is not adequate, we would expect linkages between the state and the agricultural sector (Waldner, 1999, p. 84).

However, the creation of state-market ties has a cost and is risky. Linkages are inconsistent with liberal governing principles because linkages involve discrimination and breaching of private property rights. From a liberal perspective, linkages are detrimental to the long-term public interest and to economic growth because they create "distortions" in the price mechanism. Additionally, links can be interpreted as a manifestation of "crony capitalism" in which the state takes advantage of its political position—its sovereignty—in order to provide privileges to its political allies or to powerful interest groups, simply to ensure its political survival. In other words, linkages can be interpreted as mere corruption.

Therefore, mainstream economists reject not only the economic rationale of state-market linkages—that is, that claim that such linkages are increasing welfare, compared to their absence—but they also perceive linkages as a symptom of corruption, crony capitalism and predatory practices. In practice, as this study will demonstrate, state-market linkages can be a highly effective governing tool in certain circumstances, despite the fact that they are inconsistent with the liberal principle of the rule of law and fairness.

The fact that linkages are effective but inconsistent with the liberal notion of fairness poses a challenge to late-developing economies in terms of their strategy of legitimization. Policy-makers have to justify their choices to privilege certain market or societal actors on the basis of non-liberal ideologies, such as national ideologies. Therefore, the market-building project in late-developing economies is justified by a special hybrid of liberal market ideas and national sentiments.

The distinction made here between liberal economies and late-developing economies is of course an over-simplification. In practice, state-market linkages do prevail, to some degree, also in liberal economies. However, in late-developing countries governing through state-market linkages is more common.

The working hypothesis of this book is that the pattern of linkages determines the state's capacity: that the state, as a rational actor, nurtures, dismantles and re-creates state-market links in order to develop certain state capacities to realize its preferences. As the preferences of the state change over time, state actors—policy-makers—have an incentive to nurture a certain pattern of linkages in a particular period, and dismantle them when the political, economic and institutional circumstances change. It is the job of the economic historians and the political economists, as undertaken in this book, to trace the evolution of state-market linkages, along with the development of the economic discourse that legitimized these linkages. Tracing the linkages and the discourses enables us not only to identify the structures and institutions, which formed Israeli capitalism, but also to understand the motives of the state in shaping them.

The argument presented in this book

The aim of this book is to trace the evolution of the Israeli capitalism, while at the same time to identify the elements that remained constant. The element that remained constant, the book argues, is the supremacy of state preferences as the single most significant factor that shaped policy, economic strategy and economic structure. In the long run, state preferences were changed, and were followed by a change in policy, strategy and structure.

The dependent variable is the local policy paradigm, which includes an ideational and an institutional aspect: state preferences and state market linkages. Over the long time span, from the 1930s to the 2000s, the book identifies four local policy paradigms: (1) the agrarian paradigm; (2) the paradigm of rapid development; (3) the paradigm of economic independence; and (4) the neoliberal paradigm. The book argues that state preferences affected a change in linkage patterns and not vice versa.

The change in the local policy paradigms is explained on the basis of three types of intervening variables. First, policy-makers respond to changing political and institutional conditions at the domestic and international levels: as policy-makers within the state apparatus face new conditions, which affect their capacity to realize the state preferences, they respond by updating policy instruments, policy objectives or both.

Second, policy-makers respond to changing conditions on the basis of the prevailing policy ideas that are available to them. These ideas provide policy alternatives to frame and address domestic policy problems. To gain access to prevailing policy ideas, politicians interact with economic experts, who play a role in importing and localizing policy ideas.

Third, policy-makers respond to changing conditions within political constraints, imposed by the powerful local actors. The interaction between politicians and experts leads to the consolidation of local policy paradigms based on imported and altered policy ideas. Given the dictates of the local policy paradigm, state actors take action to reconstruct linkages between the state, market and societal actors as well as to change economic policy strategy. Figure 1.1 presents a very schematic visualization of the historical process which is, of course, in reality more complex and iterative.

The structure of the book

Economic history, like history in general, is not a linear process, which means that change, most often than not, takes place in bursts rather than continuously. In most cases, relatively extended periods of incremental and gradual change are followed by shorter periods of accelerated change.[5] Nevertheless, in order to

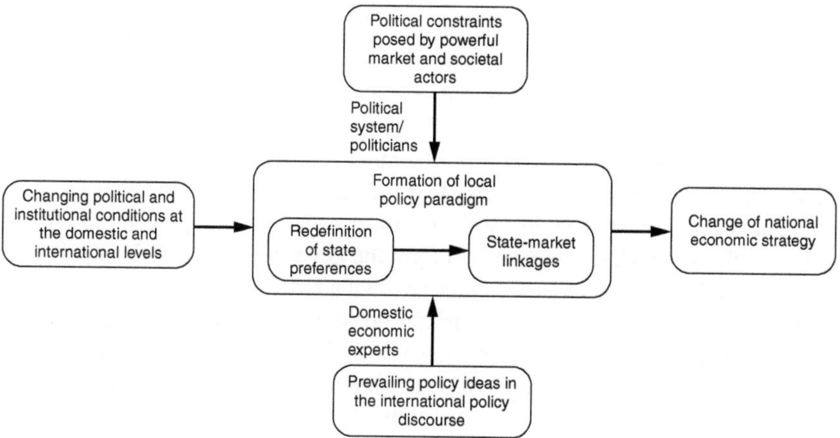

Figure 1.1 The mechanism of change.

understand the shorter periods of accelerated change, one must understand the dynamics of the incremental change that preceded it.

This book, therefore, does not aim to present the reader with a chronology of Israel economic history. The book focuses on certain critical periods and on certain chains of events within those periods. The selection of relevant events was made in an attempt to capture how policy-makers perceived the economic conditions and their response to it. This choice determined also the type of documents used for the purpose of conducting the research: the research made use of documents produced by government institutions and economists within and outside the formal state institutions.

Chapter 2 focuses on the period from 1929 to 1937, when the Peel Commission arrived in Palestine, and it will be argued that it was during this period that the Zionist leadership abandoned the old *agrarian policy paradigm* that prioritized agrarian development through small collectivist settlements, in favor of what is referred to throughout this text as the *paradigm of rapid development*, which prioritized urban settlements and the industrialization of the economy. It was in this period that elements of Keynesian economic ideas penetrated the Zionist policy discourse in order to legitimize the policies of industrialization and mass immigration. The thrust of this chapter revolves around the argument that this transition was not driven by economic calculation per se, but rather by a redefinition of the Zionist movement's primary political objective, that is, the creation of a Jewish majority in Mandatory Palestine.

Whereas, in the 1930s the paradigm of rapid development was expressed in words, in the 1940s, it was consolidated into the administrative structures of the future state. Chapter 3 focuses on a concrete historical entity: *the Planning Committee*. The Planning Committee, established in 1942, was a massive planning project by contemporary standards, promoted by David Ben-Gurion, the indisputable leader of the Jewish Labor Movement of the World Zionist Organization, to design and implement the transportation of one million Jews to Palestine within a few years. The process that led to the establishment of the Committee, the choices regarding the individuals who chaired it, as well as the content of its reports, provide us with more than just a glimpse into the process by which state preferences are shaped by policy-makers and experts. This chapter argues that the paradigm of rapid development was institutionalized during the 1940s, and it became an economic road map for policy-makers during the early years of statehood. The chapter also demonstrates that the interventionist policies of the government were not shaped by socialist ideas, but by the perception of the policy-makers, which then went on to form the key preferences of the state.

Once the Jewish population in Israel reached a critical mass, the policy-makers started to be concerned by Israel financial position. Chapter 4 traces the gradual demise of the paradigm of rapid development and the rise of the paradigm of economic independence, which endured until the enactment of the austerity policy in 1965, which was designed to boost exports. The emergence of the paradigm of economic independence was driven by a collaboration of politicians from the center and the center-right, and professional economists from the newly established

Economics Department at the Hebrew University. Whereas many observers have portrayed the paradigm of economic independence as consistent with liberal values and market economy principles, Chapter 4 argues that the new paradigm was legitimized on the basis of a new definition of state preferences rather than by a liberal ethos. While professional economists advocated less state intervention in the creation of jobs, they legitimized state intervention in subsidies to exporters.

Thus far, the financial aspects of economic development in Israel have been left in the background. Chapters 5–8 discuss the role of the central bank and the banking system in Israel's economic development. These chapters trace the process that led to the establishment of the Bank of Israel, its operation during years 1954–1959 and the transformation that the Israeli banking system went through during this period as it underwent a metamorphosis into a highly centralized system. These chapters trace and explain how and why Israeli policymakers shaped an imported model of central banking and altered it in a way to better serve Israel's developmental strategy.

In the 1980s, Israel, as in many other economies, went through a transformation in response to the globalization of the world economy. Hence Chapter 9 focuses on the period from 1977, when the Labor Party, for the first time in 29 years, lost the election to the Likud Party, to the year 1985, when the unity government of the Labor and Likud Parties implemented the Stabilization Plan, an event that marks the beginning of the neoliberal era. Whereas many scholars portrayed this transition as a shift from socialism to a free market economy, the chapter argues that the Stabilization Plan was designed by state actors to adjust Israel's economic strategy to new political economic conditions.

Chapter 10 concludes the book by arguing that Israel's economic policy during the neoliberal era does not reflect an ideational change toward liberal governing principles, but rather it reflects a new strategy by which the state realizes its preferences, given Israel's unique national security and socio-economic policy situation.

Notes

1 Katznelson and Weingast distinguish between the approach of "imputed preferences," in which preferences are calculated from theoretical assumptions regarding the behavior of the state and the historical approach, in which preferences are extracted empirically (see Katznelson and Weingast, 2005).

2 OECD: Glossary of Statistical Terms. Available at: https://stats.oecd.org/glossary/detail.asp?ID=3295 (accessed December 2016).

3 David Waldner (1999) shows that late-developing countries may either mobilize labor unions through a political exchange, which is manifested in higher wages, or confront labor unions when the government is concerned by their power.

4 Ryan Saylor demonstrates the policy dilemma of export-oriented state intervention: export-oriented coalitions "propel gains in state capacity and thereby indirectly facilitated good things, such as economic growth. But ruling coalition members did so by harnessing their disproportionate power for narrow gain" (Saylor, 2014, p. 214).

5 This view is embraced by Historical Institutionalists, who called the period of rapid change *critical junctures* (Capoccia, 2015).

References

Abdelal, R., 2001. *National Purpose in the World Economy: Post-Soviet States in Comparative Perspective*. Cornell University Press, Ithaca, NY.

Abdelal, R., Blyth, M. and Parsons, C., 2010. Introduction: Constructing the International Economy. In: Abdelal, R., Blyth, M. and Parsons, C. (Eds.) *Constructing the International Economy*. Cornell University Press. Ithaca, NY, pp. 1–19.

Acharya, A., 2004. How Ideas Spread: Whose Norms Matter? Norm Localization and Institutional Change in Asian Regionalism. *International Organization* 58, 239–275.

Barber, W.J., 1990. Government as a Laboratory for Economic Learning in the Years of the Democratic Roosevelt. In: Furner, M.O. and Supple, B. (Eds.), *The State and Economic Knowledge: The American and British Experience*. Woodrow Wilson International Center for Scholars, Washington, DC, pp. 103–137.

Blyth, M., 2007. Powering, Puzzling, or Persuading? The Mechanisms of Building Institutional Orders. *International Studies Quarterly* 51, 761–777.

Blyth, M., 2012. Paradigms and Paradox: The Politics of Economic Ideas in Two Moments of Crisis. *Governance* 26, 197–215.

Braithwaite, J., 2008. *Regulatory Capitalism: How It Works, Ideas for Making It Work Better*. Cheltenham, Edward Elgar.

Buchanan, J.M., Tollison, R.D. and Tullock, G. (Eds.), 1980. *Toward a Theory of the Rent-Seeking Society*. Texas A&M University, College Station, TX.

Campbell, J.L., 2002. Ideas, Politics, and Public Policy. *Annual Review of Sociology* 28, 21–38.

Campbell, J.L. and Pedersen, O.K., 2014. *The National Origins of Policy Ideas: Knowledge Regimes in the United States, France, Germany, and Denmark*. Princeton University Press, Princeton, NJ.

Capoccia, G., 2015. Critical Junctures and Institutional Change. In: J. Mahoney and K. Thelen (Eds.), *Advances in Comparative Historical Analysis*. Cambridge University Press, Cambridge, pp. 194–237.

Checkel, J.T., 2007. *International Institutions and Socialization in Europe*. Cambridge University Press, Cambridge.

Eichengreen, B., 1992. *Golden Fetters: The Gold Standard and the Great Depression, 1919–1939*. Oxford University Press, New York.

Eichengreen, B.J., 1996. *Globalizing Capital: A History of the International Monetary System*. Princeton University Press, Princeton, NJ.

Epstein, R.A., 2008. *In Pursuit of Liberalism: International Institutions in Postcommunist Europe*. Johns Hopkins University Press, Baltimore, MD.

Evans, P.B., 1995. *Embedded Autonomy: States and Industrial Transformation*. Princeton University Press, Princeton, NJ.

Gerschenkron, A., 1962. Economic Backwardness in Historical Perspective. In: Gerschenkron, A., *Economic Backwardness in Historical Perspective, A Book of Essays*. Belknap Press of Harvard University Press, Cambridge, MA, pp. 5–30.

Hall, P.A., 1989. *The Political Power of Economic Ideas: Keynesianism Across Nations*. Princeton University Press, Princeton, NJ.

Hall, P.A., 1993. Policy Paradigms, Social Learning, and the State: The Case of Economic Policymaking in Britain. *Comparative Politics* 25, 275–296.

Helleiner, E., 2002. Economic Nationalism as a Challenge to Economic Liberalism? Lessons from the 19th Century. *International Studies Quarterly* 46, 307–329.

Hirschman, A.O., 1958. *The Strategy of Economic Development.* Yale University Press, New Haven, CT.

Hirschman, A.O., 1984. A Dissenter's Confession: "The Strategy of Economic Development" Revisited. In: Meier, G.M. and Seers, D. (Eds.), *Pioneers in Development.* Published for the World Bank, Oxford University Press, New York, pp. 87–111.

Hobson, J.M., 1997. *The Wealth of States: A Comparative Sociology of International Economic and Political Change.* Cambridge University Press, Cambridge.

Katznelson, I. and Weingast, B., 2005. *Preferences and Situations: Intersections between Historical and Rational Choice Institutionalism.* Russell Sage, New York, pp. 1–26.

Levi, M., 1989. *Of Rule and Revenue.* University of California Press, Berkeley, CA.

Levi-Faur, D. and Jordana. J., 2005. *The Rise of Regulatory Capitalism: The Global Diffusion of a New Order.* SAGE Publications, London.

Nordlinger, E.A., 1981. *On the Autonomy of the Democratic State.* Harvard University Press, Cambridge, MA.

North, D.C. and Weingast, B.R., 1989. Constitutions and Commitment: The Evolution of Institutions Governing Public Choice in Seventeenth-Century England. *The Journal of Economic History* 49, 803–832.

Nowotny, H., 2003. Democratising Expertise and Socially Robust Knowledge. *Science and Public Policy* 30, 151–156.

Pickel, A., 2003. Explaining, and Explaining with, Economic Nationalism. *Nations and Nationalism* 9, 105–127.

Pickel, A., 2005. Introduction: False Oppositions: Reconceptualizing Economic Nationalism in a Globalizing World. In: Helleiner, E. and Pickel, A. (Eds.), *Economic Nationalism in a Globalizing World.* Cornell University Press, Ithaca, NY.

Risse-Kappen, T., 1994. Ideas Do Not Float Freely: Transnational Coalitions, Domestic Structures, and the End of the Cold War. *International Organization* 48, 185–214.

Robinson, J., 1962. *Economic Philosophy.* Aldine Publications, Chicago.

Saylor, R., 2014. *State Building in Boom Times: Commodities and Coalitions in Latin America and Africa.* Oxford University Press, Oxford.

Scharpf, F.W., 1997. Economic Integration, Democracy and the Welfare State. *Journal of European Public Policy* 4, 18–36.

Thatcher, M. and Sweet, A.S., 2002. Theory and Practice of Delegation to Non-Majoritarian Institutions. *West European Politics* 25, 1–22. doi:10.1080/713601583.

Trentmann, F., 1998. Political Culture and Political Economy: Interest, Ideology and Free Trade. *Review of International Political Economy* 5, 217–251.

Waldner, D., 1999. *State Building and Late Development.* Cornell University Press, Ithaca, NY.

Weingast, B.R., 1995. The Economic Role of Political Institutions: Market-Preserving Federalism and Economic Development. *The Journal of Law, Economics & Organization* 11, 1–31.

Weir, M. and Skocpol, T., 1985. State Structures and the Possibilities for "Keynesian" Responses to the Great Depression in Sweden, Britain, and the United States. In: Evans, P., Rueschemeyer, D. and Skocpol, T. (Eds.), *Bringing the State Back In.* Cambridge University Press, Cambridge, pp. 107–163.

Weiss, L., 1995. Governed Interdependence: Rethinking the Government-Business Relationship in East Asia. *The Pacific Review* 8, 589–616.

Part I

The formative period

Economic ideas and state preferences

2 Toward an industrial revolution

In 1935, David Horowitz published a short article entitled "Arguments against the Theory of Productivization," in the *Cooperative Bulletin* (*Hameshek hash-itufi*), the semi-weekly supplement of *Davar*, a daily newspaper owned by the Jewish Labor Movement in Mandatory Palestine.[1] In this article, the author, in his mid-thirties with no formal academic background in economics, leveled a harsh attack against one of the cornerstones of the Jewish national ethos: the ideology of productivization, which stipulated that the Jewish leadership should prioritize agricultural labor and agrarian settlements over other economic sectors such as industry, trade or services. The article would not have had any historical significance had not the Labor Movement's dominant leader, David Ben-Gurion, nominated Horowitz Secretary of the Economic Department of the Jewish Agency immediately after its publication. Two years later, Horowitz was chosen by Ben-Gurion to represent the Jewish Agency in the Palestine Royal Commission—the Peel Commission. What was it in this article that drew Ben-Gurion's attention to Horowitz? To answer this question, it is necessary to identify the policy problems Ben-Gurion faced as the leader of the Zionist movement.

The perception of David Horowitz's publication must be understood against the background of the economic and political trends that took place during the 1930s. The 1930s was a transformative decade from economic, political, national and ideational perspectives. Economically, during that decade, the private-urban-industrialized sector of the Jewish economy in Palestine thrived, and this trend called for a reconsideration of the economic strategy of the World Zionist Organization (WZO). Politically, *Mapai*—the dominant Labor Party within the Jewish Labor Movement—strengthened its position when David Ben-Gurion, the party leader, was nominated the chairman of the Jewish Agency, the local branch of the WZO. From a political-national perspective, during the 1930s, an escalation of the Jewish–Arab conflict took place, a process which affected the Jewish leadership's perception of the conflict as well as the definition of the key objective of the Zionist movement. Finally, during the 1930s, new policy ideas emerged in the United States in response to the Great Depression: according to these new lines of thought, market economies could be governed, regulated and managed rather than being completely self-regulated.

Horowitz's article touched upon each of those four aspects. Horowitz—more than any other economic expert at the time—was able to translate the new policy ideas emerging in the United States, and use them in order to offer a new economic rationale that would be able to serve the Zionist objectives more than the old economic ideas. Ben-Gurion recognized this potential, and promoted Horowitz. This was the basis of a relationship of cooperation between the two men that lasted for almost two decades, until 1952, when the two split over the austerity policy of 1952. During these two decades, the cooperation between Ben-Gurion and Horowitz gave rise to a new policy paradigm, the policy of rapid development. Chapters 3 and 4 will the story of the emergence of this local policy paradigm.

Agriculture or industry?

During the early decades of the twentieth century, the Zionist leadership[2] faced two fundamental political economic dilemmas concerning the economic strategy of the Zionist endeavor in Palestine. The first dilemma was economic, and it concerned the choice of the WZO to finance agrarian-based settlements or industry-based settlements. The second dilemma was political and it concerned the extent to which the WZO should mobilize with the Jewish private sector by allocating national resources to it. The two dilemmas were linked: the private sector was mainly urban and industrial, and the national sector was mainly agrarian. The response of the WZO to these two dilemmas shaped the Zionist economic strategy and discourse at that time.

From a purely economic perspective, the agricultural sector in Palestine was performing poorly. Between 1922 and 1947, Jewish agricultural production was valued at less than 15 percent of the total Jewish National Product (JNP), compared with services, which yielded over half of the JNP, and industry and manufacturing which contributed 20–25 percent. As far as employment was concerned, in the early 1920s the agricultural sector employed 27 percent of the Jewish workers, compared with 17 percent employed in industry and manufacturing. By 1945, agriculture provided employment to only 13 percent of the workforce compared with 31 percent employed in industry and manufacturing (Metzer, 1998, p. 142, Table 5.2). Adding to the agricultural sector's economic quandary was the fact that agricultural workers' productivity was much lower than that of industrial workers.

The poor performance of the agrarian sector came despite Jewish agricultural settlements in Palestine receiving generous financial support from the Zionist organizations. In the 1925–1926 fiscal year, for example, resources allocated to agricultural settlements totaled 60 percent of the total economic expenditure of Jewish national organizations.[3] A decade later, agricultural settlements received 66 percent of economic expenditure. During the same period, resources allocated to urban settlements amounted to only 8 percent and 7 percent respectively (ibid., p. 191 Table 6.4).

Why, then, given agriculture's poor performance, did the Jewish leadership make the choice of prioritizing the allocation of national resources to the agricultural settlements rather than to industrial projects? After all, in the long run, industrial development promised more profits and more jobs. Moreover, it was clear from the outset that Jewish farmers were less productive than the Arab *fellachin* (farmers), who were more skilled and required lower wages, making economic competition problematic at best. The Jewish national organizations made several early attempts to industrialize the Jewish sector, but their impact was negligible (see Kolat, 1997, p. 142).

There were several factors that shaped the choice of the Jewish organizations to allocate the limited national Jewish resources to the Jewish agrarian sector. First, industrial development required extensive long-term credit and it involved higher levels of risk. The WZO did not possess the kind of financial resources considered necessary for such an undertaking. Moreover, the primary purpose of the WZO was not to make profit, but rather to create new jobs for the Jewish immigrants in order to increase the economic absorptive capacity of Palestine, which was a criterion used by the British government to issue immigration certificates (Bertisch, 1981, p. 30; Metzer, 1978). Agricultural settlements created more jobs per unit of investment than investment in industry. The choice of prioritizing agricultural settlements was also shaped by the conventional belief at the time that a country must produce its own means of subsistence and that the size of the agricultural sector determines the size of the population that the country can provide for.

There were also cultural or ideological reasons to prioritize agricultural settlements (Hart, 2000). Arthur Ruppin, considered one of the founding fathers of the Jewish agricultural settlement in Palestine, who also made sociological studies of the Jewish people, believed the agricultural labor had the capacity to socially normalize the Jewish people. He argued that the high percentage of Jews occupied in "non-productive" economic sectors was an abnormal phenomenon and that it represented a degeneration of the Jewish people (Ruppin, 1973). Agricultural labor, Ruppin believed, would "rejuvenate" the Jewish people in their homeland (Bloom, 2007, 2011).

The Jewish agricultural settlements also played territorial and military roles. Unlike the privately owned citrus industry concentrated along the coast, nationally funded farms were located in peripheral areas on land that was purchased from Arab land owners. The settlements were used as centers of Jewish colonies within Arab areas, and they functioned also as military outposts on the frontier (Bertisch, 1981, p. 28; Ruppin, 1922, pp. 8–9; Shilo, 1988, pp. 108–162).

This set of justifications in favor of agricultural development was at the heart of the set of ideas, norms and economic practices, which can be termed the agrarian paradigm. Until the end of the 1920s, the agrarian paradigm, or the agrarian ethos, as it is called elsewhere (Krampf, 2010), was pervasive in shaping the perceptions of Zionist leaders at the WZO, as well as the leaders of the Labor Movement.

This is not to say that there were no dissenters, who insisted on the desirability of industrial development. In 1924, as the economic conditions seemed favorable, the Labor Movement founded the Workers Corporation (*Hevrat ha-ovdim*) as a holding company of the Histadrut. The Workers Corporation owned companies, such as Sollel Boné, a construction company, and Hamashbir, a distribution company. Ben-Gurion wrote that "the time has come to build large-scale industrial enterprises of the workers, for the workers, and through the workers' efforts and means" (Ben-Gurion, 1997). Through the Workers Corporation, the Histadrut and the Labor Movement, and in turn through them, the WZO, hoped to infiltrate the sphere of economic activities traditionally dominated by the private sector. The attempt, however, failed in 1927 when the economic crisis led to the bankruptcy of Sollel Boné.

Hence, until the late-1920s, the conventional wisdom within the Zionist leadership circles was that small agrarian settlements were preferable to large-scale industrial projects. This choice satisfied both the interests of the WZO and that of the Labor Movement. The former did not have to commit to large-scale and long-term funding, and the latter turned itself into the local agent of the WZO, which executed the settlement project.

The private sector and state-building

The Jewish economy in Palestine was divided into a private sector and a "national sector." The national sector included the economic units that received financial support from the WZO and consisted mainly of agrarian farms on the periphery of the Jewish settled areas, while the private sector consisted of small manufacturing, trade and services businesses located in urban areas that received little to no financial support from the national funds. In addition, the private sector included a large and successful citrus industry, which despite the lack of public funding, was very profitable: during the period of 1921–1939 annual citrus production grew more than 26-fold, compared with a mere average eight-fold growth in other agricultural branches (Metzer, 1998, p. 150, Table 5.3,).

Given the structure of the Jewish economy, the choice of the WZO to finance the agrarian settlements had political implications: a link between the WZO and the Labor Movement and the marginalization of the private sector. This link colored the Zionist project with a "socialist" tinge. The Labor Movement, which functioned as a financial pipeline, gained power within the Jewish political system and the connection between the WZO and the Labor Movement also developed into the dependence of the WZO on the Labor Movement, which built its administrative resources. In 1920, the Labor Movement established the Histadrut, the General Jewish Federation of Workers in Palestine. This body possessed significant capacity to control and regulate the national agrarian sector, which was important to the success of the WZO's strategy. The link between the WZO and the Histadrut was the basis of what Derek Penslar calls non-capitalist constructivism, which excluded the private sector from the national project (1991, p. 130).

Despite the effectiveness of this strategy, the WZO was split regarding the approach toward the private sector. The European Zionists favored, or at least accepted, the collectivist strategy of the Labor Movement and the socialist rhetoric by which it was legitimized. The American Zionists, however, opposed it on the ground that it was inefficient from an economic perspective, claiming that national funds could be used more effectively.

Generally, the European approach prevailed, but the American Zionists were persistent and kept demanding a reconsideration of the collectivist economic strategy. In 1924, amid an economic recession in Palestine, the WZO succumbed to demands from the American Zionists and dispatched an American economic expert, Professor Elwood Mead, to evaluate the performance of the Jewish settlements in Palestine. In his report, Mead was disparaging toward the collectivist strategy of the Labor Movement. Specifically, Mead called for eliminating the collectivist contracts that had been signed between the WZO and the settlers, and recommended their replacement with individual contracts, whereby each settler would be personally liable to repay his or her own debt to the WZO. Moreover, Mead recommended appointing paid managers in each settlement to replace the current self-management approach (Rook, 2000).

Four years later, following the decision of the WZO to establish the Jewish Agency as its domestic organ in Palestine, the rift between the European and American Zionists resurfaced. The Americans demanded that Jewish settlements be designed on the basis of market-oriented and professional principles of management. "For us," they wrote it was not "a question of Zionism or not Zionism," but rather "a question of revealing the truth."[4] The ensuing debate resulted in an additional team of experts being sent to Palestine, assigned to examine the Jewish settlement strategy on the basis of "scientific standards."[5] Again, the experts' report recommended abandoning the collectivist settlement strategy in favor of an individualistic cooperative strategy. Financial support, the report asserted, should be provided as personal loans rather than through grants or philanthropy. In addition, the WZO was called to remove any limitation on immigration of capital owners and to provide them with consultation, advice and information about business opportunities in Palestine. The report also recommended encouraging the development of Jewish industry in Palestine (Palestine Commission, 1928, pp. 140–145; see also Troen, 2003, pp. 31–34).

The experts' report caused an outrage among the Labor Movement and the European Zionists, who portrayed it as an "attack against the heart of Zionism" and as a "poor and insulting document," because it ignored the national character of the Zionist project (Eylam, 1990, p. 116). Arthur Ruppin, who is considered the "architect" of the agrarian settlements, but was not part of the Labor Movement, argued that the experts "considered only the economic aspect" of the settlements while "we have to underline the Jewish and spiritual aspects [of the settlements]" (Ruppin and Bein, 1968, p. 154).

The European Zionists, as well as the Labor Movement, rejected the American "professional" approach not because it was not socialist, but rather because it was deemed inconsistent with national interests. The private sector, they argued, cares only about its own interests, not about the interests of the Jewish people as a whole. From the perspective of the Labor Movement, the economic crisis of 1927 proved this point. Following the crisis, a large proportion of Jews, mainly from the private sector, left Palestine. "The middle class came and failed," wrote Ben-Gurion. "It had to fail because it did not know the secret transformation, nor was it able to accommodate the change of values which is necessary for the realization of Zionism and the building of the country" (quoted in Sternhell, 1998, p. 277).

To understand the hostility of Ben-Gurion toward the private sector during the 1920s, it is necessary to consider the policy alternatives of the leadership regarding their capacity to govern and mobilize the private sector. Until the 1930s the international policy discourse offered two main policy paradigms that held sway concerning economic governance: (1) the paradigm of *laissez-faire*, which drew on neoclassical economics; and (2) the Marxist paradigm. *Laissez-faire* economists believed that markets are self-regulating, which means that markets, if left alone, will fluctuate around an equilibrium. Fluctuations, or business cycles, are unavoidable and the best course for governments is to avoid intervention; Marxist economists promulgated the view that markets are prone to business cycles, but they believed that markets are inherently unstable. In the Marxist view, the only way to stabilize markets is to nationalize them and replace the price mechanism with economic planning.

Faced with these two diametrically opposed policy options, Zionist policy-makers tended to embrace the collectivist policy approach. Whereas among the Labor Movement there were parties who adhered to socialist values, for Mapai, as for the WZO, the collectivist approach provided more effective policy tools to govern the nascent Jewish economy. In other words, Zionist policy-makers resisted market practices not because they opposed the private property rights on ideological grounds, but because they realized that one cannot build a nation by employing laissez-faire governing principles and then hoping a state evolves from the primordial economic soup.

What, then, made the Zionist leadership change its position regarding the private sector? It is argued here that two factors explain this change: (1) the economic success of the private sector; and (2) the penetration of new economic ideas of planned market economies. The leadership of the Labor Movement changed its approach to the private sector once it realized that those market forces could be harnessed to the national project. This realization was the product of the entry into the Zionist policy discourse of new policy ideas originating in the United States after the Great Depression. The Great Depression debunked the fantasy that free markets were self-regulating systems, and at the same time discredited the belief that the only way to govern markets is by nationalizing them. The New Deal policies and the emergent Keynesian paradigm saw the dichotomy between free markets and nationalized planned economies being superseded by a third alternative, one of regulated and governed market economies, an approach often called a "mixed economy." These ideas entered the Zionist policy discourse, opening up ways of framing urgent policy problems and designing a proper response.

It must be made clear, that it is not argued here that specific policy instruments were imported from the United States. The New Deal policies and the

Keynesian policy ideas were designed to address a concrete problem: a situation in which a skilled labor force is unemployed, production facilities stand idle, and available credit lies unused within the context of a developed economy (Barber, 1990; Collins, 1990). This was plainly not the situation in 1930s Palestine. What is argued here is that the New Deal and elements of the Keynesian paradigm inspired local policy-makers in Israel to think anew fundamental conventions regarding economic governance. Particularly, policy-makers were inclined to reconsider deterministic and static conceptions of the economy, which had been assumed both by the laissez-faire (or the neoclassical) approach and by the Marxist tradition. These approaches were replaced by a more dynamic conception of the economy, which assigned a more active role to the state or state-like institutions in governing the economy.

Objecting to the productivization ideology

The policy ideas advocated by David Horowitz objected to fundamental elements of the agrarian paradigm. One of these elements was the productivization ideology: the belief that for various reasons, the Jewish governing organizations should prioritize productive—that is, agricultural—labor. In the local Zionist-Jewish context, the debates between the "old" and "new" ideas were not concerned—as in the advanced countries—with issues of economic stability, but rather were focused on issues that concerned planning the economy for the purpose of immigration absorption. The new imported ideas inspired the new economic policy discourse within the Zionist organizations.

David Horowitz was one of the first to identify the pertinence of the new policy ideas emerging in the United States to the Jewish economy in Palestine, and he used them to disparage the old agrarian paradigm, which he called "the ideology of productivization." "So far," he wrote in his article in the *Cooperative Bulletin* in 1935, "all these analyses … have been made from a purely productive standpoint, namely the perspective of the capitalist era whose ideal was productivization" (Horowitz, 1935, pp. 156–157). Today, he argued, the national organization should "deproductivize," i.e., shift workers away from productive sectors (agriculture) to "unproductive" sectors (services and trade). This process, he claimed, was "no longer an economic anachronism" as the agrarian paradigm assumed, but it was the "most progressive capitalist phenomenon" in all advanced economies (ibid., pp. 156–157). In more succinct terminology, Horowitz called for the WZO to allocate resources to trade, services and manufacturing, instead of agriculture.

To acknowledge the significance of Horowitz's recommendations, his article must be put in context. When he put forward his recommendations, the private Jewish sector, which specialized in services and manufacturing, was flourishing. During the 1930s, the Jewish economy was going through a semi-industrial revolution: between 1930 and 1935 the Jewish population doubled as a result of the immigration of middle-class Jews from Germany.[6] The immigrants, being relatively wealthy, brought their own capital with them and they facilitated an investment boom in the private sector.[7] The engine of the economy was the construction sector, which increased six-fold in the 1931–1935 period, together with services, industry, and manufacturing which expanded 2.5-fold. During the same period, citrus production grew 2.4-fold, while the rest of the agricultural sector stood out because it only expanded 1.7-fold (see Table 2.1). Horowitz's recommendation was that the WZO should stop rowing against the current by allocating funds to agriculture.

The publication of Horowitz's article raised a controversy among economic experts. The most senior among the Jewish economic experts was Dr. Ludwig Gruenbaum (later to change his name to Arie Ga'athon), a researcher at the *Economic Research Institute* (ERI), directed by Arthur Ruppin.[8] Gruenbaum published a response to Horowitz's article in which he attempted to pull the rug from under Horowitz's argument. Gruenbaum argued that there was no sense in comparing "old" and "young" nations as Horowitz did. Yes, in nations such as Germany the size of the "unproductive" sectors was large and growing, but this took place only after years of development. The Jewish economy, argued Gruenbaum, was young and therefore needed a larger agricultural sector. Gruenbaum concluded that the "enormous share of trade (16 percent) and of professionals [Miktzo'ot Chofshiyim] (10 percent) [of the JNP], which Horowitz emphasized to be disproportionally large relative to the low share of agriculture (15.5 percent), is no doubt a sociological inheritance of the Diaspora." It was "an inorganic relic of the social composition of the Diaspora" (Gruenbaum, 1935, pp. 226–227). Gruenbaum's conclusion was that the national organizations should continue their support of the agrarian settlements.

Horowitz's notion of "Deproductivization"—the transfer of workers from the agrarian sector to trade, manufacturing and services—assumed that the governing organization could fundamentally shape the structure of the economy. This assumption was rejected by another economist, who also published a response to Horowitz's article but signed only his initials, M.Z. The capitalist economies have their "blind, stychic laws" and therefore it is impossible to "change the economic structure in order to avoid contradictions," he argued (M.Z., 1935, pp. 328–329). The issue of market governability was a hot topic in the mid-1930s, as seen by an author in the *Cooperative Bulletin* portraying "economic planning" as a "fashionable topic today" (Brumberger, 1935, p. 251).

Table 2.1 Jewish net product by branches in selected years (thousands of Palestine pounds, 1936 prices)

	Citrus	*Other agricultural branches*	*Industry and manufacture*	*Construction*	*Services*	*Total*
1931	1200	675	1528	482	4097	7149
1935	2880	1145	3785	2888	10,409	19,213
Increase (%)	240	170	248	599	254	269

Source: Calculated from Metzer (1998, pp. 226–242 Tables A11, A12, A20, A21).

At the beginning of 1934, Jewish experts still adhered to the view that "there is absolutely no way, in any kind of politics, to turn the capitalist economy, which is based on competition, free enterprise and class conflict, into a stable economy with no business-cycles" (Naphtali, 1934, p. 10). However, alternative voices became more frequent and louder. By the end of the year, another author was claiming that "only the future will prove to what extent private-capitalist economy can successfully accommodate elements of economic planning" (Cidrovitch, 1934, p. 275). Despite skepticism, the author recommended starting building mechanisms of economic planning on a small scale in the Jewish economy.

> We all hope that in the near future, with the establishment of a central institution for all supervision associations … the idea of economic planning will infiltrate our economic life, and our primitive economic conception will vanish to be replaced by higher guidance and monitoring of our economy.
>
> (Cidrovitch, 1934, p. 277)

Erwin Brumberger, a researcher at the ERI, argued that ideas of market planning originating in industrial countries to "stabilize the economy, that is, to protect price and production levels from fluctuations … to eliminate the periodic crises … and to bring the suffering masses back to the production system," could be used in Palestine for different purposes:

> We need a planned economy in Palestine today, not in order to bring the unemployed workers back to the production system or to stimulate the paralyzed production … but in order to absorb the Jewish people in the Near East economy.
>
> (Brumberger, 1935)

The planned market economy, argued Brumberger, was more useful from the perspective of the Zionist interests than either the socialist or the laissez-faire models of economic governance. An economic strategy based on laissez-faire principles would not enable the Zionist movement to promote "Jewish labor" in the private sector. "In free economic conditions of a possessive market economy the Arab worker would always prevail over the costlier Jewish worker." On the other hand, nationalizing the economy would deter investors and stifle the flow of capital. The movement toward the planning of the market economy is "strong in large and rich countries … such as the United States and England," and therefore adopting it would not deter potential investors. "The entire future of the Jewish people in Palestine depends on these new economic systems" (ibid.).

David Horowitz: from *Hashomer Hatzair* to the free market

David Horowitz (1899–1979) was born in the Galician town of Derhovich, Poland, in an upper-middle-class family. In Poland, he joined the *Hashomer*

Hatzair (The Young Guard) movement, where he claimed to have found a combination of Zionism, socialism and a type of humanism. (Horowitz, 1970, p. 45). He immigrated to Palestine in 1920 within the framework of his youth movement which in Palestine formed a relatively small socialist faction. In 1924, he joined the Labor Battalion (*Gdud haavoda*), a communist faction within the labor movement, and he took part in formulating its political precepts. He described the Labor Battalion as "a unit in the revolutionary class struggle fighting to liberate the working class" (Horowitz, 1924, p. 537). Given Horowitz's socialist background, what were the intellectual source of his ideas?

In 1927, Horowitz experienced a transformative event that changed his career and worldview. Following a series of political clashes between the far left-wing faction in the Histadrut, the Labor Battalion, and the Center-Left dominant parties, several members of the Labor Battalion, to which Horowitz belonged, left Palestine for the Soviet Union in order to realize their communist vision in a commune. Their journey ended with them being executed by Stalin. This event left a deep imprint on Horowitz and he decided to resign from the Histadrut council, to which he was elected as a representative of the Labor Battalion. He moved to the city of Tel-Aviv. "Although the country was seething with despair and bitterness," he wrote, "I resolved to resign from the public sphere and look after my own affairs" (Horowitz, 1970, p. 198). This proved to be the closing chapter of Horowitz's socialist era.

In Tel-Aviv, after working as a journalist for a short period he was employed as an economic advisor by the American Economic Bureau in Palestine, an organization founded by American Zionists aiming to promote Jewish private entrepreneurship in Mandatory Palestine. The American Economic Bureau was established following the recommendation of the *Report of the Joint Palestine Survey Commission* (1928). The report recommended establishing an organization that "would provide detailed and comprehensive information about the conditions prevailing in Palestine" for "wealthy immigrants" (Palestine Commission, 1928, p. 140). The American Zionists sought to encourage immigration of middle-class families who would develop the private Jewish sector. In June 1931, the Zionist Organization of America published "*A Program to Accelerate the Absorptive Capacity of Palestine*." The program rejected the strategy of selective immigration implemented by the WZO and the idea that the absorptive capacity of Palestine depended on the number of farmers. The program stated that there was "practically no limit to Jewish urban immigration, if industry and commerce can be developed to provide employment for the newcomers."[9] At the time, in 1931, this statement was controversial, as it undermined the settlement strategy of the WZO. However, within a few years, the leadership of the WZO and the Labor Movement had embraced it and it became one of the central claims used to legitimize the Jewish demand for mass immigration to Palestine.

Following the publication of the program, the American Zionists founded the Economic Committee, which had a "bureau" in Palestine. The task of the Economic Bureau in Palestine was to "be a source of information, advice and assistance to American settlers in Palestine" and to lay "the foundations of a wide and continuous program of Zionist education and habituating the Zionist public to think of Palestine in terms of constructive economics" (Brodie, 1935, p. 46). Horowitz was employed as a consultant in this bureau and his job was to provide aid to Jewish immigrants, who arrived in Palestine with some initial capital and production expertise, and assist them in obtaining information in their field. In his own words, he "provided data, analyzed it and supplied it objectively for entrepreneurs and investors" (Horowitz, 1970, p. 209).

It seems most plausible that Horowitz's ideas in his 1935 article were shaped during the years he spent as an economic consultant at the Economic Bureau. Horowitz's recommendation regarding the prioritization of the development of non-agrarian sectors were ideas he most likely absorbed from the views of the American Zionists. However, what makes Horowitz a key figure in the reception of these new policy ideas is not the mere fact that he expressed innovative policy ideas and an essay but that he also played a meaningful role in injecting these ideas into the inner circle of policy-makers. Shortly after the publication of his controversial article, Horowitz was nominated by David Ben-Gurion to be the Secretary of the Jewish Agency's Economic Department, a position comparable to that of Director General in a Ministry of Finance. He also became Ben-Gurion's economic advisor and represented the Jewish Agency in international forums.

The economic consequences of the national conflict

The factors that made Horowitz's policy ideas so essential to Ben-Gurion were not only economic, but also political-national. Perhaps the political-national implications of Horowitz's ideas were more pertinent than the economic ones. Horowitz's article was published during a period of the escalation of the conflict between the Jewish and Arab communities in Palestine. Ben-Gurion believed that the conflict could not be resolved peacefully: he believed that only by creating a Jewish majority in Palestine, would the objective of a Jewish state be realized. The problem for Ben-Gurion was that most of the Zionist experts, who adhered to the agrarian paradigm, rejected the viability of mass immigration. Horowitz's policy ideas, however, explained why mass immigration was viable. Horowitz, therefore, solved Ben-Gurion's political problem.

From the beginning of the British Mandate in Palestine in July 1922 and until the appointment of the Peel Commission in 1937, the British government followed the assumption that the main factors limiting Jewish immigration to Palestine were economic rather than political. The government restricted Jewish immigration according to the principle of the economic absorptive capacity of the country (Halamish, 2003, p. 180). This criterion was accepted by the WZO, which shared the view that massive immigration beyond the country's absorptive capacity would be detrimental to the Zionist cause.[10] Based on this view, the WZO employed a selective immigration policy. The WZO, with the cooperation of the Labor Movement, restricted the immigration of Jews to Palestine on the basis of age, health, status and ideological commitment of the potential immigrant. During the British Mandate, up to 80 percent of those who wished to immigrate were rejected by the WZO. As Ruppin wrote, “It would of course be preferable if only strong and healthy persons came to settle in Palestine, so that we would be assured of a strong and healthy succeeding generation” (1936, p. 78).

The selective immigration policy was part and parcel of the perception that the conflict between the Jews and Arab communities would be able to be settled peacefully because Jewish colonization did not threaten Arab interests. As long as Jewish immigration was selective and restricted, the WZO could argue that the Jewish settlements did not pose a threat to the interests of the Arab community. This was one of the reasons why the left-wing faction in the Zionist Movement, *Brit Shalom*, which promoted a bi-national state in Palestine, insisted on selective immigration. During the 1920s, conflicts between the Jewish and the Arab communities occurred but they were not perceived as a fully-fledged national conflict.

The event that changed the perceptions of both Jewish and Arab leaders regarding the nature of the conflict was the outburst of violent clashes in 1929. Hillel Cohen rightfully points out that it was in this year that the “relations between Jews and Arabs changed radically,” and it was this year that “shaped the consciousness of both sides for decades thereafter” (2015, p. xi). In the first half of the 1930s the Jewish economy continued to grow rapidly, outpacing the Arab economy. Between 1929 and 1933, the national product per capita of the Jewish economy grew almost three times faster than that of the Arab economy (Metzer, 1998, p. 242, Table A.22). Between 1932 and 1935, the Jewish population grew more than six times faster than the Arab population (ibid., p. 29, Table 2.1). The growing tension reached a climax point in 1936 with the economic slowdown. The view among the Arab community was that the flow of Jewish immigrants and their economic success, in addition to their massive purchases of land, endangered Arab national aspirations (Peel, 1937). As a result, the Arab leadership announced a general strike and Arab groups conducted attacks on Jewish and British targets.

The escalation of the conflict strengthened the militaristic school within the Zionist movement, which interpreted the conflict between the two communities as a national conflict that would be resolved by military means (Ben-Eliezer, 1998). This interpretation of the relationship between the two national communities in Palestine required a reconsideration of the selective immigration policy and a shift to a mass immigration policy in order to create a Jewish majority in Palestine.

Demand-side economics and the economic absorptive capacity

In the early 1930s, with the escalation of the national conflict between the Jewish and Arab communities, the Zionist leadership, headed by Ben-Gurion, sought a transition from selective to mass immigration. The change opened up a conflict of economic ideas between the British government and the Jewish Agency: the British argued that mass immigration was an economically unrealistic policy, whereas the Jewish Agency claimed otherwise. The Jewish Agency's ammunition in this conflict of ideas were ideas of demand-side economics.

The concept of economic absorptive capacity was embraced in 1922 by the British government as an official criterion for determining the pace of Jewish immigration to Palestine (Halamish, 2003, p. 180). During the 1920s, there was conflict between the British government and the WZO regarding the immigration policy: both had an interest in restricting Jewish immigration to Palestine. According to the agrarian paradigm, the numbers of immigrants the country could have absorbed each year were limited. A higher rate of immigration could have created a crisis.

During the 1930s, Ben-Gurion pressed for a change, and the Jewish Agency now argued that the economic absorptive capacity was unlimited. Horowitz was among the key economic experts who provided Ben-Gurion's political objective with a sound economic foundation.

In a document dated 1936, Horowitz mocked the British experts, who had claimed six years earlier that Palestine would not be able to feed a much larger population size than that already residing in Palestine. "Since the experts delivered themselves of this verdict," wrote Horowitz,

> the Jewish population of Palestine has more than doubled, the Arab population has increased by 30%, and the general increase in the country's wealth has surpassed by several times the total progress of the post-war [World War I] decade, on which the inquiries were based.... It would appear that the static notion of "economic capacity of absorption," on which all analysis was based, is in need of re-consideration.
>
> (Horowitz, 1936)

Horowitz argued that the economic absorptive capacity of a country cannot be reliably calculated because immigration itself is a catalyst for economic development and therefore creates the conditions for its own absorption. Immigrants bring with them capital, labor, skills and purchasing power, all of which boost the economy:

> In a world in which an increase in purchasing power becomes the main condition for any form of economic growth, the mere existence of a high immigration rate, which implies in practice an increase in purchasing power, is a sufficient basis for the expansion of production.

In other words, "the conditions for absorption are created not by natural factors but by immigration itself" (ibid.).

It is difficult to fully ascertain Horowitz's sources of influence. The significance he assigned to purchasing power as a catalyst of development echoes Keynes' ideas of demand side economics. However, there is no direct evidence for such a link. As Yuval Yonay has shown, ideas of demand management were not unique to Keynes and similar policy practices were common in many countries (1998, p. 64).

Horowitz's archive offers some evidence that his views were influenced by Imre Ferenczi, an American Keynesian economist. Ferenczi was a world-reknowned expert on immigration economics, and in 1929 he published *International Migration*, which was based on research he had conducted in cooperation with the American National Bureau of Economic Research and the International Labor Organization. Ten year later Ferenczi published another title, *The Synthetic Optimum of Population* (1938), in which he presented a new method to calculate the optimal size of a population that a given territory could support. A copy of the publication reached Horowitz, as we learn from an excerpt of the text found in his archive.

In *The Synthetic Optimum of Population*, Ferenczi distinguished between four types of "population densities": the first three—arithmetic density, physiological density and agrarian density—all depend on natural resources. These indices are important in under-developed economies in which agriculture is the dominant sector and in which international trade is under-developed. Contrariwise, in developed economies, the fourth type of density—the general economic density—is more significant. According to Ferenczi, as quoted by a document prepared by Horowitz and the economist Rita Hinden, the general economic density is determined by a large number of variables, which include the quality of the labor force, the level of industrialization, technological development and investment patterns (Horowitz and Hinden, 1938a).

Fereczi's conceptualization of the notion of economic absorptive capacity provided Horowitz with a solid intellectual basis to support his own position, regarding the absorptive capacity of Palestine. Horowitz's argument regarding the significance of the quality of the labor force, of technical progress and industrialization, would go on to become a central discourse of the Jewish Agency, which was designed to legitimize its political demands on solid economic foundations. As early as November 1938, Ben-Gurion wrote in his diary:

> The view that Mandatory Palestine is too small and that it cannot absorb a mass of refugees is false and shallow. This view ignores the personal factor: the settlements in Palestine include 450,000 [Jews], each of which possess a farm which is ready to expand through absorption of immigrants. 30 years ago, we needed 250 dunam [acres, a.k.] per family, like the Arabs, now only 20 dunam.
>
> (Ben-Gurion Diaries, November 22, 1938)

The Peel Commission

The event that signifies the institutionalization of the rapid development paradigm and the demise of the agrarian paradigm, was the creation of the Peel Commission that investigated the situation in Palestine following the Arab revolt.

Ben-Gurion ensured that all the representatives of the Jewish Agency presented a narrative based on the idea that, if industrialized, there would be no upper limit to the economic absorptive capacity of Palestine.

The conflict between the Jewish and Arab communities deteriorated in 1936 with the outbreak of the Arab Revolt, which lasted three years until its final suppression in 1939. According to the representatives of the Arab community, the revolt and the strike were a response to the economic and political expansion of the Jewish community. They argued that the rising influx of Jewish immigration, their economic success and their policy of land purchasing endangered the national interests of the Arab community (Peel, 1937). Contrary to the riots of 1929, this time the violence was also directed against the British with a demand that they restrict the massive influx of Jewish immigrants and renege on the Balfour Declaration.

In response to instability in the region, the League of Nations mandated the British government to establish the Palestine Royal Commission in 1937—known as the Peel Commission—in order to "ascertain the underlying causes of the disturbances which broke out in Palestine in the middle of April" and to inquire into the manner in which the Mandate for Palestine was being implemented "in relation to the obligations of the Mandatory towards the Arabs and the Jews respectively."[11]

Within the Zionist leadership there was no agreement as to the way the Arab demand to restrict the Jewish immigration should be countered. Ruppin, the Director of the ERI, and Gruenbaum, still adhered to the agrarian paradigm, whereas Ben-Gurion and the Jewish Agency, opted to embrace Horowitz's new ideas.

Arthur Ruppin established the ERI in 1935. The objective of the Institute, which was financed by the WZO, was to "investigate methodically economic life in Palestine, examine the possibilities of its development, and provide Executives [of the Jewish Agency] with the necessary material for its economic and practical operation."[12] The Institute had an independent budget, and Ruppin was a member of the board of directors. This meant that Ruppin enjoyed a high level of managerial independence and he was not restricted by the local political leadership of the Labor Movement. Ruppin assembled a group of young economists who had recently arrived in Palestine from Germany, among whom Ludwig Gruenbaum was the most senior. Several months after its establishment, the ERI was already busy with the preparations for the arrival of the Royal Commission. Ruppin, as the architect of the agrarian paradigm, continued to advocate it and most of the researchers in the Institute followed his tune.

Ruppin expected the Institute to take an active role in the preparations for the Peel Commission. After all, the Institute employed the most senior economists operating in Palestine at the time: Arthur Ruppin, Ludwig Gruenbaum and Alfred Bonné. However, at that stage, Ben-Gurion had lost trust in Ruppin. "Ruppin's testimony poses a difficult question," Ben-Gurion wrote in his diary. "I believe his testimony could be dangerous because Ruppin does not distinguish between conversing with Zionists and conversing with the British, and he does not take into consideration the political conclusions that a non-Jew may draw from his arguments" (BGD, November 15, 1936). Ben-Gurion's issue with Ruppin was not only personal. Ben-Gurion's objective was to "fight in the Commission for large-scale immigration." He wanted to prove "not only the necessity of immigration—but also its viability" (BGD, August 11, 1936).

When Ben-Gurion marginalized Ruppin, he already had an alternative economic consultant: David Horowitz, whom he had appointed as the Secretary of the Economic Department at the Jewish Agency in 1935. The Economic Department was created in 1933 and Eliezer Kaplan was appointed to head it. Unfortunately, the archives do not reveal the exact process that led Ben-Gurion to the decision to appoint Horowitz to this position. However, we do know that in October 1935 Ben-Gurion met with Horowitz for a conversation "about the economic situation and the political steps that must be taken to increase employment opportunities, and especially to secure the position of existing industry and to grant preferential terms for new industry" (BGD, October 10, 1935). Ben-Gurion asked Horowitz to put his ideas in writing. A few days later Ben-Gurion had a meeting in London with the British High Commissioner for Palestine, Sir Arthur Wauchope, and with the Secretary of State for Dominion Affairs, Malcolm Macdonald. Macdonald urged Ben-Gurion to do more to encourage industrial development in Palestine. "Palestine cannot do without industry. If we want a large Jewish settlement, industrial development is necessary. Industry could absorb many [immigrants] and fast. It is inconceivable that the whole country depends on oranges" (BGD, October 16, 1935). Ben-Gurion reported on his visit to the Jewish Agency's Executive Committee saying that:

> There was a clear impression that the [British] government maintains a positive view of this issue [industry]. They regard industrial development and its expansion as necessary for the absorption of mass immigration.... Following our discussion with the [British] government ... I was informed by confidential sources that the High Commissioner believes an immigration of 60,000 requires the government to provide active and systematic support for industrial development.
>
> (Jewish Agency, November 10, 1935)

This sequence of events provides a plausible explanation as to Ben-Gurion's considerations: Horowitz's understanding of the political economic situation in Palestine was consistent with the perceptions of the British government, as well as with Ben-Gurion's own aspirations for the Zionist vision.

The Economic Department operated as a quasi-Ministry of Finance, and Horowitz operated as its quasi-general manager. In this position, he developed close contacts with all the key leaders of the Jewish community: Ben-Gurion, Chaim Weizmann and Moshe Sharet. By the time the Peel Commission arrived, all the policy-makers at the Jewish Agency embraced Horowitz's concepts.

In his testimony to the Commission, Ruppin focused on the unique role of agriculture in the Zionist project. In a very long speech, he unfolded the history of Jewish agricultural settlements from the beginning of the twentieth century, the obstacles they faced, the successes they enjoyed, and the ideological foundation on which they were based. "All Jews came from cities; they did not have rural habits or agricultural training." The Zionist movement established "collective farms," the aim of whichwas to "improve the skills of the settlers" and to "provide our workers cheap accommodation." Ruppin attempted to persuade the Committee that "we could transform small Palestine into a large Palestine without territorial expansion, only by increasing the productivity of the land" (Kleiman, 1987, pp. 144–148). Ruppin was the only representative of the Zionist organizations still adhering to the agrarian paradigm.

Chaim Weizmann, the President of the WZO, explained that "the development of industry in Palestine represents the creation of an entirely new source of wealth [that] Palestine would never have had at its disposal" (ibid., p. 220). Segfried Hoofien, Director General of the Anglo-Palestine Bank, began his testimony by saying that:

> It is only natural that when we speak about general economic aspects, our evidence is likely to centre around urban settlements, and again, inasmuch as industry stands at the centre of urban settlement, we must pay a very fair amount of attention to it.

The strategy of industrial and urban development, continued Hoofien, rejected the "idea that it is possible to put an ultimate limit, calculable today in exact figures, on the possibilities of urban colonization." He concluded his statement by claiming that "there is room for a large urban population to come in" (ibid., pp. 227–232). This conceptualization was the hallmark of the paradigm of rapid development: there was no calculable limit to the economic absorption capacity of the country. Moshe Shertok, Director of the Political Department of the Jewish Agency, also followed the same line of argument, claiming that the immigrants themselves brought the means of their own absorption.

> The absorptive capacity of Palestine is in far greater measure due to the fact that the Jews are now returning to the country and bringing with them their capital, their scientific resources and their physical power, rather than to the natural condition in which the Jews found Palestine originally.
>
> (Ibid., pp. 227–232)

The testimony of the Zionist delegates before the Peel Commission was a milestone in the consolidation of the new Zionist policy paradigm, the paradigm of rapid development and mass immigration, which provided the ideational foundation for a new developmental strategy. Within three years, Horowitz's controversial ideas expressed in a supplement of a daily newspaper became the official position of the WZO in an international forum.

International recognition

The testimonies of the Zionist leaders at the Peel Commission marked the discursive victory of the paradigm of rapid development over the agrarian paradigm within the Zionist policy discourse. In the following years, Horowitz's ideas also won the recognition of foreign experts.

After the Commission published its report, the ERI of the Jewish Agency, published a collection of David Horowitz's and Rita Hinden's memoranda and studies under the title *Economic Survey of Palestine: With Special Reference to the Years 1936 and 1937* (Horowitz and Hinden, 1938b). Despite the fact that the authors were associated with a political organization, it was received as a scientific and reliable document in academic circles. A review published in the *Journal of the Royal Central Asian Society*, stated: "It is a relief to find a book dealing with recent events in Palestine which is so free from all trace of the controversies associated with that subject." The author described the survey as a "dispassionate account" and "a serious attempt to apply scientific methods to the study of certain economic phenomena of great interest." According to the review, it was Horowitz's "realist" analysis that convinced the members of the Royal Commission that there was no upper calculable limit to the absorption capacity of the country, which led them to abandon the previous calculative method to determine the scope of immigration to Palestine (Street, 1939).

Conclusion

The 1930s was in several senses a transformative decade in the political economy of the Jewish settlement in Palestine. The escalation of the conflict between the Jews and the Arabs—with the riots of 1929 and the Arab Revolt of 1936—led to a reconsideration of the Zionist national-economic strategy of selective immigration and gradual development. This change, along with the desire to rapidly achieve a Jewish majority population in Palestine, created a demand for a new economic strategy, which would enable the Zionist leadership to enhance the pace of immigration and settlement. In addition, the private sector had already developed a fledgling industrial base without any assistance from the national organization, a fact that led many to question the exclusion of the private sector from the national project and the exclusive focus on agricultural settlement.

Internationally, the economic policy discourse changed, with the emergence of new ideas regarding the feasibility of governing market economies. The response of the United States to the Great Depression was based on these new policy ideas, which later entered into Zionist policy discourse and were used to frame and offer new solutions to domestic policy problems. Particularly, the new policy ideas enabled local policy-makers to think about the economy in dynamic terms, which were consistent with the overarching policy objective of creating a Jewish majority in Palestine.

The combination of the economic prosperity of the private sector, the intensification of the conflict and the arrival of new economic ideas of market planning, gave rise to a new set of policy ideas regarding Jewish statehood, regarding the possibilities of economic governance, as well as about the framing of the interaction between the Jewish and the Arab population. The arrival of demand-ideas—even in their nascent form—was essential for the Zionist movement to imagine the viability of Jewish statehood.

It would be erroneous to argue that Israeli capitalism was formed in the 1930s. As many scholars have shown, Israeli capitalism certainly had its roots in the early twentieth century (Gozansky, 1986). However, it was in the 1930s that the Israeli capitalism acquired certain features, that would characterize it in the future. It was during the 1930s that the Zionist leadership—including the leadership of Mapai—recognized the opportunities that a planned market economy would provide for nation-building. Market forces, it was acknowledged, could be molded and mobilized to be used as another instrument by which the Jewish polity would fight its way to statehood.

Notes

1 The journal *The Cooperative Bulletin* (*Ha-meshek ha-shitufi*) was issued fortnightly. Its first editor was Berl Katzenelson, followed by Itzhak Galfat. The journal was a venue for experts from the labor movements and the Jewish Cooperative bodies. Also, experts form the national Jewish organizations published in the journal.

2 Throughout, this book will use interchangeably the terms "Jewish leadership," "Zionist leadership" or "national organizations." These terms signify the quasi-state institutions that governed the Jewish economy in Palestine.

3 Economic expenditure did include expenditure on security and social services. The "national budget" included that of the International Zionist Federation, and from 1929 on, the budgets of the Jewish Agency, the National Committee, the Zionist Women Organization, Hadassah, and the Histadrut Trade Union Federation.

4 Louis Marshal to James Marshal, May 9, 1927, quoted in Eylam (1990, p. 95).

5 The delegation consisted of British, American and German Jewish businessmen. It included Lord Melchett (Alfred Mond), British industrialist and financier, Lee K. Frankel, who was involved in Jewish American welfare and health organizations, Felix M. Warburg, an American banker of German descent, and Oscar Wassermann, a German banker (Palestine Commission, 1928, p. 9).

6 At the end of 1931, the Jewish sector consisted of 168,410 Jews and at the end of 1935 it consisted of 355,157 Jews (Metzer, 1998, p. 215, Table A.1).

7 In 1934, capital inflow was 3.5 times greater than in 1931 (ibid., p. 254, Table A.24).

8 Ludwig Gruenbaum had immigrated to Palestine shortly after receiving his PhD in political-economy from the University of Berlin.

9 The full citation is:

> The resources of private initiative in this field will have to be looked to for its further development. Then again, there is definite limit, even though it is remote, to Jewish agricultural immigration. Land which is arable and can be made arable in Palestine is, after all, limited and the fellaheen must be considered in the ultimate division of it. There is practically no limit to Jewish urban immigration, if industry and commerce can be developed to provide employment for the newcomers.
>
> (Brodie, 1935, p. 14)

10 On the debates on the concept of the economic absorptive capacity of Palestine, see Halamish (2003) and Troen (2003).
11 "Mandates Palestine Report of the Palestine Royal Commission (July 1937)." Available at: www.jewishvirtuallibrary.org/jsource/History/peel1.html
12 Report to the 20th Congress, pp. 416–418, CZA, K66.

References

Barber, W.J., 1990. Government as a Laboratory for Economic Learning in the Years of the Democratic Roosevelt. In: Furner, M.O. and Supple, B. (Eds.), *The State and Economic Knowledge: The American and British Experience*. Woodrow Wilson International Center for Scholars, Washington, DC, pp. 103–137.

Ben-Eliezer, U., 1998. *The Making of Israeli Militarism*. Indiana University Press, Bloomington, IN.

Ben-Gurion, D., 1997. Charoshet [Industry]. In: Gorny, Y. and Grinberg, I. (Eds.), *The Israeli Labor Movement*. Open University Press, Tel Aviv, pp. 1093–1096 (in Hebrew).

Bertisch, A.M., 1981. *A Study of the Political-Economic Philosophy of Arthur Ruppin and His Role in the Economic Development of the Zionist Settlement in Palestine from 1907 to 1943*. University Microfilms International, Ann Arbor, MI.

BGD, various dates. Ben-Gurion's diary. Ben-Gurion Archive, Section: Diaries.

Bloom, E., 2007. What "The Father" Had in Mind? Arthur Ruppin (1876–1943), Cultural Identity, Weltanschauung and Action. *History of European Ideas* 33, 330–349.

Bloom, E., 2011. *Arthur Ruppin and the Production of Pre-Israeli Culture*. Brill, Leiden.

Brodie, I.B., 1935. *A Retrospect and a Program; The Acceleration of the Absorptive Capacity of Palestine*. The American Economic Committee for Palestine, New York.

Brumberger, E., 1935. The Jewish Enterprise and Economic Planning in Palestine. *Cooperative Bulletin* 14–15, 252–254 (in Hebrew).

Cidrovitch, G., 1934. Planned Economy and the Supervision Association. *Cooperative Bulletin* 19, 166–169 (in Hebrew).

Cohen, H., 2015. *Year Zero of the Arab-Israeli Conflict 1929*. Brandeis University Press, Waltham, MA.

Collins, R.M., 1990. The Emergence of Economic Growthmanship in the United States: Federal Policy and Economic Knowledge in the Truman Years. In: Furner, M.O. and Supple, B. (Eds.), *The State and Economic Knowledge: The American and British Experience*. Woodrow Wilson International Center for Scholars, Washington, DC, pp. 103–137.

Eylam, I., 1990. *The Jewish Agency*. The Zionist Library, Jerusalem (in Hebrew).

Gozansky, T., 1986. *Development of Capitalism in Palestine*. Haifa University Publishing Company, Haifa (in Hebrew).

Gruenbaum, A.L., 1935. More About the Question of Productivization. *Cooperative Bulletin* 12–13, 224–227 (in Hebrew).

Halamish, A., 2003. Immigration According to the Economic Absorptive Capacity. In: Bareli, A. and Karlinsky, N. (Eds.), *Economy and Society During the Mandate*. The Center for Ben-Gurion Legacy, Sdeh-Boker, pp. 179–216.

Hart, M.B., 2000. *Social Science and the Politics of Modern Jewish Identity*. Stanford University Press, Stanford, CA.

Horowitz, D., 1924. About Our Position in the Histadrut. In: *Me'cha'iyeynu* [From Our Life] (in Hebrew).

Horowitz, D., 1935. Arguments Against the Theory of Productivization. *Cooperative Bulletin* 9–10, 154–158 (in Hebrew).

Horowitz, D., 1936. Jewish Colonization in Palestine, May, Central Zionist Archive, S25/5818.

Horowitz, D., 1970. Ha-Etmol Sheli [My Early Days]. Shoḳen, Jerusalem (in Hebrew).

Horowitz, D. and Hinden, R., 1938a. *The Synthetic Population Optimum* (Ferenczi). The Economic Research Institute, Tel Aviv, June 1938, Central Zionist Archive, S3/1787/6.

Horowitz, D. and Hinden, R., 1938b. *Economic Survey of Palestine, with Special Reference to the Years 1936 and 1937*. Economic Research Institute of the Jewish Agency for Palestine, Tel-Aviv.

Jewish Agency, various dates. *Minutes of the Jewish Agency Executive Meetings*. Central Zionist Archive.

Kleiman, S.A. (Ed.), 1987. *The Palestine Royal Commission 1937*. Garland Publishing, New York.

Kolat, I., 1997. Ha'poel Ha'tza'ir—from Conquer of Labor to Consecration of Labor. In: Gorny, Y. and Grinberg, I. (Eds.), *The Israeli Labor Movement*. Open University Press, Jerusalem, pp. 137–169 (in Hebrew).

Krampf, A., 2010. Reception of the Developmental Approach in the Economic Discourse of Mandatory Palestine, 1934–1938. *Israel Studies* 15 (2), 80–103.

Metzer, J., 1978. Economic Structure and National Goals: The Jewish National Home in Interwar Palestine. *The Journal of Economic History* 38, 101–119.

Metzer, J., 1998. *The Divided Economy of Mandatory Palestine*. Cambridge University Press, Cambridge.

M.Z., 1935. More About the Question of Productivization. *Cooperative Bulletin* 18–19, 327–329 (in Hebrew).

Naphtali, P., 1934. Is Anti-Cyclical Policy Possible in Palestine? *Cooperative Bulletin* 1–2, 10–12 (in Hebrew).

Palestine Commission, 1928. *Reports of the Experts Submitted to the Joint Palestine Survey Commission*. Press of Daniels Printing, Boston.

Peel, 1937. *The Peel Commission Report*, Secretary of State of the Colonies to the United Kingdom Parliament, (July 1937), Jewish Virtual Library. Available at: www.jewishvirtuallibrary.org/text-of-the-peel-commission-report (accessed April 5, 2017).

Penslar, D.J., 1991. *Zionism and Technocracy: The Engineering of Jewish Settlement in Palestine, 1870–1918*. Indiana University Press, Bloomington, IN.

Rook, R.E., 2000. An American in Palestine: Elwood Mead and Zionist Water Resource Planning, 1923–1936. *Arab Studies Quarterly* 22, 71–89.

Ruppin, A., 1922. Economic Activities in Palestine: report submitted to the XIIth Zionist Congress held at Carlsbad. World Zionist Organization, Jerusalem.

Ruppin, A., 1936. The Selection of the Fittest. In: *Three Decades of Palestine: Speeches and Papers on the Upbuilding of the Jewish National Home*. Schocken Press, Jerusalem, pp. 74–78.

Ruppin, A., 1973. *The Jews in the Modern World*. Arno Press, New York.

Ruppin, A. and Bein, A., 1968. *Pirke ḥayai* [My Life]. Am Oved, Tel-Aviv (in Hebrew).

Shilo, M., 1988. *Experiments of Settlements*. Yad Yitzhak Ben Zvi, Jerusalem (in Hebrew).

Sternhell, Z., 1998. *The Founding Myths of Israel: Nationalism, Socialism, and the Making of the Jewish State*. Princeton University Press, Princeton, NJ.

Street, S.H., 1939. A Review of an *Economic Survey of Palestine*. By D. Horowitz and R. Hinden. *Journal of the Royal Central Asian Society* 16, 518–520.

Troen, S.I., 2003. *Imagining Zion: Dreams, Designs, and Realities in a Century of Jewish Settlement*. Yale University Press, New Haven, CT.

Yonay, Y.P., 1998. *The Struggle Over the Soul of Economics: Institutionalist and Neoclassical Economists in America Between the Wars*. Princeton University Press, Princeton, NJ.

3 Constructing state capacities

During World War II, the state-building process entered a new phase: the phase of building quasi-state capacities. The main issue was no longer *persuading* the international community that a Jewish state was an economically viable project, but rather *planning* a viable Jewish state. It was acknowledged by the Zionist leadership that international legitimacy and recognition—formal sovereignty—would not be a sufficient condition for realizing its principal objective—creating a Jewish majority in Palestine by transferring Jews to Palestine. To realize this aim, administrative state-like capacities had to be forged.

During the period between 1941 and 1952, the World Zionist Organization (WZO) and the Jewish Agency focused on one concrete policy objective: the transplantation of hundreds of thousands of Jews to Palestine/Israel. This objective was driven by two factors: the Jewish majority in Palestine was perceived as a necessary condition for Jewish statehood, and at the same time, Jewish statehood was perceived to be a necessary condition for the survival of the Jewish people, physically and symbolically.

In 1941, the WZO approved Ben-Gurion's plan for the creation of a Jewish majority in Palestine, as detailed in his *Outline of Zionist Policy* (Ben-Gurion, 1941). This schematic plan guided the Jewish national organizations/the Israeli government until February 1952, when the government announced the first New Economic Policy, an austerity policy, and put on hold the mass immigration policy.[1] In the period that separated the two events, the Israeli state was planned and crafted as an institutional instrument for the transplantation and absorption of Jewish immigrants.

This chapter traces the process by which the paradigm of rapid development was translated from words to institutions, and in which the Jewish Agency constructed administrative state-like capacities, that would enable it to realize the mass immigration policy. The state of Israel, it is argued, was not formed as an attempt to emulate an abstract model of statehood, but rather as an attempt to build an instrument to solve a domestic policy problem. The chapter focuses on the activity of the Planning Committee, an extensive political-administrative project for the planning of the transplantation and absorption of one million Jews within a year or two. The Planning Committee was initiated by Ben-Gurion and organized by David Horowitz between 1942 and 1945. The chapter focuses on three aspects of the project: (1) the economic policy ideas it was based on; (2) the type of policy network it created; and (3) its impact on the foreign relations of the Jewish Agency.

Domestic trends

World War II, perhaps ironically, created favorable economic conditions from the perspective of the Zionist organizations. The Jewish economy flourished due to the protectionist regime imposed on Palestine by the British government, which boosted domestic investment in industry. During the years 1939–1945, the Jewish Domestic Product (JDP) expanded at an average annual rate of 11.2 percent, a rate higher than that of the United States during the same period (Gross and Metzer, 1999, p. 302, Table 1). The industrial sector, which had been the largest before the war, became even more so. The share of industrial product grew from 24.2 percent of the JDP in 1939 to 33.1 percent in 1945, while agricultural production grew only mildly in value, from 9.7 percent of the JDP to 10.7 percent (ibid., p. 310, Table 4). The strengthening dominance of industry was obvious when observing the size of the respective sector workforces. The war years saw the number of Jews employed in industry grow from 22.8 percent to 30.8 percent, while the number of Jews employed in agriculture fell from 22.2 percent to 13.1 percent (ibid., p. 310, table 5). Among other factors, this trend was the product of rising private investment in industry in the Jewish sector: the annual investment in industry between 1940 and 1944 was eight times higher than in the late 1920s and four times higher than in the early 1930s.[2]

During these years, the governing institutions of the Jewish community became more centralized and coherent. Due to the war in Europe, the balance of power from the WZO shifted to its local arm, the Jewish Agency. Domestically, Mapai, led by its charismatic leader, David Ben-Gurion, began its dominance over the Jewish Labor Movement in Palestine and it established control over the Jewish Agency and the Histadrut—the General Jewish Federation of Workers in Palestine—and its holding company, the Workers Corporation. This institutional triangle gave Mapai significant structural power and quasi-state capacities. Mapai adjusted well to its new position and no longer perceived itself and acted as a class party, but transformed itself into a party that represented all "Jewish people."

The population as an object of governance

The notion of Israeli statehood has its own internal history. The history of Israel is not only the material and institutional changes, but it also includes the transformation of the perceptions of the Israeli leadership regarding Israeli statehood. The year 1941 was transformative in the sense that it gave rise to a more concrete perception of Israeli statehood. This perception was shaped in response to events that shook the world.

As early as the 1930s, following the escalation of the Jewish-Arab conflict, Ben-Gurion sought to define the key objective of the WZO as the creation of a

Jewish majority in Palestine. By 1941, the Jewish Agency's leadership had sufficient information about the unfolding catastrophe for the Jewish populations in Europe, which provided another reason to hasten the immigration process. In October 1941, two years after the publication of the British White Paper in which the British government restricted Jewish immigration to Palestine to "some 75,000 immigrants over the next five years" (White Paper, 1939), Ben-Gurion submitted a document entitled *Outlines of Zionist Policy* to the Executive Board of the Jewish Agency.

The *Outlines of Zionist Policy*, consisting of around 30 pages, provides a glimpse of the way the Zionist leadership conceived of statehood in the decade preceding the establishment of the state. Its uniqueness lies in the detailed technocratic language in which Ben-Gurion portrayed the state, with reference to military, legal, administrative and economic aspects. In this document, the state was no longer referred to as a visionary lofty idea, but as a concrete administrative project. At the center of the project was the issue of population and the necessary means by which it must be governed:

> A large-scale Jewish immigration and colonisation in Palestine cannot be secured otherwise than through a Jewish Administration, having power and responsibility for creating in Palestine such economic, administrative and political conditions as may be necessary for the absorption and free development of a large new population.... That such colonisation is possible in Palestine and that we are capable of achieving it has been proved by our work there. Large-scale colonisation, without which large-scale immigration into Palestine is impossible, makes it necessary to have in Palestine an Administration whose main purpose is to carry out such colonisation and immigration. It requires a political regime expressly for this end and the whole system of land legislation requires to be changed; so does the industrial and labour legislation, and indeed the whole fiscal system of the country. However, the personnel of the Administration must be entirely and wholeheartedly devoted to the achievement of this aim.
>
> (Ben-Gurion, 1941, pp. 8–9)

Within a year, by May 1942, Ben-Gurion's program had been discussed and approved by the WZO in the Biltmore Hotel in New York. The Biltmore Program defined the core interest of the Zionist organizations as the attainment of a Jewish majority in Palestine through mass immigration:

> The Conference urges that the gates of Palestine be opened; that the Jewish Agency be vested with control of immigration into Palestine and with the necessary authority for upbuilding the country, including the development of its unoccupied and uncultivated lands; and that Palestine be established as a Jewish Commonwealth integrated in the structure of the new democratic world.
>
> (JVL, 1942)

The clear definition of the Zionist goal in administrative terms exposed the weakness of the Zionist organizations' institutional capacities. The Zionist movement had no experience of planning such a massive endeavor. In fact, most of the Jewish Agency's experts and advisors precluded the viability of this project. Therefore, in order to realize the plan, the Jewish Agency's political leadership had to create a community of experts, technocrats and men of practice and to disseminate a new way of thinking about economy, the state and the relationship between the two. It had to turn mass immigration from an impossible objective into a possible one, by offering a new way of thinking about the economy, which would be consistent with the prevailing and legitimate bodies of knowledge. This crucial undertaking was to be done by the Planning Committee.

Zionism and developmental economics

If the economic event that shaped economic thinking during the 1930s was the Great Depression, the economic thinking of the 1940s was shaped by the war economy, as well as by a nascent form of developmental economics. Both types of economic ideas entered the Zionist economic discourse, and shaped the way they perceived the local situation and its potentials.

During the period between the two world wars, the British government managed its colonies according to laissez-faire policy principles, which implied minimal intervention in the local economy for whatever reason. With the onset of the war, the British government had to shift its policy drastically. According to Nahum Gross, in the years 1940–1945 the British government "completely mobilized the resources for the needs of the war economy." The government eliminated the controls on international trade and implemented capital control, it imposed restrictions on production and trade, it restricted competition and it established a system for supply, rationing and price control (Gross, 2000, pp. 221–225). The United States also used interventionist policies to mobilize the national economy and to control the allocation of resources (Koistinen, 2004), an approach that affected the West as a whole (Nash, 1990). The interventionist global trend opened new possibilities in terms of economic governance for the Zionist leadership. The state-building project did not have to be planned in terms of either free market practices or a socialist planned economy. It could be planned in terms of a market planned economy: Just as the allies mobilized their national economies without fully nationalizing them for the purposes of wining the war, the Zionist organization would be able to use the same policy instrument to build a state.

In addition, during the 1940s, the seeds of another new type of economic idea emerged on the world's periphery. In hindsight, this new type of ideas was called developmental economics, but in the 1940s it did not have a name. One of the harbingers of developmental economics was the British-Australian economist Colin Clark, whose ideas entered the Zionist economic discourse. In his books, *Conditions of Economic Progress* (1940) and *The Economics of 1960* (1942),

Clark stressed the *dynamic* aspect of economic development. Developmental economics differed from the other three economic schools that had prevailed in the 1940s: the Neoclassical, the Marxist and the German Historical School. Despite the deep differences between these schools, they all shared a belief in immutable economic regularities: these were either the laws of markets, the trans-historical laws of class struggle, or the evolutionary laws of economic institutions.

The developmental school rejected the existence of immutable economic regularities. Specifically, the developmental school argued that there are ways in which economic progress can be accelerated by, for example, "increasing production per head in the sphere of primary, secondary or tertiary industry; or by transferring labor from less to more productive spheres" (Clark, 1940, p. 11).

A key element in Clark's notion of economic development was the significance of the quality of human capital for economic development. He was among the first to point out the correlation between high GDP per capita and a large service sector (Arndt, 1990). This argument was essential in order to justify the Zionists' demands to the British government to allow mass immigration. Horowitz quoted Clark's assertion that "the average income per capita is linked in most cases to a greater proportion of the population that is employed in tertiary branches" (Horowitz, 1944a, p. 117). Hence, shifting workers from agriculture to industry, trade and services, would increase not only the absorptive capacity of the country, but also its standard of living.

Within the Zionist policy-making circles, Ben-Gurion and Horowitz were among the first who recognized the merits of this new economic policy approach. Whereas other experts were still thinking in terms of the economic determinism dictated by the laissez-faire and the Marxist textbooks, Horowitz and Ben-Gurion looked at what government actually did, and they realized that the new world order would be based on a new way of thinking about the possible and the impossible from an economic perspective.

The Planning Committee

Early in 1941, Arthur Ruppin pointed out to Ben-Gurion that the drafting of the "facts and recommendations" to be handed over to the international community at the expected post-war peace conference would be an essential step for the Jewish Agency. He believed that the representation of the Zionist interest would be deficient without "a rich factual basis and detailed plans." Ben-Gurion liked the idea, but he instructed Ruppin to aim for a more specific plan. "I hope," he told Ruppin, "that you will show that it is possible to bring five million Jews to Palestine" (Troen, 2003, p. 179). In March, the Executive Committee of the Jewish Agency decided to "establish committees and teams of experts to investigate, collect—and publish when needed—any material in reference to the absorptive capacity of the country and its economic possibilities." The team of experts would also "prepare plans and recommendations—financial and administrative—for the establishment of a country, urban, and maritime economy that would absorb the massive immigration following the war" (quoted in Gal, 1985, pp. 118–119). Four years later, in October 1945, David Horowitz handed in the final report of the Planning Committee to Ben-Gurion, under the title *Absorption of One Million of Jewish Immigrants in Palestine.*

The first meeting of experts called by Ben-Gurion took place at Beit Hakerem, a suburb in Jerusalem, on September 17, 1942. Attending the meeting were the most senior experts within the Zionist organizations, with the Economic Research Institute (ERI) being represented by Ruppin, Ludwig Gruenbaum, Alfred Bonné and Erwin Brumberger. Eliezer Siegfried Hoofien, Director of the Anglo-Palestine Bank also attended, as did Yitzhak Galfat, the Marxist editor of *Cooperative Bulletin.* Also present were Eliezer Kaplan, a member of the Jewish Agency Executive Committee and its treasurer, Dr. Emil Shmorek, a member of the Jewish Agency Executive Committee and Director of the Department of Commerce and Industry of the Jewish Agency, and David Horowitz, the Secretary of the Economics Department.

Ruppin, the Director of the ERI, set the agenda and, together with Arié Ga'athon, as the senior economists from the ERI, he was the most dominant figure in the meeting. The aim of the meeting was to design a plan for the absorption of as many Jews as possible within the shortest possible period of time. Ruppin and Gruenbaum opened the meeting, arguing that the Jewish Agency could hope to absorb 60,000 immigrants within the first year and a total of 150,000 immigrants in the tenth year, which meant that it would take around 10 years to absorb one million Jews. Ruppin and Gruenbaum based their calculation on two conservative economic assumptions: that a constant ratio of 1 to 5 between the number of farmers and the entire population must be kept, and that the annual population growth rate of 11 percent should be kept constant (Ruppin, 1942).

Alfred Bonné and David Horowitz rejected Ruppin and Gruenbaum's conservative calculations, arguing that the new world order brought new possibilities. After the war, argued Bonné, the world would enter "a period of instability that will alter prevailing beliefs of economic and social life." He predicted that the economic methods that governments used during the war—monopolies and state-owned companies—would persist after the war for different purposes (Bonné, 1942). Horowitz predicted that in the future governments would play a decisive role in governing the economies:

> Whether we like it or not, the trend in the world is toward *etatism.* It is still not clear if *etatism* or socialism will prevail; but there is no chance of going back to a free market economy as before the war.
>
> (Horowitz, 1942)

The Atlantic Charter Treaty, signed between the United States and Britain, had recognized the right of nations to self-determination: the international community will "respect the right of all peoples to choose the form of Government under which they will live; and they wish to see sovereign rights and self-government restored to those who have been forcibly deprived of them." The declaration, they predicted, would play a decisive role in the future of the Jewish national movement. "Palestine will play an important role in the new constellation that might result from these tendencies," argued Bonné (1942).

Horowitz and Bonné were in the minority among the group of experts. All the others supported the position of Ruppin and Gruenbaum. Dr. Ludwig Samuel, Director of the Agricultural Research Station in the Rehovot, argued that "our analysis is fully consistent with the analysis of Dr. Gruenbaum." Dr. Irwin Brumberger supported Gruenbaum, arguing that his plan "is based on our knowledge and our experience regarding Palestine" (ERI, 1942a).

Expertise and statehood

It is tempting to portray Ruppin, Gruenbaum and those who supported them as scientists who stood firm in their autonomy and integrity vis-à-vis pressure from the political leadership. This interpretation is reinforced by the fact that Kaplan, the Head of the Economic Department of the Jewish Agency, explicitly demanded that the experts provide "scientific fictions" for the purpose of waging political warfare.

However, this interpretation misses the fact that Horowitz and Bonné—as well as Ben-Gurion—did not reject science, but only a specific way of economic thinking. They offered an innovative economic position which had much in common with developmental economics. While traditional experts assumed the constancy of economic regularities, irrespective of political institutions, Horowitz, Bonné and Ben-Gurion brought institutions into the mix and they acknowledged that institutional changes affect "the laws of the economy."

In his book, *Ben-Gurion and the Intellectuals*, Michael Keren argues that Ben-Gurion was not skeptical concerning all science per se, but rather doubted scientific knowledge derived from statistics and probability alone (Keren, 1988, pp. 59–64). The reason was that statistical regularities are merely based on experience and as such cannot accurately predict all possible events in the future. This interpretation of Ben-Gurion's philosophy of science is consistent with the explanation he provided at the next meeting, which took place two months later. Ben-Gurion explained to the experts: "There is a view that in fact there are only chemical laws, physical and physiological laws. All other sciences are fabricated." As far as the laws of economics were concerned, he continued:

> The last twenty years revolutionized economics, and now everything is done contrary to scientific laws ... I want to talk about the possibility ... that all these [Jewish] people could be brought to Palestine not according to the laws of economics that prevailed at the time when economics book were written, but at the time when the world fixes itself.
>
> (ERI, 1942b)

To make his approach clearer, Ben-Gurion compared the transplantation of Jews to Palestine to the invasion of the United States to Europe. When the Americans were considering their participation in the war, asked Ben-Gurion, did they ask the statisticians how many Americans go each year to Europe?

> Nobody is interested in how many people travel each year from America to Europe, because the travel is done for different reasons, not for the individual need of the traveler. When the war came, the problem was this: how many people can the United States of America transfer to Europe, for its own needs, of its own power—organizational power, financial power, industrial power, legal power?

The instruments of war, argued Ben-Gurion, could be used in times of peace to achieve large-scale national goals. Just "as the army is sent from America … not by the individual will of each person, but by a calculated plan for the purpose of the masses, with state capacity and with state means" (ibid.).

Cooperation between the expert and the politician

The response of the experts to Ben-Gurion's words ranged between amusement and hostility. Galfat, a Marxist economist, argued that "Ben-Gurion was a doctrinaire today because he made an abstraction of reality. He assumed not only ideal conditions but also fictitious ones." Dr. Avraham Granovsky, Director of the Jewish National Fund (Keren Kayemet), an organization that purchased land from the Arabs in Palestine, was also skeptical: even "if we have full sovereignty, don't we still have natural restrictions on the issue of land?" Professor Volkani, an agricultural expert, rejected Ben-Gurion's figures, exclaiming that "I am a Zionist and I say definitively: if someone submits this material to me I will not accept it" (ibid.).

Horowitz, arrived at the second meeting well prepared: he had on the table an outline of a plan for the absorption of one million Jews within a few years, well beyond the numbers Ruppin and Gruenbaum had talked about. He dismissed the minimalistic forecasts on the grounds that through economic planning, "it is possible to do many things that seemed hitherto impossible." Ruppin and Gruenbaum had based their calculations on the assumption that economic laws and regularities are constant over time. Horowitz, on the contrary, assumed that "it is possible to change them … the war proved that a planned economy has different possibilities" (ibid.).

Horowitz's outline consisted of three key principles, which are essential in order to grasp the economic rationality of the state-building project between 1941 and 1952.

1 *Industrialization (rather than agricultural development)*: to increase the number of immigrants and the pace of their absorption, the Jewish sector must be rapidly industrialized, because in industry productivity is higher than in agrarian sectors: "economic absorption capacity is a function of productivity: how much you can produce." Horowitz dismissed Ruppin and

Gruenbaum's insistence that a constant ratio between farmers and non-farmers must be kept. In modern economies, he argued, workers must create new value, irrespective of the type of goods or services they produce. In Palestine, he concluded, "there cannot be too many farmers" (ibid.).

2 *Immigration is a precondition for development and should precede development*: whereas other Zionist experts had argued in the past that the creation of jobs must precede immigration, Horowitz reversed this, arguing that immigration is the fuel of economic development because it creates demand for goods and demand is a precondition for economic development. This principle was based on the rationale that immigrants create a higher demand for goods and services, thus boosting the economy. "To a large extent," he explained, "the absorptive capacity is a function of the market … if we can create a concentration of people, which consume certain things, this is the functionality of the market" (ibid.).
3 *Transplantation first, absorption later*: According to his plan, immigrants would be transferred to Palestine within a very short period of time, but their absorption in the economy would be carried out gradually over a longer period. During the transition, they will be accommodated in "enclaves" which "will be, in a way, separated from the economic life in the country." During this period, the immigrants will not be employed but will be supported by external financial sources. "If we have the means to keep these people here rather than in Poland, it is an enormous economic advantage" (ibid.). In hindsight, this proved to be a very precise description of the way the mass immigration policy was actually carried out.

Horowitz's outline well suited the political vision of his patron, Ben-Gurion. However, one should not infer that Horowitz simply legitimized Ben-Gurion's political vision for the purpose of promoting himself. Such an interpretation would completely miss the nature of the interaction between ideas, power and interests. If ideas have any impact on economic history, it is precisely because they are not reduced to a legitimization strategy. Horowitz and Ben-Gurion needed each other, in order to change the institutional and political reality by bringing together ideas, power, and interests.

Did Horowitz provide "scientific fictions" that simply served his patron's political needs?

Following the experts meeting, Ben-Gurion appointed Horowitz as the organizer of the Planning Committee and he referred to him as the "author of the plan."[3]

The exclusion of the ERI

With the death of Ruppin in January 1943, Alfred Bonné was appointed the Director of the ERI. Bonné made attempts to restore the relationship between the ERI and the Jewish Agency, but to no avail. He wrote to Ben-Gurion and pleaded with him to allow the ERI to take a more active role in the Planning

Committee, arguing that the prestige of the ERI would contribute to the clout of the final report (Bonne, 1943). The Committee, he wrote to Ben-Gurion, will probably face "a fierce struggle with foreign experts and criticism will certainly be voiced" (Bonné, 1944). He suggested that the ERI would imbue the recommendation of the Committee with more scientific prestige. Other researchers at the ERI, who still believed Horowitz's plan was based on faulty assumptions, made individual attempts to warn the other participants about Horowitz's line of argument. Eliyahu Margalit claimed that he "analyzed Mr. Horowitz's memorandum sentence for sentence … and found that his political line of argument is wrong and dangerous" because it is "far from reality" (Margalit, 1944). Gruenbaum also sent a letter directly to Horowitz pointing out all the mistakes in his approach (Gruenbaum, 1944).

However, these efforts all proved fruitless. While the ERI researchers participated in some of the meetings, they had no impact on the final outcome. Out of the 90 reports prepared by the Planning Committee, only two were written by ERI researchers, and even those did not deal with significant issues.[4] When Horowitz submitted the final report to Ben-Gurion, he thanked certain persons and institutions for their help and support. He mentioned the Water Ministry, the Jewish National Fund (Keren Keyemet) and a list of ten researchers. The ERI was not mentioned anywhere, nor were any of its researchers (Horowitz, 1944b).

It is difficult to tell whether the exclusion of the ERI was driven by personal politics—Horowitz's concern that the more reputable economists of the ERI would not respect his authority as the organizer of the Planning Committee—or by the concern that the ERI researchers would try to undermine the economic rationale on which the emerging Zionist development strategy was based. In any case, the exclusion of the ERI was effective and by the 1940s the agrarian paradigm which had shaped the Zionist settlement strategy during the 1920s had lost not only its domestic political appeal but also its scientific credibility. The notion that only agricultural production is a productive economic activity and the idea that economic progress takes place according to immutable laws—be they economic or institutional—were obsolete. The policy discourse, both in Palestine and worldwide, entered into a new era of economic planning, in which governments played a large role. This new trend thoroughly permeated Zionist policy discourse and profoundly changed it from within.

Informal linkages

Sovereignty is not a sufficient or necessary condition for economic governance. Formally, a sovereign state may lack the capacities to govern, and economic governance can be practiced without formal sovereignty, at least partially. The capacity of certain actors to govern other actors depends on the ability of the former to shape the behavior of the latter. When the governing actors lack sovereignty, or if their sovereignty is incomplete and porous, they can govern by creating policy networks, linkages and dependencies (Evans, 1985; Gerschenkron, 1962; Hobson, 1997; Waldner, 1999; Weiss, 1995). When formal state institutions lack capacities, then the cooperation and coordination between state and non-state actors play a more central role in governing the economy. The Planning Committee played a key role in constructing such policy networks and linkages among diversified actors, organizations and individuals, which were part of an institutional complex that was to become the Israeli state.

The Planning Committee operated for two years and during this period it employed more than 90 researchers from various policy areas. It consisted of 20 sub-committees, which were chaired by politicians of the highest rank.[5] In order to estimate the extent to which the Planning Committee contributed to the creation of linkages between governing institutions and to the state-building process, this section will trace the occupational biography of all its participants in the period after the establishment of the state. The governing institutions will be classified into eight categories: (1) the public sector (government, state agency and the bureaucracy and government companies); (2) the Histadrut sector (the Histadrut and the Workers Corporation); (3) the Jewish Agency; (4) the private sector; (5) research institutions; (6) political organizations (parties); (7) local government; and (8) civil organizations. This classification will enable the reader to assess the type of institutions that shared common perceptions regarding the objectives of the state and the best means to realize them.

Among the researchers of the Planning Committee, 38 were employed in the public sector after the state was established: five in the government, 15 in the bureaucracy and 18 in government companies. The Histardut sector employed 13 researchers: three in the Histadrut itself and 10 in the Workers Corporation. Five of the researchers were employed by the Jewish Agency, four of which were in financial institutions. Nine researchers were employed in the private sector, both in industrial companies as well as in financial institutions. Only a small number of researchers were employed in research institutions, political organizations and local governments. Finally, six researchers were involved in civil organizations (Table 3.1 and Appendix).

This analysis suggests that the Planning Committee contributed to links between four types of institutions: the public sector, the Histadrut sector, financial institutions, and the private sector. It must be kept in mind that the Histadrut sector included the Workers Corporation, which owned a large number of enterprises in various industries such as construction (Sollel Boné), water (Mekorot), agriculture (Yachin), supply and distribution (Hamashbir and Tnuva), as well as financial institutions (Bank Hapoalim and various saving and loans cooperatives) (Greenberg, 2004, pp. 17–39). During the 1950s, the Histadrut sector accounted for around a fifth of the economy.

The linkage between the government and the financial institutions of the Jewish Agency is consistent with the dependency of the state during its first years upon foreign funding, channeled through the Jewish Agency, which continued to support the state after its establishment. The linkage with the private sector in the early years of the state was not as developed as with the Histadrut sector. However, in the second half of the 1950s and into the 1960s, the state nourished its links with the private sector (Bichler and Nitzan, 2001) (Figure 3.1).

Table 3.1 Planning Committee participants in post-independence institutions

Sector or type of institution	*Number of members*
Public sector	
• Government companies	18
• State bureaucracy	15
• Government	5
Histadrut sector	
• Workers Corporation	10
• Histadrut	3
Jewish Agency	5
Private sector	9
Research institutions	3
Political organizations	2
Local government	3
Civil organizations	6
Total	79

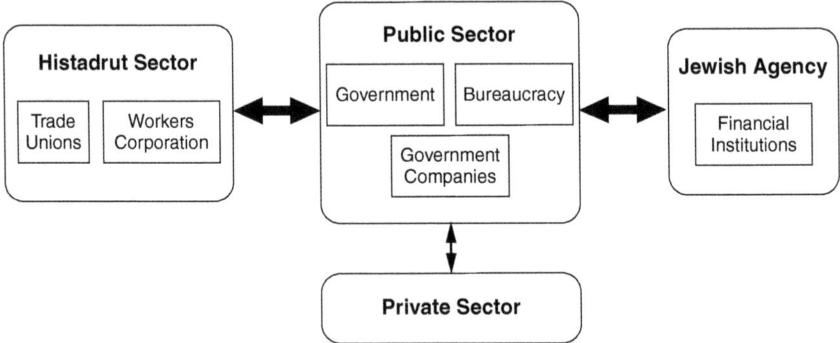

Figure 3.1 Links created by the Planning Committee.

The Jewish Agency and American Jewry

The Planning Committee affected not only internal linkages but also external ones. In particular, an unintended consequence of the Planning Committee's operation was its impact on the relationship between the Jewish Agency, the American Jewry and the United States in general. Up to the time of World War II, the national Jewish organizations had invested most of their diplomatic efforts in Europe and particularly in Britain. Europe was the center of world politics and the European Zionists had more clout than the American Zionists. Moreover, the European and American Zionists were divided on ideological grounds: the European faction in the WZO felt more comfortable regarding cooperation with the Labor Movement than the American faction, which resisted the collectivist settlement strategy, as well as the socialist rhetoric of the Labor Movement.

The conflict between the two approaches surfaced when the WZO arranged for experts to evaluate the settlement strategy in Palestine in the 1920s.[6]

In the 1940s, however, an ideological convergence took place between the American economic policy discourse and the Zionist one: in the United States, economists shifted toward Keynesianism, and Zionist leaders were open to consider various types of cooperation between national capital and the private sector. This ideological convergence was a key political asset for the Zionist leadership during the 1940s and the 1950s, as it enabled closer cooperation not only with the American Zionists, but also with the US administration (Gal, 1991).

The new spirit of cooperation between the Jewish Agency and American Jewry was manifested in the cooperation between the researchers of the Planning Committee and a team of researchers dispatched to Palestine by the American Palestine Institute, with the purpose of preparing a report about the economic feasibility of a Jewish state in Palestine. Contrary to the experts in the 1920s, this time the American Jewish experts were welcomed.

The leading researcher of the American team was Robert Nathan, a student of Symon Kuznets. This was a critical fact: Kuznets was an American-Jewish economist and a Nobel Laureate, who had been influenced by the American Institutional School, through his teacher, Wesley Mitchell. Prior to his visit to Palestine, Nathan served as the director of the National Income Division of the US Department of Commerce during the New Deal and as the chairman of the War Production Board's Planning Committee (Troen, 2003, p. 117). The other two experts were Daniel Creamer, who had been a researcher for the Social Security Board and the National Income Division in the US Department of Commerce, and Oscar Gass, who worked as an economist in the Treasury Department before World War II and during the war joined the War Production Board.

The researchers of the Planning Committee cooperated closely with the American team. In fact, the American team based their own analysis on studies conducted by the Planning Committee's members. The cooperation was most significant in the American report's chapter about industry, a policy area which was essential from the perspective of the paradigm of rapid development. In this chapter the American economists quoted no less than 23 reports prepared by the Planning Committee, each of them focused on a different industry (Nathan *et al.*, 1946, p. 60). The chapter particularly quoted the research of Alfred Marcus, a member of the sub-committee for industry and the economist for the Israel Manufacturers' Association. In addition, the Americans held talks with Eliezer Hoffien, Avrahm Zbarsky, Dr. Yeshayahu Foerder and others.

Not surprisingly, the two teams reached very similar conclusions and recommendations. As Nahum Gross put it, the American experts' report "outlined a plan for mass immigration and development" and it was characterized by "an interventionist tone." Moreover, he added, "It may very well be that the local experts were the ones who raised some of these ideas. What is important is the fact that the American team embraced them" (Gross, 2000, pp. 327–328). The American report endorsed the view that despite limited natural resources in

Palestine, the economy could thrive on the basis of the quality of the labor force (Troen, 2003, pp. 177–178).

If the cooperation between the two groups was intended to remain restricted to the preparation of the report, this did not have a historical significance. Quite the opposite, the ties persisted after the establishment of the state, and Oscar Gass fulfilled a central role in mediating between the Israeli government and the American administration in various policy areas. He took part in planning the transition to an Israeli currency; he assisted Israel in managing its foreign exchange reserves in the United States and he mediated between Israeli and American officials in relation to loans and grants. In 1953, Gass headed the Economic Advisory Staff in the Prime Minister's Office. Furthermore, in 1954, Daniel Creamer was also appointed as the head of the Falk Center for Economic Research, where his first task was to prepare the Israeli system of National Accounts.

International committees

The Planning Committee also had a significant impact on the Jewish Agency's capacity to legitimize its demand for a Jewish state in Palestine. Following the war, two international committees were assigned the task to investigate the feasibility of such a state. The Jewish Agency was expected by both committees to persuade the international community that a Jewish state was economically feasible. Shortly before the arrival of the Anglo-American Committee in 1946 and the United Nations Special Committee on Palestine (UNSCOP) in 1947, the Economic Department of the Jewish Agency was occupied preparing empirical data to support the Zionist argument. A key question that was discussed was the economic absorptive capacity of the area assigned to the Jewish community. Many of the researches prepared by the Planning Committee, and quoted by Nathan, Gass and Creamer, were also used in the preparation for the international committees.

In his testimony at the UNSCOP, Horowitz presented the Jewish Agency's economic argument, according to which the economic absorptive capacity of a country is practically incalculable because it does not have an objective upper limit:

> The first question with which we have to deal is: what is the concept of economic capacity of absorption of the country? It certainly is not a problem of arithmetic. The economic capacity of absorption of the country cannot be gauged in terms of arithmetic and there is no such thing as a fixed constant, rigid, concept of capacity of absorption per se inherent in a country. The economic capacity of absorption is a function of a number of factors, such as natural resources, capital, skill, the determination of the population to take roots in a country, productivity of labour, and a number of imponderablesé Transformation of economic conditions, technical discoveries and inventions, development of economic conditions, development of potential resources, all have a bearing on economic capacity of absorption.
>
> (Horowitz, 1947)

Horowitz presented his detailed conception regarding immigration and economic development, laboriously put together for the last decade and a half, to the United Nations committee.

Conclusion

During the 1940s, the emphasis within the Zionist organizations shifted from a conflict over the international legitimacy of a Jewish state in Palestine, to planning and constructing the administrative capacities of the state. As far as economic ideas was concerned, the issue was no longer only to persuade the international community that a Jewish state was viable politically and economically, but rather to use legitimate and acceptable economic ideas in order to plan what the state was going to look like.

Theories of the state tend—naturally—to underline the universal features of states. Rightfully, they argue that the very idea of statehood as well as the idea of sovereignty is an international norm. However, the way each state is formed may diverge from the abstract model. The notion of Israeli statehood, as shaped in the period between 1941 and 1952, was constructed around the objective of mass immigration and rapid development. The national organizations—and later the Israeli government—mobilized resources for this purpose. This was obviously not the only purpose to which resources were allocated—military spending also took a significant chunk—but in terms of civil objectives, the transplantation and absorption of the Jewish population formed a purpose that defined the structure of the state and its interaction with market actors and the civil society.

The Planning Committee was a milestone in the process of the institutionalization of the rapid development paradigm. The Planning Committee translated the general economic policy ideas that emerged during the 1930s within the Zionist policy discourse, and translated them into concrete and administrative terms. The Planning Committee created a kernel of a network that shared ideas, interests and purpose, which was able to put these ideas into action within a few years. After the state was established, these institutions enabled the execution, largely as planned, of the mass immigration project (Hacohen, 1994).

The rapid development paradigm, which gained the status of the Zionist/state policy strategy, can be defined by three elements. The first element was the prioritization of the creation of a Jewish majority in Palestine: Jews must be brought to the territory of Palestine/Israel, at all financial costs. Second, to sustain the Jewish population in Israel, the production capacities of the economy must be expanded and jobs must be created, even if the value created by workers is lower than their wages. Finally, as the previous two principles imply, the scarcity of financial resources would not limit the government's expenses. Rather, the national needs would determine how much money must be mobilized externally. This was perhaps the most controversial element in the rapid development strategy, and therefore many economists interpreted it as an "ideology" rather than part of an economic rationale. However, one must keep in mind that this principle had its internal logic: the Jewish state was not perceived as a state of its citizens, but as a state of the Jewish people, including the Jews who did not reside in the territory of Israel. Therefore, the financial burden required to sustain the state must not fall only on the shoulders of those Jews, who reside in the territory of Israel.

The Reparation Agreement between Israel and West Germany in 1953 was a demonstration of this principle: West Germany paid Israel the amount of four billion marks—450 millions of which went to the World Jewish Congress—both as the heir of the victims who did not have family, and as the country who absorbed the Jewish refugees. Having said this, though, the rationale of the rapid development paradigm was based on the fact that during the first decade even the expenses deemed to be absolute necessities, food, housing and security, meant the country literally struggled for its survival. Given this reality, policy-makers had to find the resources for these necessities.

However, the paradigm of rapid development had two blind spots which had a long-lasting impact on the economic history of Israel, and which, eventually, led to its demise. First, the paradigm of rapid development had severe social consequences. When Horowitz, Bonné and Ben-Gurion argued against Ruppin and Gruenbaum, they ignored one essential problem: the low standard of living of the immigrants during the period between their arrival in Israel and their actual absorption into the economy. Horowitz, Bonné and Ben-Gurion thought about the Zionist cause, not the welfare of the individual citizens. In practice, the process of "absorption" took many years and it created a deep social division between the veterans, who had resided in Palestine before the establishment of the state, and the new immigrants. Here then are the roots of the socio-economic division between Mizrachim (Arab Jews) and Aschkenazim (European Jews) as well as between the center and the periphery.

The second blind spot of the rapid development paradigm concerned the issue of Israel's balance of payments and labor productivity. The strategy of rapid development, with its emphasis on full employment and expansion of production, required constant foreign financial support and/or isolation of the Israeli economy from international markets. Soon after the establishment of the state, voices began calling for the abandonment of this strategy as it was not sustainable, it did not allow Israel to reach economic independence and its low labor productivity was blamed. Thus began the gradual transition to the paradigm of economic independence, which is the topic of Chapter 4.

Appendix

List of institutions where former members of the Planning Committee served as senior staff after the establishment of the State of Israel

After the establishment of the State of Israel, members of the sub-committees of the Planning Committee were active in various political, social and economic institutions in Israel. This list presents the institutions and organizations in which they operated and the functions they filled. The list of people who participated in the research projects of the Planning Committee is based on the work of Ari Bar'el (2004, 2014). The names of the institutions in which the people served are derived from their professional biographies, most of which are found in various volumes of *Who's Who in Israel* (Cornfeld and Aurel, various years) from the years 1949–1958. In several cases the biographies were taken from *Personalities in Eretz Israel* (Shavit *et al.*, 1983).

The following list provides a detailed account of the roles in which the people served in senior positions.[7]

The Public Sector (38)

Government Ministries (5)

1 Agriculture (two ministers).
2 Finance (minister).
3 Rationing and Provisions (minister).
4 Trade and Industry (minister).
5 Transportation (two ministers).

State Agencies and Bureaucracy (15)

1 Agriculture and Settlement Planning Authority in the Ministry of Agriculture (Member).
2 Bank of Israel (Governor; Members of the Advisory Board).
3 Central Bureau of Statistics (Founder and General Manager).
4 Commission for Central Urban Planning (Member).
5 Government's Central Advisory Committee on Economics (Chairman; Member).
6 Hydrological Agency (Manager).
7 Israel Standards Institute (Vice-President).
8 Ministry of Defense (Treasurer; Purchasing Director of the Procurement Department).
9 Ministry of Finance (Director General).
10 Ministry of Health (Director of the Health Department).
11 Ministry of Trade and Industry (Director of the Department of Industrial Development).
12 Ministry of Transportation (Supervisor of Land Transportation; Director of the Department of Air and Maritime Mail).
13 The Advisory Committee on Protective Duties, Ministry of Trade and Industry (Director General).
14 War Production Authority (Chairman, 1947–1949).
15 Water Department in the Ministry of Agriculture (Director).

Government Companies (18)

1 Amidar Residences Corporation (Manager; Member of the Board of Directors).
2 Bank for Industrial Development (in cooperation with Hapoalim Bank, Leumi Bank, and Discount Bank) (Chairman; Member of the Board of Directors).
3 Bizur Bank Ltd. (Member of the Board of Directors).
4 Bonds and Securities Corporation (Member of the Board of Directors).
5 Building Corporation, The Israeli (Palhouse) (Manager).
6 Delek, Israeli Fuel Corporation (Manager; two Members of the Board of Directors).
7 The Corporation for the Development of Jerusalem, Ltd. (General Manager).
8 Fertilizer and Chemicals Corporation (Director; Member of the Board of Directors).
9 The Corporation for Funding Industry and Building Ltd. (Buildco) (General Manager).
10 General Mortgage Bank of Israel (General Manager; Chairman of the Board of Directors).
11 Jaf-Ora Plant for Citrus Products (Technical Manager).
12 Mehadrin (Chairman).
13 Mekorot (Manager; Member of the Board of Directors) (in cooperation with the Jewish Agency).
14 The Israeli Corporation for Milling and Trade (Manager).
15 Negev Phosphates (Chairman).
16 The Israeli Sugar Corporation (Member of the Board of Directors).
17 The Israeli Cotton Industry Ltd. (Manager).
18 The Israeli Ship Renovation Corporation (Manager).

Histadrut Sector (13)

Histadrut (3)

1 Histadrut Economic Council (Member).
2 The Histadrut (Economic Advisor; Director of the Research Institute of the Executive Committee).

Workers Enterprise (10)

1 Gmul (Manager).
2 The Central Hamashbir (General Manager; Member of the Board of Directors.
3 Hapoalim Bank (Manager; Member of the Board of Directors).
4 Hasneh Insurance Company (Chairman).
5 The Israeli–American Industrial Development Bank (General Manager).
6 Koor (Manager).

7 Secretariat of the Workers Corporation (Member).
8 Shemen (Member of the Board of Directors).
9 Shikun, Workers' Residential Building Company (Manager).
10 Zim Shipping Company (Manager).

Companies Owned by the Jewish Agency (5)

1 Igud Bank (Manager).
2 Jewish National Fund (KKL) (Chief Engineer and Director of the Technical Department; Chairman of the Board of Directors).
3 Leumi Bank (two Chairmen of the Board of Directors).
4 Otzar Hahityashvut Hayehudit Bank (Chairman).
5 Otzar Lataasiya Bank (Chairman).

Private and Public Companies (9)

1 Argaman Plant (Owners and Manager).
2 Assis (Owners and Manager).
3 Ata Textile Works (Founder and Manager).
4 Kitan Ltd. (Manager).
5 Kupat Am Bank Ltd. (Manager; Member of the Board of Directors).
6 Lodzia (Owners and Manager).
7 Mizrahi Bank (Chairman).
8 The Residential Home Bank (Chairman).
9 Teva (Manager).

Research and Academic Institutions (3)

1 Hebrew University in Jerusalem (Associate Professor in the Department of Meteorology and Climatology; Professr of Statistics and Demography).
2 Technion (Professor Engineer of Roads and Trains; Professor of Food Technology; Professor of Civil Engineering).
3 Tel-Aviv University (Member of the Board of Directors);

Political Organizations (2)

1 General Council of Mapai (Member).
2 General Zionists Party (President of the Party's Federation; MK).

Local Government (3)

1 Architect and City Planner.
2 Bnei-Braq Municipality (Municipal Engineer and Adviser).
3 Tel-Aviv Municipality (City Engineer).

Civil Organizations (6)

1 Engineers' and Architects' Association (President).
2 General Merchants' Association (President).
3 Israel Center of Consumer Cooperation (Chairman; Manager).
4 Israel Land Council (Member).
5 Israel Manufacturers' Association (President; Council Member).
6 Tel-Aviv Museum (Member of the Board of Directors).

Banking and Financial Institutions (including all ownerships) (15)

1 Bank for Industrial Development.
2 Bizur Bank.
3 Bonds and Securities Corporation.
4 General Mortgage Bank of Israel.
5 Gmul (Manager).
6 Igud Bank (Manager).
7 The Israeli-American Industrial Development Bank (General Manager).
8 Kupat Am Bank Ltd. (Manager; Member of the Board of Directors).
9 Leumi Bank (two Chairmen of the Board of Directors).
10 Mizrahi Bank (Chairman).
11 Otzar Hahityashvut Hayehudit Bank (Chairman).
12 Otzar Lataasiya Bank (Chairman).
13 The Residential Home Bank (Chairman).
14 The General Mortgage Bank of Israel.
15 The Residential Home Bank.

Notes

1 See Chapter 4 for details.
2 In nominal terms. Calculated from (UN, 1947).
3 In a letter Ben-Gurion sent to one of the researchers he wrote: "You are required to prepare your assignments in contact with D. Horowitz, the author of the plan" (Ben-Gurion, 1944).
4 One research report, on temporary employment after World War II, was co-authored by Brumberger and Gruenbaum. Another research report, on the economy of the Middle East,was prepared by Alfred Bonné (List, NA).
5 Ben-Gurion was the Chairman of the Planning Committee and headed the Central Committee for Immigration, and International Transportation; Eliezer Kaplan headed the Central Committee for Agriculture and the Sub-committee of Demobilization; Dr. Shmorek headed the Sub-committee of Industry and the Central Committee of Trade. Eliezer Hoofien headed the Central Committee of Finance (Proposal, 1943).
6 See Chapter 2 for more discussion.
7 One of the following is considered to be a senior position: in the case of government or public corporations: General Manager, Deputy General Manager, Chairman of the Board of Directors, and member of the Board of Directors; in the case of private corporations: owner; in the case of academic institutions: professor and researcher; in the case of political parties: at least MK.

References

Arndt, H.W., 1990. Colin Clark as a Development Economist. *World Development* 18, 1045–1050.

Bar'el, A., 2004. Ben-Gurion's Approach to Science and Technology, 1935–1948. Master's thesis Hebrew University of Jerusalem (in Hebrew).

Bar'el, A., 2014. *King-Engineer: David Ben-Gurion, Science and Nation Building.* Sdeh-Boker: Ben-Gurion Institute (in Hebrew).

Ben-Gurion, D., 1941. Outlines of Zionist Policy. October 15. Ben-Gurion Archive, Section: Speeches and Articles.

Ben-Gurion, D., 1944. Ben-Gurion to G. Cidrovitch. July 16. Central Zionist Archive, S90/880.

Bichler, S. and Nitzan, Y., 2001. *From War Benefit to Peace Dividends.* Carmel, Jerusalem (in Hebrew).

Bonné, A., 1942. Theses from Dr. A. Bonné's lecture. September 17. Central Zionist Archvie, S7/2392.

Bonné, A., 1944. A letter from A. Bonné to D. Ben-Gurion, June 22, 1944, Central Zionist Archive, S90/875.

Bonné, Alfred., 1943. A Report on the Research Effort of the Economic Research Institution towards the Peace Committee, September 23. Central Zionist Archvie, S90.916.

Clark, C., 1940. *The Conditions of Economic Progress.* Macmillan and Co., London.

Clark, C., 1942. *The Economics of 1960.* Macmillan and Co., London.

Cornfeld, P. and Aurel, A.M. (Eds.) (various years). *Who's Who in Israel.* M. Shoham's Press, Jerusalem.

ERI (Economic Research Institute). 1942a. Economic Research Institute Convention. November 24. Ben-Gurion Archive, Lectures and Papers.

ERI (Economic Research Institute). 1942b. The Debate after Dr. Gruenbaum's lecture. Economic Research Institute, September 17. Central Zionist Archive S7/2392.

Evans, P.B., 1985. Transnational Linkages and the Economic Role of the State: An Analysis of Developing and Industrialized Nations in the Post-World War II Period. In: Evans, P., Rueschemeyer, D. and Skocpol, T. (Eds.) *Bringing the State Back In.* Cambridge University Press, Cambridge.

Gal, A., 1985. Dayid Ben-Guryon—Towards a Jewish State, 1938–1941. Ben-Gurion University, Ḳiryat Śedeh Boḳer (in Hebrew).

Gal, A., 1991. The Sources of Ben-Gurion's American Orientation, 1938–1941. In: Zweig, R.W. (Ed.), *David Ben-Gurion: Politics and Leadership in Israel.* Frank Cass, London, pp. 115–123.

Gerschenkron, A., 1962. Economic Backwardness in Historical Perspective. In: Gerschenkron, A., *Economic Backwardness in Historical Perspective*, Belknap Press of Harvard University Press, Cambridge, MA, pp. 5–30.

Greenberg, Y., 2004. *Anatomy of a Crisis Foretold: The Collapse of Labor Owned Enterprises in the 80's.* Am Oved, Tel Aviv (in Hebrew).

Gross, N.T., 2000. The Economic Policy of the British Mandate in Palestine. In: Gross, N.T. (Ed.), *Not by Spirit Alone: Studies in the Economic History of Modern Palestine and Israel.* The Hebrew University Magnes Press and Yad Izhak Ben-Zvi Press, Jerusalem, pp. 172–227 (in Hebrew).

Gross, N.T. and Metzer, J., 1999. Palestine During the Second World War. In: Gross, N.T. (Ed.), *Not by Spirit Alone: Studies in the Economic History of Modern Palestine and*

Israel. The Hebrew University Magnes Press and Yad Izhak Ben-Zvi Press, Jerusalem, pp. 324–300 (in Hebrew).

Gruenbaum, A.L., 1944. To Horowitz from Gruenbaum, April 16, Central Zionist Archive. S90/875.

Hacohen, D., 1994. *Immigrants in Turmoil*. Jerusalem: Yad Ben-Zvi Press (in Hebrew).

Halevi, N., 1983. The Political Economy of Absorptive Capacity: Growth and Cycles in Jewish Palestine under the British Mandate. *Middle Eastern Studies* 19, 456–469.

Hobson, J.M., 1997. *The Wealth of States: A Comparative Sociology of International Economic and Political Change*. Cambridge University Press, Cambridge.

Horowitz, D., 1942. Summary of D. Horowitz's Lecture on the Economic Problems of the Transition Period, September 17. Central Zionist Archive, S7/2392.

Horowitz, D., 1944a. Palestine at a Crossroads. *Cooperative Bulletin* 13–14, 117–120 (in Hebrew).

Horowitz, D., 1944b. A letter from D. Horowitz to D. Ben-Gurion, September 4. Central Zionist Archive, S90/80.

Horowitz, D., 1947. Minutes of an Open Session Before UNSCOP. April 4. Yad Yaari Archive, Division 74–95, Box 2, File 3.

JVL (Jewish Virtual Library). 1942. Declaration Adopted by the Biltmore Conference. Jewish Virtual Library. Available at: www.jewishvirtuallibrary.org/the-biltmore-conference-1942 (accessed June 6, 2017).

Keren, M., 1988. *Ben-Gurion and the Intellectuals*. Ben-Gurion University, Qiryat Sde Boker (in Hebrew).

Koistinen, P.A.C., 2004. *Arsenal of World War II: The Political Economy of American Warfare, 1940–1945*. University Press of Kansas, Lawrence, KS.

List, NA. n.d. List of Publications and Studies in Connection with Post-War Planning. Central Zionist Archive, S90/847.

Margalit, E., 1944. Margalit's Lecture, March 13. Central Zionist Archive, S90/880.

Nash, G.D., 1990. *The American West Transformed: The Impact of the Second World War*. University of Nebraska Press, Lincoln, NE.

Nathan, R.R., Gass, O. and Creamer, D.B., 1946. *Palestine: Problem and Promise, an Economic Study*. American Council on Public Affairs, Washington, DC.

Proposal, 1943. A Proposal for the Division of Planning between Central Committees and Sub-Committees. September 17. Central Zionist Archive, S90/879.

Rook, R.E., 2000. An American in Palestine: Elwood Mead and Zionist Water Resources Planning, 1923–1936. *Arab Studies Quarterly* 22, 71–89.

Ruppin, A., 1942. Dr. Ruppin at the Conference of the Economic Research Institute. September 17. Central Zionist Archive, S7/2392.

Shavit, Y., Goldstein, Y. and Beer, H. (Eds.), 1983. *Personalities in Eretz Israel*. Tel-Aviv: Am Oved.

Troen, S.I., 2003. *Imagining Zion: Dreams, Designs, and Realities in a Century of Jewish Settlement*. Yale University Press, New Haven, CT.

UN, 1947. *United Nations Special Committee on Palestine: Report to the General Assembly*. United Nations, New York.

Waldner, D., 1999. *State Building and Late Development*. Cornell University Press, Ithaca, NY.

Weiss, L., 1995. Governed Interdependence: Rethinking the Government-Business Relationship in East Asia. *The Pacific Review* 8 (4) 589–616.

White Paper, 1939. British White Paper of 1939: The Avalon Project. http://avalon.law.yale.edu/20th_century/brwh1939.asp (accessed: July 20, 2017).

Part II

From full employment to economic independence

Production and finance

4 Economic independence

Reality, policy and rhetoric

The enactment of the austerity policy—the recession policy, as it is often called—which ran from 1965 to 1966, was a milestone in the economic history of Israel. On this occasion, the Israeli government, with broad support from the Knesset, implemented an economic policy that caused unemployment and recession. The enactment of the austerity policy ended almost two decades of rapid growth and full employment policies, and almost four decades of a strategic alliance between the state (or the national institutions during the Mandate period) and the General Labor Union, the Histadrut.

This dramatic change of policy had both economic and social impacts on Israel's historical path. From an economic perspective, Israel's policy changed from an inward-oriented industrialization strategy, designed to create jobs and increase production, to an export-oriented industrialization strategy, designed to promote Israeli goods and services in the global marketplace. The change had social consequences: to promote exports the government had to liberalize the labor market and curtail its job creation support policy and reallocating this support toward export-oriented businesses. Moreover, the government had to abandon its full employment policy and not only accept, but actually promote, a higher level of unemployment.

The literature on the austerity policy focuses on the immediate causes of the austerity policy. Economists argue that the policy was a response to the rising current account deficit: in 1964, the trade deficit widened from 40 percent of GDP to 46 percent, after several years of steady decrease (Figure 4.1). In response, the government decided to cool the economy and put a brake on investment, production and consumption (Greenwald, 1972). Political economists explain the austerity policy as a response to the crisis in industrial relations caused by over-employment that brought a spiral of wage rises, frequent strikes and eventually a loss of control over the labor force (Grinberg, 1991; Shalev, 1992).

The two explanations, however, leave some open questions. Both make the tacit assumption that the existence of a policy problem is a sufficient explanation for the government response, as if any policy problem had one and only one policy solution. In practice, responses of governments follow a longer process during which the policy problem is framed, defined and policy responses are dis-

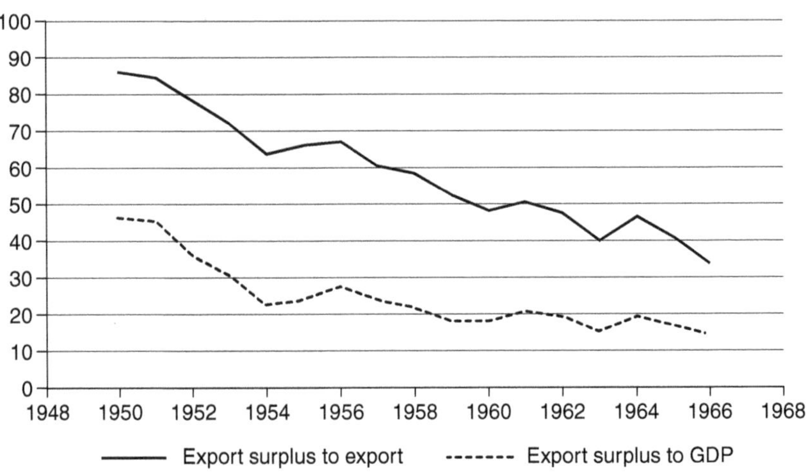

Figure 4.1 Export surplus to export and to GDP, 1949–1966 (%).

Sources: Krampf (2015, p. 93, Figure 2). Based on Halevi and Klinov-Malul (1968, p. 115, Table 50; p. 194, Table 74).

cussed, assessed, rejected or accepted. Therefore, the question why the government enacted an austerity policy includes the underlying question, why policy-makers believed that an austerity policy was the best response to the prevailing policy problems. The answer to this question requires a longer-term perspective on the ideational, institutional and political economic changes, that took place in the years preceding the enactment of the 1965 austerity policy.

The austerity policy, it is argued here, was the culmination of a long-term gradual process of policy paradigm change that started with the enactment of the New Economic Policy in February 1952. The process took place at three levels: (1) an ideational level that consisted of the arrival of new policy ideas; (2) an institutional level that consisted of the emergence of new state agencies within the state; and (3) a structural-political level that consisted of a change in the linkage pattern between the state and non-state actors. Whereas over time, each of the three levels affected the others, the key driver of change of this process was the change in the external political economic conditions, and the response of the state to this.

The politics of the current account deficit

A key feature of the paradigm of rapid development was the assumption that financial constraints should not restrict the attainment of national objectives. In practical terms, it meant that the scarcity of foreign reserves and the trade deficit should not pose any constraint on the key policy objectives of immigration, industrialization and the attainment of full employment. In other words, money should not impose constraints on national objectives. However, over time, during the 1950s and the 1960s, policy-makers, politicians and economists started to express their concern regarding the problem of the current account, and the need to reconsider the prioritization of rapid development. The demand for this change had political implications: it implied a friendlier policy toward businesses and less friendly policy toward the workers. The process of transition, therefore, had both elements of social learning as well as political elements of political conflict. To tell the historical story, it is necessary to dwell on the political economy of the current account.

The *current account* forms part of the *balance of payments* which records the transactions that take place between an economy and the rest of the world. The current account includes three items: the trade balance—the gap between exported and imported goods and services—the yield on foreign investment, and, finally, net transfers, which are unilateral transfers of capital, such as foreign aid. In many cases, the yield on foreign investment is negligible and therefore the trade balance plus net transfers are almost identical to the current account.

Having a trade deficit implies that the value of the nation imports exceeds the value of its exports. When a country imports more than it exports, it has to find a source of foreign currency to finance its net imports. This can be done through "gifts"—unilateral transfers or by long-term loans. Logically, it is impossible for all countries in the world to have a trade surplus: for every country that has a surplus of one dollar, another county must have a deficit of one dollar. Therefore, the question arises whether governments should perceive their trade deficit as a problem, or rather, as a blessing: the fact that they can run a trade deficit implies that they can raise loans or receive grants. The answer to this question depends on several factors.

First, the national value of the deficit depends on the uses to which the imported goods are put. Given that a state may have a preference for long-term growth and industrialization, a trade deficit would contribute to attaining these goals if the import surplus is channeled into productive purposes rather than into consumption. Productive purposes include developing infrastructure, industrialization, and in some cases an intensification of agriculture and housing. The capacity to control the allocation resources, however, requires an effective bureaucracy and significant control over the banking and the financial systems.

A second factor that affects the national value of a trade deficit is the price of foreign capital and the domestic yield on investment. As a rule of thumb, a trade deficit is desirable if the price of foreign credit—the interest rate charged to obtain it—is lower than the domestic yield on its investment. However, this is only part of the story: even in cases when the price of foreign capital is higher than domestic yield, a trade deficit may be justified if the government use it for investment in infrastructure, the contribution of which to social welfare cannot always be quantified in purely monetary terms.

A trade deficit also affects the country's international position: a country running a trade deficit becomes dependent on foreign loans and financial aid, thus making it dependent on the institutions that provide such international credit: other states, banks or international institutions. The resultant political dependency may then be manifested by events such as the intervention of foreign actors in domestic policy-making processes (Cardoso and Faletto, 1979).

The existence of a trade deficit may also have other domestic political implications. In small economies, an attempt to increase exports through lower levels of real wages may result in higher levels of socio-economic inequality. Attempts by the government to lower the trade deficit will require lower real wages and higher levels of unemployment. Hence, such a policy would be consistent with the interests of employers rather than of workers. On the other hand, a country which prioritizes full employment is likely to have higher real wages but lower labor productivity. This approach would require the government to use alternative means to restrict imports, such as taxes and subsidies. A government's preference for one of the two strategies is likely to be affected by the incentive structure created by international factors.

Finally, the national value of a trade deficit can also be affected by the prevailing international trade and money regimes. In an international regime that includes capital controls, the costs of a high trade deficit are lower than in a more liberalized regime. If the government can control capital movement, it can run higher levels of public debt without the risk of a damaging capital outflow. For example, during the period of the Bretton Woods system, capital controls were common (Ruggie, 1982). They shielded small economies from international financial markets and the costs of running a trade deficit were lower. In the transition to the global economy, global financial markets proved more likely to "punish" countries with severe or chronic deficits.

Hence, the current account balance—or the trade balance—is a controversial issue both economically and politically. The size of the deficit is not determined only by "economic fundamentals" but it is also the product of a policy choice. A government may prioritize the reduction of its trade deficit, but it may also choose to maintain a high deficit and prioritize other policy objectives.

Israel is a relatively small state operating in the global market, and therefore its decisions in the economic policy domain must take into account the implications of these choices on its current account. This chapter argues that during the period between the establishment of the state until the implementation of the austerity policy in 1965, the government gradually changed its prioritization regarding reducing the trade deficit. This choice required the political leadership to reprioritize the state's interests.

The trade deficit in the pre-state era

In the pre-state era the national institutions discussed the trade deficit of the Jewish economy and aimed at persuading the international community that a Jewish state in Palestine was a realistic possibility. During the 1930s, an era of economic prosperity, the trade deficit of the Jewish sector in Palestine reached one-third of the total value of imports. Despite this high ratio, the deficit, however, was not considered a problem because the import of capital counteracted this. Jewish economists argued "not only that the balance of payment *can* be passive, it *should* be passive" (Avramovitz, 1938, p. 35). The deficit was financed mainly by assets imported into Palestine by the immigrants themselves (70 percent), as well as by capital mobilized by the World Zionist Organization (20 percent) (Michaely, 1963, pp. 1–3).

During World War II, the Jewish economy was in surplus as the economy of Palestine was largely isolated and the British Army had no other choice but to purchase most of its needs from Jewish manufacturers and farmers. The transactions with the British Army were treated as exports. The foreign reserves that were accumulated on behalf of the Jewish economy by the Palestine Currency Board during this period were transferred to the Israeli government after the establishment of the state.

After the war, when the Anglo-American Committee and the UNSCOP discussed the idea of a Jewish state, the Jewish Agency had to prove the economic viability of the idea. The agency had to explain how the Jewish economy would survive with such a high trade deficit as was seen during the 1930s. Horowitz, in his testimony, explained that the trade deficit of the Jewish economy was caused by the import of capital and therefore posed no problem:

> It is not so much that the deficit in the Palestine trade balance is covered by capital import. This would be an erroneous definition of the situation. Jewish capital import into Palestine is causing the deficit in the trade balance. Of course, capital import must find its expression in the import of goods and commodities.
>
> (Horowitz, 1947)

The question of the direction of causality also concerned the policy-makers at the Jewish Agency. Eliezer Kaplan, the Treasurer of the Jewish Agency, confessed that the high current account deficit posed a "danger" that was "concealed by large financial reserves, the import of capital, and military expenditure" (ibid.). After the state was established, in his capacity as Director General of the Ministry of Finance, Horowitz presented both interpretations of the Finance Committee in the parliament: one could argue that the current account deficit was "covered" by the import of capital; or that "because we have an enormous import of capital, it creates a negative trade balance." Both definitions are, he claimed, "quite valid" (Finance Committee, 7 December 1949, p. 5).

The question concerning the direction of causality between the trade deficit and the import of capital persisted within Israeli policy discourse for some time. Those who supported the continuation of rapid development and mass immigration argued, that as long as Israel had foreign financial sources, it should use them and expand them as much as possible. In contrast, those who believed that the government should restrict its intervention in the economy, advocated a policy that prioritized economic independence.

Trade deficit, war and immigration

Sovereignty brought with it new responsibilities and new policy problems. First, there was the security policy problem: between 1947 and 1949, Israel engaged in a war of survival with its Arab neighbors, which, according to estimations, consumed around 40 percent of GDP (Gross, 2000, p. 331). The second policy problem was the transplantation and absorption of immigration: between 1948 and 1951, the domestic Jewish population grew from 630,000 to 1.4 million. (Halevi and Klinov-Malul, 1968, p. 40, Table 7). The vast numbers of immigrants entered the underdeveloped economy, were housed in transition camps—*Maabarot*— isolated from the local economy. As was planned, they were only gradually absorbed into the mainstream economy.[1] During the transition period the immigrants were dependent on the state for their survival. This strategy involved a very high level of unemployment. In 1949, the unemployment rate reached 14 percent according to official estimates.

The financial burden both of waging war and the absorption of immigration placed an enormous strain on the trade deficit, which reached 50 percent of the GDP in 1950. In the early years the trade deficit was financed by the foreign reserves accumulated during World War II. As these reserves dwindled, the government faced a tough dilemma.

Trade deficit, inflation and the standard of living

Another policy problem that the government faced in its very early years was inflation. Israeli policy-makers had little experience with dealing with inflation. During the British Mandate, the local currency was fixed to the British pound, and therefore inflation could not have been caused by monetary expansion. During World War II, prices rose due to limited supply, a phenomenon which was dealt with by rationing and price control (Gross, 2000; Seikaly, 2016). With independence, the government issued its own currency and it had the capacity to finance its expenses through the issuance of money. In the first years, a quarter of the state budget was financed through the issuance of new money (Halevi and Klinov-Malul, 1968, p. 154, table 63).[2]

Nevertheless, the Treasury did not associate the problem of inflation with the expansionary monetary policy of the government, but with the scarcity of goods. This interpretation was probably shaped by the British response to the inflation shocks in Palestine during the war, which was dealt with by rationing and price control (Seikaly, 2016, p. 85). The Treasury, therefore, tried to fight inflation by increasing the supply of goods, that is, by expanding imports. "The war on inflation," argued David Horowitz, the Director General, "requires introducing as many products as possible to the consumer market at the lowest prices possible" (Finance Committee, December 7, 1949, p. 5). It must be kept in mind that inflation had socio-economic implications: given constant (and low) wages, the inflated prices significantly lowered the capacity of a large proportion of the population—many of them new immigrants—to purchase basic goods. However, lowering prices by increasing imports widened the trade deficit.

The Treasury framed the situation as a choice between the risk of dwindling foreign reserves and "cruelty": "The size of the reserve depends upon our cruelty. Increasing reserves means a worse standard of living and public hardship" (ibid., p. 5).

The first to demand a change of policy were the right-wing parties. As early as 1949, they demanded the government change its monetary course. Both Herut and the General Zionists, who represented the private sector and the middle class, and were not included in the government coalition, argued that the deteriorating levels of foreign reserves posed a threat to the national interest as it undermined the confidence of foreign investors in the Israeli currency. The argument based on "confidence" was rejected out of hand by Horowitz as "pure psychology that is opposed to the national interest." The current account deficit, he claimed, "is a consequence of Zionism and of absorbing many [immigrants] who are largely consumers, and whom we must turn into producers.... The problem is not merely confidence and prestige" (ibid., p. 11).

However, within a year or two, the position of the Ministry of Finance began drifting toward that of the liberal parties and a gap opened up between the position of the Ministry of Finance and the Prime Minister's Office, which still adhered to old paradigm. At that stage the Treasury embraced the monetarist interpretation of inflation: "We throw banknotes and coins into the money market to a much greater extent than is desirable," argued the minister of finance. As long as they persisted in doing so, "the disease [of inflation] will continue to spread" (Finance Committee, September 11, 1950, p. 1).

The monetarist interpretation of inflation implied a different causal link between inflation and the trade deficit, and therefore a different policy response. According to the new interpretation, the trade deficit and inflation were positively correlated, and therefore the government, it was argued now, should restrain its spending. Horowitz explained that when the domestic money supply increases, given that "our production costs are extremely high by international comparison," we of course see that "our prices can by no means compete with international prices" (Finance Committee, November 28, 1950, p. 6). Obviously, this analysis excludes the option of a devaluation of the exchange rate. These claims imply that the government did not seriously consider the option of currency devaluation.

Horowitz's technical assertion had a hefty policy implication: the government had to make a choice between low inflation and a low trade deficit, on the one hand, and the continuation of the mass immigration policy, on the other. "As long as each year more people enter the country," he explained, "the chances for a real absorption of the immigrants is reduced. This is the internal secret of our balance of payments" (Finance Committee, December 4, 1951). This framing of the policy choices the government faced can be taken as the first cracks in the ideational edifice of the paradigm of rapid development. If there is a trade-off between the absorption of the immigrants and reducing the trade deficit, and if reducing the trade deficit is a strategic objective, then there might be the case for the government having to reconsider its priorities.

As the state's foreign reserves were deteriorating, a split was created between the Prime Minister Office and the Finance Ministry.[3] Whereas the prime minister defended the continuation of the mass immigration policy, the Ministry of Finance started to implement austerity measures without the formal approval of the Knesset. Horowitz, the Director General, presented his position to the Finance Committee of the Knesset:

> I have only one criterion for absorption: how it affects the balance of payments ... There is a simple mathematical formula that no slogan can change: if more Jews are brought into the country, and one cannot increase income correspondingly—there is less integration and capital is consumed. If we strip ourselves of our brains as Jews and become simple economists, this, then, is our main point.
>
> (Ibid.)

What made the Treasury change its position regarding austerity? By 1951, the continuation of mass immigration was no longer of vital interest to Israel. Until July 1949, Israel was at war and immigration was still perceived essential to the survival of the state. After a truce was reached, the policy concerns shifted from short-term security issues to long-term economic issues. Moreover, by the end of 1949, the number of Jewish immigrants had reached around 700,000 per year and the economic and social costs of the mass immigration policy had surfaced. At this point, there was a growing demand to re-examine the continuation of the mass immigration policy and with the rising power of the liberal parties acting as a catalyst, even the Prime Minister, David Ben-Gurion, began supporting the austerity policy.

Between liberalism and socialism

The tension between the prime minister and the Treasury was accompanied by a growing political competition between Mapai and the liberal opposition from the right. In the local municipalities elections of November 1950, the liberal right had an astonishing success, which threatened the dominance of Mapai. The General Zionists, a party that represented the middle class, won 24.5 percent of the votes in comparison to only 5.2 percent in the previous elections. This achievement positioned the party in the second place after Mapai that won 27.3 percent of the votes. The General Zionists repeated its success in the general election of July 1951, in which it won 20 seats in comparison to the seven they held from the previous election, which likewise turned them into the second largest party in the parliament (Rozin, 2008).

The demand to terminate the mass immigration policy was a key item in the General Zionists' platform. In 1949, Peretz Bernstein, one of the party's leaders, declared: “At this point in time I am not sure whether immigration strengthens our position or weakens it” (Knesset, March 17, 1949, vol. 1, p. 152). Bernstein argued that the resources allocated to the immigrants had not contributed to “development.” Rather it was money that was wasted on “welfare work” (Knesset, September 18, 1951, vol. 1, p. 85).

The government’s policy faced opposition also from the socialist left in the Knesset. The socialist and communist parties argued that Israel was losing its independence to the United States, which was portrayed as an imperialistic power. The high level of government expenditure were financed partly by loans and grants from the United States. During the period from 1949 to 1951, the US administration transferred more than US$300 million to Israel in loans and grants. This represented 35 percent of the accumulated current account deficit during those years.[4] The first loan for the amount of US$100 million was received in 1949 from the American Import-Export Bank. Two years later another US$35 million loan was received, and a third loan of US$185 million was received in 1951 (Halevi and Klinov-Malul, 1968, p. 134).

The Communist Party—Maki—condemned the government for sacrificing Israel’s economic and political independence. A member of the Communist Party, Shmuel Mikonis, argued that the US support was motivated by the desire to “expand the American markets into different parts of the world” (Knesset, March 17, 1949, vol. 1, p. 151). The loans from US banks, they argued, should be invested in agriculture rather than in industry: “We shall have to account for our foreign trade, our gold reserves, wages, prices, the national and public budget, international investments and debts—in short, for everything” (ibid., p. 152). The socialist parties believed that American support was a means to intervene in Israel’s internal affairs. The timing of the loans, they argued, was proof that Ben-Gurion’s decision to exclude the socialist party, Mapam, from the coalition and to take into the government the General Zionists, was the result of American pressure. “The turn of the government to the right was the first impact of the American loan,” argued a member of the Communist Party (ibid., p. 152).

The dependence thesis propounded by the left gained credibility when the idea of Israel joining the Middle East Command was made public. The Command, as it was called, was a military organization intended to be an arm of the North Atlantic Treaty Organization (NATO). The socialist daily newspaper, *Al Hamishmar*, reported that the socialist movement in Israel was an obstacle to Israel joining the Command. The Mapam Party, which was more cautious than the Communist Party in its attacks on the government, also opposed what was perceived as an attempt by the United States to turn Israel into its military base. Moshe Sneh, one of the party’s leaders, declared: “The Israeli Defense Force would never submit to the command of Atlantic generals, even if their orders were translated into Hebrew” (Sneh, 1951).

When the US administration granted the Israeli government the right to sell Israeli bonds to American citizens—the Independence Loan (Milve Ha’atzmaut)—the Communist Party presented it as yet another manifestation of the infiltration of American influence into Israel. It was “nothing but another form of enslavement of the Israeli economy by American monopolistic capital. It is nothing but another shackle binding Israel to the bandwagon of American imperialism," argued Tufik Tobi (Knesset, February 20, 1951, vol. 8, p. 1135). Therefore, the real purpose of the loans was not to help Israel but to "prepare the ground for turning our country into a strategic and economic base for American warmongers" (ibid., p. 1135).

Hence, despite the political dominance of Mapai, as expressed in its position at the Knesset—in the election of 1951, Mapai maintained its dominance in the Knesset by securing 45 seats (out of 120)—the government faced severe opposition from both the liberal right and the socialist left.

Toward the New Economic Policy

The political success of the liberal right, as well as the position of the Ministry of Finance, increased the pressure on the government to end the mass immigration policy and to employ an austerity policy. In 1951, the Ministry of Finance started to implement the New Economic Policy. By the end of the year the New Economic Policy became a *fait accompli* and in February 1952, Ben-Gurion himself presented, advocated and defended it in the Knesset.

In terms of content, the New Economic Policy was fully consistent with the liberal right demands. It included three key elements: (1) a balanced budget; (2) a curtailing of consumer credit; and (3) a devaluation of the Israeli lira. Three exchange rates were set: US$2.80 per lira for the import of essential food products; US$1.40 per lira for fund raisers, tourists, the diplomatic corps, and several commodities such as meat, fish, coffee, tea, medication, and fertilizers; and US$1.00 per lira for capital investors. The differential exchange rate was common practice during the 1950s and was intended, as Ben-Gurion explained, to "encourage the flow of capital from abroad, stabilize the currency, strengthen the export of agricultural and industrial products while simultaneously preventing the prices of vital necessities from rising" (Knesset, February 13, 1952, vol. 11, p. 1321).

The rhetoric by which the New Economic Policy was legitimized was not less important than its content. Ben-Gurion faced a difficult task: how to legitimize an austerity policy the principles of which ran counter to the core values that he himself had created and promoted for at least a decade, including values that had become intrinsic to the very definition of Israel's national identity? A key concept in Ben-Gurion's speech was that of "economic independence."

"Economic independence is not in the sky," Ben-Gurion declared from the podium in the parliament. And he continued:

> First, we must secure our food supply from the product of our land.... Locally produced food is not merely an economic and financial necessity, as we do not have the foreign currency to buy food abroad, but it is also a primary security need. We are still under siege, and the siege imposed upon us by our neighbors is not likely to be lifted any time soon.
>
> (Ibid., p. 1319)

There is no doubt, he asserted:

> that if we persist in our agricultural and industrial development project, at the rate and the extent at which we have pursued it so far, and we obtain the means necessary for it, within a few years we shall reach the haven of a strong, stable economy.
>
> (Ibid., p. 1317)

The innovative aspect in Ben-Gurion's speech concerned the means of achieving economic independence: the price mechanism, high productivity and the right of employers to profit: "The price and the profit will be determined by the efficiency of the market and the refinement of production techniques that is likely to reduce production costs, increase productivity, and improve the quality," explained Ben-Gurion. Moreover,

> the right to employment is binding. But we also recognize the right of the entrepreneurs and of capital owners, who contribute to the development of the country and to the absorption of immigrants, to a fair profit. This [right] is also binding.
>
> (Ibid., pp. 1319–1321)

The New Economic Policy lasted for no more than two years, until the Reparation Agreement with West Germany came into force in March 1953. However, the rhetoric of the New Economic Policy created a new policy legacy that offered an alternative to the paradigm of rapid development. Ben-Gurion demonstrated that economic independence—a strong state preference—could only be achieved by market practices and through cooperation between the state and the private sector. This idea was the seed of the new policy paradigm, which would be consolidated in the following years.

The notion of economic independence became a token used by policy-makers and economists from both the political left and right as they all accepted the objective of economic independence as a key state interest. The first volume of the Israeli *Economic Quarterly* (*Rivon Lekalkala*) came out in 1953 and stated that the objective of the journal was to become "a free venue, constructive and critical, designed for economists and men of action, to contribute to our progress toward *economic independence*."[5] Whereas the objective of economic independence was accepted by both socialist and liberals, workers and employers, there was no consensus regarding either the meaning of the term or how to attain it.

Defining economic independence

During the 1950s, professional economists attempted to define and quantify economic independence, as well as to provide policy recommendations on how to achieve it. Abba P. Lerner, the American-Jewish Keynesian economist, who had been invited to join the Economic Advisory Staff (EAS) headed by Oscar Gass, at the Prime Minister's Office, was the first to make such an attempt (Krampf, 2010). In the first volume of the *Economic Quarterly*, Lerner published an article on the attainment of economic independence. Lerner's point of departure was that, in the future, Israel would inevitably exhaust its foreign resources and therefore economic independence will be imposed on it anyway. The government, therefore, must "prepare the way towards economic independence" (Lerner, 1954, p. 3). To reach sustainable independence, Lerner recommended that the government use three policy instruments: cut real wages, subsidize exports while taxing imports, and devalue the lira (ibid., pp. 10–11).

A few years later, Daniel Creamer, an American-Jewish economist, who was the Research Director of the Falk Institute in Jerusalem, proposed a method to quantify and then measure Israel's economic dependence during its first decade. He defined economic dependence as the ratio of the import surplus (trade deficit) to the sum of the national economic resources, which is equal to the sum of the national product plus the import capital. Creamer's study concluded that during its first decade, Israel had made progress and came close to economic independence (Creamer *et al.*, 1957). Using the same index a few years later, Dan Pines, an economist in the Planning Authority of the Prime Minister's Office, found that between 1950 and 1959, the ratio of import surplus to the available national resources had reduced from 33 percent to 15 percent (Pines, 1961, p. 250). In simple terms, both economists favorably judged the government policy, which brought the economy closer to the goal of economic independence.

The positive evaluations of the government policy by Creamer and Pines did not satisfy Don Patinkin, who believed that the government should abandon the full employment policy. Patinkin, at the time the head of the Economics Department at the Hebrew University and the Research Director of the Falk Institute (replacing Creamer), published his book, *The First Decade* in 1960—a comprehensive book about the Israeli economy which was an overarching condemnation of the government's policies of rapid development strategy and full employment. These policies, argued Patinkin, were a failure. Patinkin made his own calculations and he reached the conclusion that "since 1953 the Israeli economy has not come significantly closer to economic independence.... Here lies the key failure of the economic policy during the first decade" (ibid., pp. 114–115). To reach economic independence, argued Patinkin, the government must change course and abandon the full employment policy. Patinkin believed that the solution to the current account deficit was to expose the labor force to market forces and to accept higher levels of unemployment.

Patinkin's argument provoked hostile responses from those local economists, who were not part of the Economics Department or the Falk Institute. Dan Pines, an economist at the Planning Authority at the Prime Minister Office, argued that Patinkin's econometric analysis was flawed because he used *current prices* instead of *constant prices*. This choice, argued Pines, "distorts … the direction of change, that is, the trend" (Pines, 1961). The editor of the *Economic Quarterly*, Yosef Ronnen, was skeptical regarding the whole attempt to quantify the concept of economic independence, which to him was "a policy slogan" rather than “a concept with clear economic-scientific content.” The problem was that, on the one hand, policy-makers see in economic independence “a desired situation … a central goal, a supreme and final purpose for our economic policy,” but, on the other hand, this is a situation which policy-makers fear as the “import of capital is abolished.” Therefore, he argued that it is better to make an effort to find “alternative sources for the import of capital in addition to the promotion of exports and the production of import substitutes” (Ronnen, 1960, p. 163).

Similarly, David Golomb, Director of the Economic Research Institute of the Histadrut,[6] argued that it made no economic sense to reduce the import surplus as long as Israel had cheap available foreign financial resources. Israel, he argued, “would rely on import of capital for many years to come.” Any attempt to restrict imports required an increase in Israel’s foreign exchange reserves, which were quite large at the time and had reached the international average. Moreover, the cost of long-term international credit was lower than the yield on domestic investment and, even from a purely economic perspective; there was no reason to repay debt rather than investing available capital. Golomb’s conclusion was clear: “The size of the import surplus cannot serve as a goal of economic policy, and it cannot serve as a criterion for its success” (1961, pp. 150–151).

Patinkin’s interpretation was rejected by many economists. Nevertheless, he succeeded in injecting his ideas into the policy-making circles in the Ministry of Finance and the Bank of Israel and eventually helped shape the government’s austerity policy (the Recession Policy) in 1967.

Patinkin’s boys

The success of Patinkin in shaping government policy is a historical puzzle: Patinkin was a graduate of the Economics Department at the University of Chicago, known for its pro-market policies. Policy-makers in Israel during the 1950s and the 1960s were known to have no tolerance for abstract ideas such as “free markets,” and they were known to aspire to control anything that could be controlled. How, then, can the collaboration between Patinkin and his “boys” and the Israeli political echelon be explained?

There are two complementary factors that can explain this puzzle. First, an institutional factor: Patinkin succeeded, in ways that will be demonstrated below, to monopolize the academic economic field in Israel and to crowd out any potential competitors as producers of economic knowledge. Second, an ideational factor: Patinkin advocated free market practices, but he did not advocate liberal ideas and therefore he did not pose a threat to the legitimacy of the state to intervene in the economy.

A useful starting point for Don Patinkin’s story is his graduation in 1947 from the Economics Department of the University of Chicago, where he studied under the supervision of Oskar R. Lange (Mehrling, 2002; Patinkin, 1995). In 1949, he immigrated to Israel after the Hebrew University offered him the position of a founding director of the Economics Department (Gross, 2004a, 2004b). In 1954, an American philanthropic foundation named after Morris Falk decided to establish a research institute for economic policy studies in Israel. The American economist Simone Kuznets was invited to oversee the project. Kuznets had in mind an institute that would "furnish independent competent analysis of economic facts, upon which more rational decisions affecting national policy may be based" (Kuznets, 1953a). This would then in turn "develop trained economic analysts for careers in government, teaching and industry" (Kuznets, 1953b). The first director of research was Daniel Creamer who laid the foundation for Israel's National Account System and was the first to develop a quantitative index for Israel's economic independence (Krampf, 2010).

Toward the end of the Creamer contract in 1956, Kuznets offered Patinkin the job of directing the Falk Institute. Kuznets wanted the Institute to be directed as an independent unit, but Patinkin insisted that the Falk Institute be affiliated with the Economics Department of the university. Patinkin was by far the most prestigious economist in Israel at the time and Kuznets had no choice but to accept Patinkin's conditions (ibid.), and his position as the Director of the Falk Institute enabled him to provide his students from the Economics Department with employment and research experience and to nurture connections between the department and state institutions, especially government ministries (Kleiman, 1981). Patinkin's simultaneous control over both the Economics Department and the Falk Institute enabled him to create a hierarchical and cohesive community of economists—Patinkin's boys. His students were dependent on him financially and professionally, meaning the incentives to follow his intellectual path were strong.

Monopolizing the academic economic discourse was a necessary but by itself not a sufficient condition for Patinkin's success in injecting his ideas to the policy-making circles. The question still arises why pro-interventionist policymakers took advice from Patinkin, who constantly criticized the government policy and who advocated free market policy principles, which were allegedly inconsistent with the government's economic approach.

A detailed analysis of Patinkin's writings, however, demonstrates that his views were closer to the government than one would expect. Whereas Patinkin criticized the government's policy, he did not question the basic assumption, according to which economic policy should prioritize the interests of the state, rather than the interests of the individuals. Patinkin did not advocate economic liberalism, which relegates weight to individual rights and freedom, but he advocated a kind of state-centered market economy, in which markets are instruments that serve the collective.

As a graduate of the Economics Department of the University of Chicago, Patinkin saw in the price mechanism a means for the efficient allocation of resources and therefore principally he opposed any intervention that might distort prices. A detailed analysis of Patinkin's world view, however, reveals that Patinkin's position was not based on a liberal world view, according to which markets are designed to serve individual interests and to guarantee economic freedom. He believed that the efficient market economy should serve the aggregated political body, that is, the state. Patinkin's conception of the role of the state in governing a market economy was probably influenced by his teacher, Henry Simons, who believed that the state must play an essential role in "opposing with equal rigor all forms of monopoly, business as well as labor unions" (Simons, [1934] 1948). Hence, whereas Patinkin opposed socialism, he was not a liberal. Perry Mehrling argued that for Patinkin the dilemma was not a choice between social control and laissez-faire, "but rather how practically to use social control to implement and sustain liberalism" (2002, p. 164).

Patinkin's unique world view can explain the enigma of why Patinkin was embraced and respected by the local political elite in Israel, despite his critical policy views. Unlike liberals who questioned the legitimacy of the government to intervene in the allocation of resources, Patinkin's nuanced argument was that the government did not intervene in the right way. He opposed the government's full employment policy and argued that it should expose the labor force to market forces. However, he—nor any of his students—did not oppose the intervention of the government to promote exports.

Patinkin's view differed fundamentally from economists such as Milton Friedman or Friedrich Hayek, who perceived markets not only as efficient mechanisms for the allocation of resources, but as political mechanisms that protect individuals against the power of sovereigns. In Patinkin's world view, the rights of individuals and economic freedom were not discussed. Therefore, there was a common understanding between the political leadership of Mapai and Patinkin's boys, regarding the prioritization of the state interests over the interests of individuals. This common understanding facilitated the pervasive entry of Patinkin's ideas into policy-making circles.

The Workers Corporation and the government

With the advent of the paradigm of economic independence, the government had to reconsider the traditional link with the Histadrut sector. The state allocated resources to the Histadrut sector, which in turn used the resources in ways that were consistent with the government's economic strategy. Over time, however, the tie to the Histadrut turned into a liability: the dependence of the state on the Histadrut undermined the autonomy of the state. The state was restricted in its capacity to implement policies that were not consistent with the interests of the Histadrut and it was restricted in nurturing ties with other market and societal actors. In particular, the situation was made worse by the fact that the Histadrut—in its traditional form—increased the political and economic costs associated with a policy change toward export-oriented development.

The Histadrut—the General Jewish Federation of Workers in Palestine—was established in 1920 by the Jewish socialist parties. Its role exceeded that of a conventional labor union given that the Jewish national organizations did not have sovereignty. Hence the Histadrut filled the institutional gap and performed functions, including in the field of economic and social policy. Moreover, due to the national conflict between the Jewish and Arab populations, the Histadrut was not a “universal” labor union but was rather a national organization. A milestone was the establishment of the Workers Corporation (*Chevrat Ha'ovdim*) in 1923, a holding company owned by the Histadrut, which established and owned various economic enterprises and had a status comparable to that of government companies. The Histadrut therefore had a central role in building the economy during the pre-state period and it maintained close ties with the political leadership of the Jewish Agency (Gorny, 1996; Greenberg, 2004).

By the time the state was established, the Workers Corporation had become a powerful economic and political entity. In terms of size, it contributed around 20 percent of the GDP, equal to that of the government sector. It owned a large number of companies in diverse economic sectors: Sollel Boné (construction); Mekorot (water supply); Yachin (citrus production); Shikun (urban housing); Tnuva (dairy and fresh food); and Hamashbir Hamerkasi (distribution and logistics). In addition, the Workers Corporation owned Bank Hapoalim (The Workers Bank), the second largest bank in Israel along with a large number of credit associations (Greenberg, 2004).

The hierarchical ownership structure of the Workers Corporation, its centralized managerial style and the ties to the government turned it into a highly effective instrument of economic control. In particular, through the Workers Corporation, the government could control the allocation of resources. Zeév On, the Director of the Workers Corporation, described how it worked:

> If the government wants to maintain the productive credit, and to distinguish between productive and consumer credit, between essential credit and non-essential credit, … I think that this forum [the Economic Committee of the Labor Movement], through its management institutions and the Workers Corporation as a central institution that coordinates between the members and the governments, can do so more successfully, than any other sector will do it some other way.

The policy of the Histadrut and of the Workers Corporation, he argued, “complements the government policy and supports it, in that it enables rationing and the control [of prices]” (Economic Committee LM, April 1, 1954, p. 6).

The Histadrut and the Workers Corporation also enabled the government to more effectively govern the labor force. This was urgently needed during the mass immigration period when the government faced the prospect of dealing with hundreds of thousands of unskilled laborers who had to be absorbed into the economy and had to be provided with paying jobs. The Workers Corporation was the largest employer in Israel. Sollel Boné, the construction company, was the largest of its companies. Between 1948 and 1958, Sollel Boné trained 86 percent of Israel's construction workers and many of them were employed by the company once they had completed their training (Greenberg, 2004, p. 49). Halevi and Klinov-Malul describe the position of the Workers Corporation as a monopoly in labor force supply. The monopolistic position of the company enabled the government to use it in order to achieve its socio-economic goals, but at the same time it restricted the government's capacity to liberalize the labor market (Halevi and Klinov-Malul, 1968, pp. 52–53). The Histadrut, in its capacity as the labor union, had managed the Labor Offices since 1940, the aim of which was to train and place workers and to implement the work relief programs (Adut, 2005). The Histadrut continued to manage the Labor Offices until they were nationalized in 1959 and the Ministry of Labor took control (Gal, 1994, 1997; Rosenhek, 2002). Given the central role of the Histadrut in Israel's economic development, it had vested interests in the paradigm of rapid development and full employment: so long as the government prioritized the objective of full employment, the Histadrut sector enjoyed privileged access to cheap credit.

The relationship between the Histadrut sector and the government had also a clientelistic basis. Mapai was the dominant party in the government, and it had deep political, cultural and personal ties with the Histadrut. Moreover, through the Histadrut and the Workers Corporation Mapai channeled resources to its constituencies and sustained its political survival (Shalev, 1992; Shapira and Grinberg, 1988). This pattern of ties between the state, Mapai and the Histadrut, which had both clientelistic-political and economic-institutional foundations was at the heart of the paradigm of rapid development. The strong ties between the institutions were based on a common national vision, on short-term opportunistic interests and cultural affinities.

The rise of the economic ministries and the Bank of Israel

The changing pattern of the ties between the state and non-state actors was accompanied by a transformation of the state itself. Whereas the paradigm of rapid development was carried out by the Prime Minister's Office and by the Ministry of Development, the transition to the paradigm of economic independence was associated with the rise of new state actors: the Ministry of Finance, the Ministry of Trade and Industry and the Bank of Israel. These three state agencies were unified by a local network of economists, who were employed by all three of them, and they were not as dependent as the other ministries on the Histadrut. Therefore, they had both the drive and the capacity to push for change.

In the early 1950s, the Director of Sollel Boné, Hillel Dan came up with the initiative to expand the company's heavy metal section by establishing the Steel District Project. Initially the project was supported by the Ministry of Development, headed by Dov Yosef, as it was consistent with his and Ben-Gurion's idea that the Israeli economy should be industrialized, jobs should be created, and that issues of economic efficiency were of a secondary nature (Levi-Faur, 2001, pp. 150–155). In 1952, Hillel Dan was appointed the Director of the Reparation Company, which was established in order to allocate the reparations paid by Germany. This appointment provided Dan with the capacity to influence the use of the reparation payments.

However, the project had to be approved by the Ministry of Finance as well as the Ministry of Trade and Industry, and the ministers of the two ministries, Levi Eshkol and Pinhas Sapir, respectively, had different plans. Eshkol and Sapir did not approve of Hillel Dan's request for a loan and this put an end to the Steel District project. Instead, they initiated a plan to weaken the monopolistic position of Sollel Boné by dividing it up into smaller companies: Sollel Boné, the part that kept the original name, focused on construction, the Kur company focused on industry and the Ports Company was in charge of Sollel Boné's business interests abroad (Frenkel, 2008; Greenberg, 2004; Grinberg, 1991; Levi-Faur, 2001).

The division of Sollel Boné did not decrease the market size of the Histadrut sector, which remained around one-fifth of GDP. However, it changed the structure of the company and its economic strategy.[7] The identity of the Workers Corporation was gradually changed from an agent of the state to that of an oligopolistic company that operated within a more competitive—but obviously far from free—market economy. As Lavon put it, the Workers Corporation had been changed into a "holding company" (Greenberg, 2004, pp. 57–59).

The Ministry of Finance employed another strategy to restrict the expansion of the Workers Corporation: it nationalized its financial sources. In 1950, the government approved the establishment of *Gmul*, a financial company owned by the Workers Corporation with the purpose of handling the reserves of the Workers Corporation's banking institutions, which included Bank Hapoalim and a large number of saving and loan cooperatives. The reserves were channeled through Gmul to the Workers Corporation. In 1953, more than 60 percent of Gmul's reserves were allocated to the Histadrut sector, that is, to various Workers Corporation companies.

This situation had changed by 1957 when Pinhas Sapir initiated new directives that forced Gmul to invest 65 percent of its reserves in recognized investment instruments, 60 percent of which were government bonds. In 1965, the share of recognized investments was raised to 80 percent of Gmul's reserves (Aharoni, 1991, pp. 164–165; Sarnat, 1966, p. 82) "These funds," argued Levi-Faur in his book, "empowered the state and made it into a dominant actor in industrial development" (2001, pp. 164–165).

How did the government use these resources? During the 1950s, the Ministry of Trade and Industry nurtured the development of private industry in the textile sector (ibid., p. 194). In the years 1956–1957, the ministry launched a plan for the development of the industry in Israel in order to expand local textile production, both for export and import substitutes. The Ministry of Trade and Industry mobilized local and foreign entrepreneurs to establish textile factories with the financial support of the state.

Hence, during the second half of the 1950s, the government took several measures in order to weaken its dependence on the Histadrut sector and to shift resources from the Histadrut sector into the private sector. From 1954 onward, argue Shimshon Bichler and Jonathan Nitzan, "the big bourgeoisie was differentiated from the small bourgeoisie, as it linked to new initiatives of the government and the large Histadrut companies that were managed by the new network of statist directors" (2001, pp. 153–154). This was an essential phase in the gradual but consistent change from the inward-looking development and full employment to export-oriented industrialization.

The Treaty of Rome

The transition in the second half of the 1950s was accompanied by the consolidation of the autonomy of certain state institutions, primarily, the economic ministries which included the Ministry of Finance and the Ministry of Trade and Industry. The process not only involved more power and autonomy, but also new types of policy ideas regarding economic development.

In 1960, the Ministry of Finance and the Bank of Israel initiated a common program for "economic planning" (Susman, 1960, p. 337), a term often associated with socialist policy and state intervention. The Ministry of Finance and the Bank, however, viewed and used the term in a new way. The Director of the Research Department of the Bank of Israel argued that economic planning should aim at "eliminating distortions in the economic system," such as "legal restrictions on the interest rate, multiple exchange rates, the indexing of wages to price levels, and continuous inflationary pressures" (Kochav, 1959, p. 45). This type of economic planning did not "ignore the price system" and did not try "to act against it. Rather, it operated through the price system" (ibid., p. 46). In general, "the main principle of [economic] planning is the creation of conditions and infrastructure for private and public economic enterprises, rather than initiating and executing detailed plans" (ibid., p. 47). The goal of economic planning, according to its new usage, was improved efficiency and productivity and the exposure of the Israeli economy to international trade (Aharoni, 1962).

A catalyst for the emergence of the new policy ideas was external: in 1957, the Treaty of Rome was signed and the European Economic Community was established a year later. The establishment of the European Common Market marked a milestone in the evolution of the Bretton Woods regime. The United States signaled that it would scale down its aid programs in the near future and that developing countries would have to finance themselves by means of their own foreign exchange earnings (Wade, 1990, p. 117). All the signs indicated that the leaders of the international community were pushing for more trade liberalization. Economists in Israel were concerned by the implications of this trend for the Israeli economy as it "put a burden on Israeli exports" (Bach, 1959, p. 205).

In response to the international trend, the Economic Department of the Ministry of Foreign Affairs convened a meeting with policy-makers and economists to discuss the implications of the establishment of the European Common Market on the Israeli economy. Don Patinkin, Nadav Halevi, one of Patinkin's students, and David Kochav, the Head of the Research Department in the Bank of Israel, were all invited. The ministry staff framed the choices of Israel in the following way: "either remaining an isolated economic island or assimilating into the 'market' and the 'region' " (EEU, 1957a). All the participants agreed on adopting "a more liberalized policy" (EEU, 1957b). "Joining the Common Market," Nadav Halevi explained, "would force the economy to go through a process of restructuring and would bring us closer to economic independence" (EEU, 1957c). The participants at the meeting agreed that if Israel sought to benefit from the new European arrangement, it would have to expose itself to international trade and to adjust its economy accordingly.

The collaboration between the economists and the staff of the Ministry of Foreign Affairs demonstrated the growing link between economic policy-making and foreign policy issues. The sociologist Baruch Kimmerling argues that this link was designed only to invite external pressure on domestic societal actors who resisted change:

> [The] technocrats, who were filling more and more power positions in the Israeli economic political structure, viewed the creation of ties with the European Common Market as a means for creating exogenous pressure for change and modernization in the Israeli economic structure. It seemed to them that only by means of external pressure of this type would it be possible to overcome the vested interests and ideological foundation on which the structure of the Israeli economy was based.
>
> (Kimmerling, 1983, p. 129)

Indeed, the emergence of new policy paradigm was inseparable from the institutional change in the Israeli political economy: the Ministry of Finance and the Bank of Israel challenged the "old" actors who had benefited from the rapid industrialization policy—the Histadrut and the Workers Corporation. This was facilitated by the fact that the Ministry of Finance and the Bank of Israel were not dependent on the Histadrut sector, as other state actors were. Their power and influence were based on their prestige and professional standing as well as on their links with international institutions. These institutional resources enabled them to confront these two traditional allies of Mapai and weaken the ties between them and the government.

From full employment to full natural employment

The change from full employment to export-oriented growth was associated with a higher level of unemployment, a fact that raised a legitimacy problem: how can the regime, which hitherto had promoted full employment, now justify a policy which deliberately creates high levels of unemployment?

The full employment policy that the government had implemented in the 1950s was probably inspired by the Keynesian paradigm, but was not identical to it. Keynesian full employment policy was designed for economies that face recession, where a government stimulates the economy by an increase in public expenditure and monetary expansion in order to boost public and household demand. In Israel, however, the situation was different. The high level of unemployment in the early 1950s was not caused by a recession, but rather by the swell of immigrants who entered the country in a very short period. The government responded to this situation by employing three complementary measures. First, an expansive fiscal policy accompanied by the intervention in the allocation of resources to labor-intensive ("productive") sectors (Gal, 1994, p. 120); second, occupational training of the workers, mainly by the Workers Corporation; and third, a work relief program for those who did not have jobs or were not trained. Mordechai Namir, the Labor Minister, explained the logic of this approach: "Hundreds of thousands of new immigrants were turned through the work relief program, from a situation of joblessness … to working people" (Namir, 1957).

The full employment policy in the 1950s, therefore, was more "interventionist" than a Keynesian-style demand-side policy. The assumption that guided this policy was a "productivist" ideology, according to which each healthy citizen must work, even if the associated salary exceeds the worker's contribution to production. Unemployment was considered the ultimate social evil that had to be avoided at all costs.

Don Patinkin was one of the first in the Israeli context who undermined the socio-economic logic of the full employment policy, as well as its normative foundation. Patinkin argued that in practice the full employment policy solved a social problem by using an economic means, and the result was not only bad economic policy but also bad social policy. The government, argued Patinkin, did not eliminate unemployment by creating real jobs, but rather it created "disguised unemployment" by creating fake jobs, such as in the work relief programs (Patinkin, 1967, p. 35). Unemployment, argued Patinkin, could not be abolished "until these workers acquire the educational characteristics necessary for a modern industrial economy" (ibid., p. 38).

Patinkin's views regarding unemployment gradually penetrated the policy-making circles. The first minister to use Patinkin's terminology was no other than the minister of labor. Giora Yoseftal advocated abandoning the policy objective of full employment in favor of "natural full employment," which meant that firms should not hire more workers than needed (Yoseftal, 1960, p. 4). Yigaal Alon, Yoseftal's successor at the Ministry of Labor, explained that "each firm and each industry must stand the test of economic criteria." This approach, which implied the exposure of the labor market to market forces, was legitimized by an appeal to the national interests:

> The Israeli economy will be stronger from the perspective of production and profitability as its chances to conquer more markets are higher: as we expand trade, we expand investment and the economy. And the expansion of the economy is the real solution for natural full employment.
>
> (Alon, 1966, p. 111)

During the first half of the 1960s, policy-makers went so far as to argue that unemployment was actually a desired phenomenon. Some economists suggested that maintaining "a reserve of unemployed in order to create competition among the workers and to increase their dependence on the employer" was a desirable situation (Alon, 1962, p. 17). The idea was also championed by David Horowitz, by that time the Governor of the Bank of Israel, who explained that "a reserve of unemployed, whose subsistence is guaranteed" is a good thing, because it provided the economy with a "capacity to maneuver to improve production" (quoted in Doron and Kramer, 1992, p. 130). It should be noted here that this suggestion was made in the context of the discussion of the unemployment insurance scheme. Horowitz supported unemployment insurance because it would provide policy-makers with greater macroeconomic flexibility as they would have the legitimacy to implement policies associated with higher levels of unemployment, knowing there was a safety net in place (Krampf, 2013).

One may say that throughout the 1960s unemployment was transformed from a social evil that must be avoided to a necessary evil that must be tolerated or even embraced to achieve economic independence. The new mindset toward unemployment implied that the state had no responsibility to prevent unemployment at all costs, but it still had partial responsibility to assist the unemployed in other ways.[8] This new mindset toward unemployment made it easier for the government to justify the radical shift from full employment policy to the austerity policy.

The austerity coalition

It is not clear whether after the election that took place in November 1965, the acting minister of finance, Pinhas Sapir, realized that the Israeli economy was sliding into an economic slowdown. What is certain is that immediately after the election—before the inter-party negotiations for coalition building had started—Sapir made public his intention to activate an austerity policy. He signaled to any potential coalition partner that the austerity policy was not up for negotiation. After the formation of the coalition, the austerity policy was supported by all its members: from the Independent Liberal Party on the right, to Mapam on the left. Only the Communist Party objected to it. It was a unique case in which all the parties in the coalition supported this unprecedented policy in Israel, a result made all the more remarkable because it abandoned the previous core policy principle of full employment. "The die is cast," exclaimed government member, Shlomo Lorentz, "those who have resided in a fools' paradise have now opened their eyes and realized that this could no longer go on" (Knesset, February 22, 1966, vol. 44, p. 717). Who could have ever imagined, he continued, that Meir Ya'ari, the leader of Mapam, a social-democrat party, "would one day warn against increases in wages" (ibid., p. 717).

The first signs of recession appeared in 1965 just as several large publicly funded construction projects were completed: the port at Ashdod, industrial projects at the Dead Sea, and the National Water Carrier. Immigration flows to Israel lessened, and as a result the investment in construction curtailed, a situation further compounded by the fact that for the first time since the establishment of the state, negative net migration, particularly of academics, became significant. GDP growth fell to 8 percent after years of an annual average growth rate of 11 percent (Kanovsky, 1970).

At the same time, foreign currency sources were expected to terminate as reparations from West Germany had dwindled significantly since the early 1960s and were expected to end in 1966. Furthermore, the proportion of grants and donations within the total import surplus fell from 86 percent in 1963 to 62 percent in 1964 (Halevi and Klinov-Malul, 1968, p. 115, Table 50, p. 128, Table 57). Hence, while the economic slowdown in the mid-1960s also had material exogenous causes, this accounts for only part of the overall situation.

After the elections of November 1965, Pinhas Sapir, the minister of finance in the previous government, declared that he would be willing to head the Ministry of Finance for another term only if his economic plan—the austerity policy—was approved. The austerity policy, therefore, was presented to potential members in the coalition as a "take it or leave it" option. The key elements in the austerity policy were the following: a balanced budget, freezing nominal wages, canceling cost of living allowances and imposing obligatory arbitration in labor disputes (Sapir, 1965). These elements were perceived as severe measures in the local context, nevertheless, there was no significant opposition to them.

The first party to join the coalition was the Independent Liberals (*Liberalim Atzmaim*), who, in the words of one of its members, Pinhas Rosen, represented the "private sector in Israel" (Knesset, January 13, 1966, vol. 44, p. 365). The party fully supported the economic platform of the *Ha'ma'arach*—a coalition of *Mapai* and *Achdut Ha'avoda*—Sapir's party. In the inauguration session in the Knesset, Rosen pointed out that "If one of our members headed the government, he would not present a different economic policy, no more liberal, progressive, or more assertive than the one presented today by the prospective prime minister" (Knesset, January 13, 1966, vol. 44, p. 365).

The negotiations with the other factions were not as easy and swift. Interestingly, the disagreements did not revolve around economic issues but rather around the relationship between the state and religion. The Independent Liberals on the right and Mapam on the left were united in their opposition to religious legislation. The religious parties tethered their entry to the coalition with the religious legislation.(Mapam, 1965). The clash between Mapam and the religious parties made it easier for Mapam's leaders to justify their entry into the coalition, adopting the economic platform of the liberal right-wing parties on socio-economic issues. The party leader, Meir Yaari, coined the term "cooperation through confrontation" [*'Shutafut derech Maavak*] to legitimize the joining of the socialist party to the austerity coalition (Yaari, 1966). The resulting coalition was very broad-based, as it included 79 of the 120 parliament members who came from both liberal right-wing and social-democrat left-wing parties.

Strikes and deficit

The coalition was assembled while the economy was besieged by strikes. The textile factories Argaman and Serina were caught up in bitter labor disputes that ended in violent confrontations with the police and the arrest of workers.[9] Similar strife swept through the transportation cooperatives (*Al Hamishmar*, 1966b), public hospitals (*Al Hamishmar*, 1966c), universities (*Al Hamishmar*, 1966d, 1966e), the Port Authority (*Al Hamishmar*, 1966f) and even among the civilian workers of the Defense Forces as well as employees of the Bank of Israel (*Al Hamishmar*, 1966a; IDF, 1966). An intense wave of industrial relations crises struck within a period of three months between December 1965 and February 1966, just as the coalition was assembled and the new government inaugurated, a factor that further contributed to the consolidation of consensus around the austerity policy.

In the parliamentary sessions during January and February 1965 the austerity policy held center-stage. The social-democratic left depicted the austerity policy as a response to the current account deficit. This framing made it easy for the left-wing leaders to justify their support for the policy to their constituency: the policy was framed as a national necessity. The liberal right, as well as the prime minister and the minister of finance, justified the policy as a response to the industrial relationship crisis.

At the government's inauguration session, the Prime Minister Levi Eshkol declared that the new government intended to implement an austerity policy in order to reduce the current account deficit. To achieve that end it would use two complementary policy instruments. The first was designed to shift the allocation of resources from consumption to investment in order to "expand production and exports." The second instrument was designed to increase the productivity of "each worker in industry, services and management, by an improvement of productivity and the efficiency of production" (Knesset, January 12, 1966, vol. 44, p. 346). Eshkol resented what he described as a "licentious class struggle" that "any labor movement that respects itself and the state, cannot accept" (ibid., p. 346).

The industrial relations crisis was also a central issue in the negotiations surrounding the annual budget. The Minister of Finance Pinhas Sapir complained that "work ethics in Israel are deteriorating.... We cannot hide our heads in the sand and ignore the fact that there is a difference between responsible negotiations and wild strikes that cause damage to essential branches of the economy" (Knesset, January 14, 1966, vol. 44, p. 613).

The Independent Liberals went further and demanded that in addition to the austerity policy, a committee for the investigation of the profitability and viability of government companies be established, to restrict the economic activities of the government, and to make wage increases contingent upon improvements in productivity, by encouraging the flexibility and mobility of the labor force and by taking firm action against "wildcat" strikes (Knesset, January 12, 1966, vol. 44, p. 365).

Parliament members from the center-left supported the policy but justified it on the basis of state interests rather than on a "class struggle" scenario. Israel Kragman, a member of the Ma'arach, explained that "everybody would have to mobilize their strength to reduce our dependence on others and attain economic independence" (ibid., p. 355). David Ben-Gurion, who established the *Rafi* Party, also supported the austerity policy arguing that "we don't have to explain that without a large-scale expansion of our exports, we would not attain economic independence and our political independence would not be complete and real" (ibid. p. 358). The left-wing social-democratic party, Mapam, approved the political and economic rationale of the policy while Meir Ya'ari stated that "We share the concern regarding the reduction of the trade deficit, the expansion of exports and the reduction of imports, the improvement of productivity and the profitability of the economy." He added, however, paying lip service to the constituency of Mapam, that "this is in order to guarantee full employment, the continuation of immigration and last but not least—the improvement of our security" (Knesset, February 22, 1966, vol. 44, p. 696).

The only voice opposing the austerity policy was that of the Communist Party. Meir Vilner, from *Rakach,* claimed that the austerity policy was a "smoke-screen" and "propaganda" aimed at creating a public "psychosis" in order to force workers to make concessions and give up their wage increases, which they duly deserved according to their existing contracts (ibid., p. 717).

Economic *Hasbara*

Despite the consensus in the parliament, the austerity policy posed a serious legitimacy problem for the government: How could a party presenting itself as a labor party justify the abandonment of the full employment policy? How could it justify a policy that ran counter to the national ethos it had promoted for more almost two decades? The center and center-left parties had to find a way to explain to their constituencies why they were embracing policies and values that so far had been promoted by the liberal right and which it had condemned in the past.

In order to legitimize the austerity policy, the government employed a unique measure—even within the local context: it initiated a massive propaganda campaign, or *Hasbara. Hasbara* is a Hebrew term that lacks a precise English equivalent. Linguistically, the root of the term is from the verb *explaining.* However, *Hasbara* assumes a hierarchical relationship between the one who explains, and the one to whom the explanation is addressed.

To legitimize the austerity policy, a suggestion was made in the parliament to establish a "Central Division for *Hasbara.*"[10] The minister of finance explained that "The proposed budget places a heavy burden on the shoulders of many circles [in Israeli society] and therefore it is desirable to bring to the awareness of the people the many new tasks that the government must accomplish." *Hasbara* should "enjoin the people to exercise self-restraint, and it should disclose openly the danger of the deterioration that is likely to occur in the wake of reckless behavior in the economic area" (*Yedioit Aharonot,* 1966). The proposal was accepted and in 1966 the government embarked on an unprecedented campaign to legitimize the austerity policy.

In March 1966, the government announced "Export Month" during which it purchased advertising space of no less than four pages in all daily newspapers.

The four pages were used to tell to the public about the Export Month and included interviews with exporters, articles by policy-makers and the advertisements of export companies. The central article, entitled "By export we live," was written by Haim Zadok, the minister of trade and industry:

> This year we exported only 60% of our imports.... We covered the gap by the import of capital from outside (personal remuneration, reparations, foreign investment, foreign loans, and the World Jewish Appeal). If we wish to eliminate the gap between imports and exports and "to eat bread we baked by our own hands," we must balance the two sides of the equation, that is, reduce imports or increase exports.
>
> (Tzadok, 1966)

The government initiated the Certified Exporter Diploma Award, which was issued to a selected group of exporters. One of the certified exporters was Max Tal, owner of Shimshon, a tire production firm. In his interview, Tal unleashed fierce criticism against the workers, pointing out their low productivity and lack of discipline. These characteristics of the Israeli labor force, he argued, impaired the national interests. "How can we be competitive ... when the actual number of working days in Israel is among the lowest in the western world?" he asked (Hasbara, 1966).

The Hasbara campaign also mobilized professional economists from the Hebrew University. In 1966, there were still no television broadcasts in Israel, which the government could have used to bring the voice of the experts into the homes of the populace. As a substitute, the government initiated "Hasbara shows" [*Bimot Hasbara*], which consisted of public events in theatre halls in the large cities involving professional economists and policy-makers publicly discussing the austerity policy.

Two such events took place at the Tzavta Club in Tel Aviv, a well-known theatre that usually hosted entertainment shows of various kinds. Participants in the first event were the minister of housing, the Director General of the Ministry of Finance, and two parliamentary members, Zeev Zur from Mapai and Viktor Shem-Tov from Mapam. The participants in the second event were academic economists from the Hebrew University and a representative of the Ministry of Finance. The *Al Hamishmar* newspaper reported that the economists discussed the questions "how to reach economic independence" and "how to reduce the deficit in the balance of payments." In what seems to be a staged discussion, the moderator presented to the economists the following question: "What is the best way to stop the process, which is dangerous to the economy and moves us further away from the long-awaited economic independence?" (Tzavta, 1966). The two economists from the Hebrew University, Haim Barkai and Ephraim Kleiman, supported the austerity policy and argued that the government should also devalue the currency, a step which would have led to a further reduction of real wages. Moshe Sanbar, from the Budget Division in the Ministry of Finance, argued that "the political and social reality does not allow for cruel, radical devaluation" (ibid.). To represent the left-wing opposition, the organizers invited Efrayim Reiner, who held only a B.A. in economics and was known for his pro-labor views. He argued that the policy placed a disproportionally heavy burden on the public. At that point, however, the austerity policy was a *fait accompli*. Even the left-wing *Al-Hamishmar* embraced the ever-growing consensus that a period of austerity was needed in order to reach economic independence.

Conclusion

The austerity policy of 1965 was a transformative event in the economic history of Israel. It ended a period of approximately three decades—starting in the mid-1930s—during which the national economic ethos had been built on the objectives of the expansion of production, creation of jobs and the Jewish demographic expansion. The strategy was made possible by two institutional features: links between the state (or the national organization during the British Mandate) and the Histadrut, and the inflow of funds which financed the expansion process. Hence, the cooperative symbiosis of the state and non-state actors contributed to the government's capacity to realize its preferences as it mobilized the non-state actors.

During the 1950s and the first half of the 1960s, domestic and international conditions changed, creating a demand for a corresponding change in state preferences and strategy. The focus shifted from job creation and expanding production to export-oriented growth, with the aim of narrowing the trade deficit and lowering the dependence of Israel on external funding. This transition had several implications. First, it had socio-economic implications, because it terminated the structural incentive that underlined the alliance between the Histadrut and the state, and more generally, between the workers and the state. The austerity policy of 1965 signified a shift toward a stronger connection between the state and the private sector. Second, it had implications for the autonomy of the state: whereas the paradigm of rapid development was embedded in the mutual dependence between the state and the Histadrut, the policy paradigm change was accompanied by the consolidation of a more autonomous state, manifested in the new position of the Ministry of Finance, the Ministry of Trade and Industry and the Bank of Israel, all became more active in shaping Israel economic policy. Finally, with the advent of the paradigm of economic independence, policy-makers embraced liberal rhetoric to legitimize certain policy instruments. However, the use of liberal rhetoric was selective, and it was always qualified by the traditional nationalistic argumentation.

In hindsight, the effectiveness of the austerity policy was limited. The trade deficit dropped from 17 percent in 1964 to 12 percent in 1966, but this reduction was the result of lower consumption and lower investment rather than the result of export expansion. The social cost of the policy was devastating. The unemployment rate surged and for the first time since the establishment of the state, the migration flow was negative.

An unintended consequence of the austerity policy was the expansion of Israel's welfare practices. Until the austerity policy, the common view among policy-makers—especially the left-wing parties—was that the government should provide employment, not unemployment benefits. In 1966, as an ad hoc response to the high unemployment rate, the government started to pay unemployment benefits and in 1972 the Unemployment Insurance Bill was approved by the Knesset (Gal, 1994; Krampf, 2013). During the 1970s, Israeli governments increased expenditure on social services and the welfare system was formalized and universalized (Rosenhek, 2002).

One can only guess what would have been the long-term consequences of the austerity policy had it lasted longer. However, the outbreak of the 1967 War (the Six Day War) in June reshuffled not only Israeli politics but also the political economy. The euphoria after the war, the "enhanced" position of Israel at the international level and the cheap labor that ensued, all contributed to lifting the Israeli economy out of recession.

Notes

1 See Chapter 3 for more details.

2 A more detailed analysis of the development of Israel monetary and banking systems is presented in Chapters 5 and 6.

3 The reparation agreement with the Federal Republic of Germany was signed only in September 1952 and came into force in March 1953. Therefore, in 1951, the government was not certain that an external source of foreign reserves would be found.

4 In early 1949, the government of Israel received the first loan from the Export-Import Bank of the United States for the sum of US$100 million. Two years later it received approval for another loan for the sum of US$35 million. Moreover, during 1951, the government of Israel received additional grants from the United States for the sum of US$185 million (see Halevi and Klinov-Malul, 1968).

5 *The objectives of the journal were printed on the first page of the first volume.* Emphasis added.

6 David Golomb underwent basic economic training in the Hebrew University in Jerusalem. He was Director of the Institute for Economic Research of the Histadrut in 1961–1965 and a member of the planning center of the Workers Corporation in 1965–1969. He was a member of parliament for the Ma'arach faction in 1965–69 and 1977–1981. He was also a member of the Board of Directors of Koor Industries.

7 The public and Histadrut sectors produced around 20 percent of the NDP during the 1950s and the private sector produced 60 percent (Levi-Faur, 2001, p. 4, Figure 1).

8 During and after the austerity policy of 1965, the government established several committees that recommended the use of unemployment insurance. The Unemployment Insurance Bill was finally approved in 1972 (Gal, 1994; Krampf, 2013).

9 The headlines in the daily newspapers reflect the intensity of the situation: "Dismissal letters were posted to 'Argaman' strikers—the *Histadrut* cut off contacts," *Al Hamishmar*, December 17, 1965; "The 'Argaman' dispute escalates," *Al Hamishmar*, December 22, 1965, p. 6; "Industrialists fear future with past experience in 'Argaman'," *Yedioth Aharonot*, December 27, 1965, p. 4; "'Kitan' workers: we'll fight to the end," *Al Hamishmar*, January 6, 1966, p. 6; "Clashes between 'Kitan' strikers, strike-breakers and the police," *Al Hamishmar*, January 9, 1966, p. 6; "12 of

Kitan strikers arrested," *Al Hamishmar*, January 13, 1966, p. 6; " 'Sarina' strikers to demonstrate in the capital," *Al Hamishmar*, January 23, 1966, p. 6.

10 The term "advocacy" is used as a translation of the Hebrew word *Hasbara*. *Hasbara*, however, means also "propaganda."

References

Adut, R.Y., 2005. Workers and Administrators: The Ethnic-Class Division of Labor in Jerusalem in the Forties and Fifties. MA thesis Tel Aviv University, Tel Aviv.

Aharoni, Y., 1962. Adaptation to the International Price Level. *The Economic Quarterly* 36, 213–223 (in Hebrew).

Aharoni, Y., 1991. *The Israeli Economy: Dreams and Realities*. Routledge, London.

Al Ha'mishmar. 1966a. Bank of Israel Employees in All 3 Major Cities to Strike Beginning Tuesday. *Al Ha'mishmar*. January 9: 6.

Al Hamishmar. 1966b. The Transportation Cooperatives Threaten a Service Standstill. January 10.

Al Hamishmar. 1966c. Government Hospital's Workers Will Hold 2-Hour Strike Today. January 16: 6.

Al Hamishmar. 1966d. Teachers at Institutions of Higher Learning Will Strike Beginning This Thursday, Al Hamishmar, January 31: 6.

Al Hamishmar. 1966e. Academic Staff to Strike Tomorrow. June 2: 6.

Al Hamishmar, 1966f. Port Authority Insists Will Not Resume Work in Ashdod Without Agreement. February 11. 1.

Alon, Y., 1962. Summaries and Trends. *Labor and National Insurance* 8, 3–17 (in Hebrew).

Alon, Y., 1966. Trends and Operation of the Ministry of Labor in 1966/67. *Labor and National Insurance* 4, 107–112 (in Hebrew).

Avramovitz, Z., 1938. "Autarchy," Industrial Center and Reality. *Cooperative Bulletin* 3–4, 36–39.

Bach, I., 1959. The European Common Market. *The Economic Quarterly* 23, 197–209 (in Hebrew).

Bichler, S. and Nitzan, Y., 2001. *From War Benefit to Peace Dividends*. Carmel, Jerusalem (in Hebrew).

Cardoso, F.H. and Faletto, E., 1979. *Dependency and Development in Latin América*. University of California Press, Berkeley, CA.

Creamer, D., Weisbrod, H., Kahane, R., Kotowitz, Y., Katz, D., Barkai, M., Noam, M., Kurzweil, Z., and Duvshani, H., 1957. *The National Income of Israel, 1950–1954*. Falk Center for Economic Research in Israel, Jerusalem (in Hebrew).

Doron, A. and Kramer, R.M., 1992. *The Welfare State in Israel*. Am Oved, Jerusalem.

Economic Committee. Various years. *Labor Party Archive*. Economic Committee of the Labor Movement.

EEU, 1957a. Minutes of the Second Meeting in Regard to European Economic Unification, June 19. *Economists' Papers Archive*, Duke University, Durham, NC, box 69.

EEU, 1957b. Minutes of the Third Meeting in Regard To European Economic Unification. August 21. *Economists' Papers Archive*, Duke University, Durham, NC, box 69.

EEU, 1957c. Minutes of the Fourth Meeting in Regard to European Economic Unification. September 30. *Economists' Papers Archive*, Duke University, Durham, NC, box 69.

Finance Committee. Various years. Minutes of Finance Committee. Knesset Archive.

Frenkel, M., 2008. The Emergence of the Managerial Field in Israel as a Dynamic in Overlapping Fields. *Israeli Sociology* 10, 133–159 (in Hebrew).

Gal, J., 1994. The Development of Unemployment Insurance in Israel. *Social Security* 3, 117–136.

Gal, J., 1997. Unemployment Insurance, Trade-Unions and the Strange Case of the Israeli Labour Movement. *International Review of Social History* 42, 357–396.

Golomb, D., 1961. The Import Surplus: An Effect or a Cause? *The Economic Quarterly* 150–152 (in Hebrew).

Gorny, Yosef. 1996. The Historical Reality of Constructive Socialism. *Israel Studies* 1 (1): 295–305.

Greenberg, Y., 2004. *Anatomy of a Crisis Foretold: The Collapse of Labor Owned Enterprises in the 80's*. Am Oved, Tel Aviv (in Hebrew).

Greenwald, C.S., 1972. *Recession as a Policy Instrument: Israel 1965–1969*. C. Hurst, London.

Grinberg, L.L., 1991. *Split Corporatism in Israel*. State University of New York Press, Albany, NY.

Gross, N., 2000. The Economic Policy of the British Mandate in Palestine. In: Gross, N., *Not by Spirit Alone*. The Hebrew University Magnes Press, Jerusalem, pp. 172–227 (in Hebrew).

Gross, N.T., 2004a. Department of Economics in the Hebrew University in the 1950s. unpublished article. Available at: www.economics.huji.ac.il/GrossHistory.pdf (in Hebrew).

Gross, N.T., 2004b. Social Sciences in the Hebrew University until 1948/9, unpublished article. Available at: www.economics.huji.ac.il/gross.pdf (in Hebrew).

Halevi, N. and Klinov-Malul, R., 1968. *The Economic Development of Israel*. Akademon, Jerusalem (in Hebrew).

Horowitz, D., 1947. Survey of Economic Conditions. April 2. Yad Yaari Archive, Division 74–95, box 2, file 2.

IDF, 1966. Civilian IDF Employees to Protest-Strike and Cut Overtime. *Al Ha'mishmar* January 11: 6.

Kanovsky, E., 1970. *The Economic Impact of the Six-Day War: Israel, The Occupied Territories, Egypt, Jordan*. Praeger, New York.

Kimmerling, B., 1983. *Zionism and Economy*. Schenkman Pub. Co, Cambridge, MA.

Kleiman, E., 1981. Israel: Economists in a New State. *History of Political Economy* 13 (3): 548–578.

Knesset. Various years. *Divrei Ha'knesset* [Minutes of Parliament Sessions].

Kochav, D., 1959. Comments on Economic Planning. *The Economic Quarterly* 23, 244–247 (in Hebrew).

Krampf, A., 2010. Economic Planning of the Free Market in Israel during the First Decade: The Influence of Don Patinkin on Israeli Policy Discourse. *Science in Context* 23, 507–534.

Krampf, A., 2013. Liberalization and Universal Unemployment Insurance in Israel. *Social Security* 91, 29–57 (in Hebrew).

Kuznets, S., 1953a. Kuznets to Ga'athon, July 10, *Israel State Archive* 1832/2-Peh.

Kuznets, S., 1953b. Kuznets to Ga'athon, letter, July 12, *Israel State Archive* 1832/2-Peh.

Lerner, A.P., 1954. Stability and Economic Independence. *Economic Quarterly* 5–6, 3–11 (in Hebrew).

Levi-Faur, D., 2001. *The Visible Hand: State-Directed Industrialization in Israel*. Yad Ben-Zvi Press, Jerusalem (in Hebrew).

Mapam, 1965. Mapam and Independent Liberals Clarify Their Opposition to Religious Legislation, to Ma'arach. *Al Ha'mishmar* December 7.

Mehrling, P., 2002. Don Patinkin and the origins of postwar monetary orthodoxy. *European Journal of the History of Economic Thought* 9, 161–185.

Michaely, M., 1963. *Foreign Trade and Capital Imports in Israel*. Am Oved, Jerusalem (in Hebrew).

Namir, M., 1957. On unemployment, the Ministry of Labor in the Knesset, 2/1/1957. *Labor and National Insurance* 1, 2–5.

Nathan, R.R., Gass, O. and Creamer, D.B., 1946. *Palestine: Problem and Promise, an Economic Study*. American Council on Public Affairs, Washington, DC.

Parliament. Various years. *Divrei Ha'knesset* [Minutes of Parliament Sessions].

Patinkin, D., 1960. *The Israel Economy: The First Decade*. Falk Project for Economic Research in Israel, Jerusalem (in Hebrew).

Patinkin, D., 1967. The Israel Economy: The First Decade. The Falk Project for Economic Research in Israel, Jerusalem.

Patinkin, D., 1995. The Training of an Economist. *BNL Quarterly Review* 195, 359–396.

Pines, D., 1961. Indices for Economic Independence. *Economic Quarterly* 31, 242–252 (in Hebrew).

Ronnen, Y., 1960. About Dan Ptinkin's Essay. *Economic Quarterly* 25–26, 162–165 (in Hebrew).

Rosenhek, Z., 2002. Social Policy and Nation-Building: The Dynamics of the Israeli Welfare State. *Journal of Societal & Social Policy* 1, 15–31.

Rozin, O., 2008. *Duty and Love: Individualism and Collectivism in 1950s Israel*. Am Oved, Tel Aviv (in Hebrew).

Ruggie, J.G., 1982. International Regimes, Transactions, and Change: Embedded Liberalism in the Postwar Economic Order. *International Organization* 6, 379–415.

Sapir, P., 1965. P. Sapir Proposes Wage Freeze, Cancellation of Cost of Living Allowances and Obligatory Arbitration. *Al Ha'mishmar* November 23: 1.

Sarnat, M., 1966. *The Development of the Securities Market in Israel*. Kyklos-Verlag, Basel.

Seikaly, S., 2016. *Men of Capital: Scarcity and Economy in Mandate Palestine*. Stanford University Press, Stanford, CA.

Shalev, M., 1992. *Labour and the Political Economy in Israel*. Oxford University Press, Oxford.

Shalev, M., 1998. Have Globalization and Liberalization "Normalized" Israel's Political Economy? *Israel Affairs* 5, 121–155. doi:10.1080/13537129908719515.

Shapira, Y. and Grinberg, L.L., 1988. *The Full Employment Crisis, 1957–1965*. Golda Meir Institute, Tel Aviv (in Hebrew).

Simons, H.C., [1934] 1948. A Positive Program for Laissez-Faire. In: Simons, H.C. (Ed.), *Economic Policy for a Free Society*. University of Chicago Press, Chicago, pp. 40–77.

Sneh, M., 1951. Moshe Sneh's speech, *Al Ha'mishmar* October 21: 5.

Susman, Z., 1960. Limitation of Economic Planning in Israel. *Economic Quarterly* 28, 337–366 (in Hebrew).

Tzadok, H., 1966. If We Export, We Live. In "Export Month 1966." *Haaretz* March 11.

Tzavta, 1966. At Tzavta—Economists on the Economy's Recovery. *Al Hamishmar* March 7, 2.

Wade, R., 1990. *Governing the Market: Economic Theory and the Role of Government in East Asian Industrialization*. Princeton University Press, Princeton, NJ.

Yaari, M., 1966. Mapam's Guideline—Partnership Through Struggle. *Al Ha'mishmar* January 9.

Yedioit Aharonot. 1966. A Central Arm of Hasbara Is Needed. February 11: 4.

Yoseftal, G., 1960. Summaries and Lines of Action: A Speech by Giora Yoseftal in the Parliament. *Labor and National Insurance*.

5 Establishing a central bank in a late-developing country

Many studies on the role of the Bank of Israel during its first decades have portrayed it as a rather weak and a politicized institution serving as a technical arm of the government in its attempts to allocate resources to powerful societal and market actors. This claim is inspired by the more general claim made by mainstream economists, that central banks in developing countries were weak, politicized and "distorted." Rather than focusing purely on maintaining the stability of the currency, central banks were used as a political instrument in order to control the banking system and to extract purchasing power from the private sector to the government through *seigniorage* (Fry, 1982; McKinnon, 1984).

The following four chapters will trace the establishment of the Bank of Israel and its operation during the first five years, and will argue that bank was not the product of a failed attempt to imitate the conventional Western model of central banking, but rather was the product of an attempt to use the central bank to address domestic policy problems in a way that was consistent with the state preferences, within the political constraints. Central banks in developing countries, it will be argued, were obviously inspired by the models of central banking in advanced economies, but policy-makers in the Global South did not simply imitate them. Rather, these central banks were designed to offer institutional solutions to the unique policy problems that were associated with late development (Krampf, 2012, 2014).

The following four chapters will trace the establishment of the Bank of Israel and its operations in the first five years of its existence and will argue that the Bank of Israel was specifically designed to assist the government execute its development strategy. For that purpose, the Bank of Israel was granted extensive powers to control the banking system. Moreover, it will be argued that in order to serve as an effective developmental instrument, the bank had to be relatively independent, not only from the government but mainly from powerful actors. Therefore, the establishment of the bank was a milestone in the consolidation of the state autonomy vis-à-vis the market and the societal actors.

The rest of this chapter presents the economic rationale of developmental central banks, and the political economic theory of developmental central banking, and will explain the considerations of the Israeli government in establishing a central bank. Chapters 6 and 7 trace the process of formulating the

Central Bank Bill, with a focus on two contentious issues: the managerial structure of the bank and the status of the banks' supervision department. Chapter 8 will trace the operation of the bank during its first five years.

Central banking and international norms

A modern central bank is a state agency established and financed by a state. However, the norms which shape the design, the instruments and the behavior of central banks are decidedly international. Therefore, any historical account of a particular central bank must start with the prevailing central banking norms.

The conventional view is that the main purpose of modern central banks is to exercise monetary policy with the aim of maintaining price stability and/or stable exchange rates (Goodhart *et al.*, 1994, p. 2). However, the objectives of central banks have changed over time and across countries and regions. During the period of the gold standard, roughly from the 1870s and until the outbreak of World War II, the role of central banks was to maintain the convertibility of notes and gold. The Bank of England, which served as a model for other central banks, acted almost automatically by maintaining a fixed exchange rate between the currency and gold. However, even within the rules of the gold standard, central banks had a discretionary ability to carry out interest rate policy through the purchasing and selling of short-term securities in order to smooth the adjustment of prices (Gallarotti, 1995).

Prior to World War I, the gold standard monetary order was almost a global one that encompassed both core and peripheral countries. The world periphery, which was colonized by the world's powers, was part of the gold standard regime through domestic currencies, which were fixed to one of the key currencies and were managed by currency boards. Currency boards operated completely automatically by converting local currency to a key currency according to a fixed exchange rate. Hence, during the gold standard, the central banks and the currency boards operated according to strict rules, they were protected from government intervention and they were not expected to respond to varying economic circumstances (Eichengreen, 1992; Gallarotti, 1995; Lindert, 1969).

Central banking policy norms changed after World War II with the consolidation of the Bretton Woods regime. Most central banks were nationalized and became an agency of the state. National currencies were fixed to the US dollar, which was fixed to gold. The exchange rate could be adjusted after approval from the International Monetary Fund (IMF). A key feature of the Bretton Woods regime was the imposition of capital controls, which lessened the pressure on exchange rates caused by the free flow of capital (Ruggie, 1982). These features of the Bretton Woods regime enabled governments and central bankers to practise more discretion than under the gold standard regime. The Bretton Woods regime protected national economies from global markets, hence enabling governments and central bankers to adjust fiscal and monetary policies to domestic circumstances (Goodhart *et al.*, 1994; Ruggie, 1982).

The political economy of central banks

Formally, the power to exercise monetary policy belongs to the sovereign—the king or the government. During the eighteenth and nineteenth centuries the emerging convention was that sovereigns should delegate the monetary powers to an independent central bank, which followed transparent policy rules. Usually, the central bank consisted of a chartered private bank. The rationale for delegation is based on a political economic exchange between the sovereign and market actors: the sovereign was willing to bind its hands and restrict its powers, in exchange for (expectations of) higher returns in terms of growth, taxes and lower costs of financing its debt. However, independence and rules also have costs. The policy dilemma central bankers face between rules and flexibility is manifested in the debate between two schools of thoughts, the origin of which can be traced back to the English discourse of the early nineteenth century.

The English economy of the early nineteenth century was characterized by high levels of inflation. Adherents of the Currency School put the blame on the central bank, which issued notes that had no cover in gold (fiat money). They recommended institutionalizing the monopoly of the central bank as the sole note issuer in the county, to institutionalize its independence from the government in law and to bind the central bank to maintain convertibility between currency and gold. Contrariwise, adherents of the Banking School believed that inflation was caused by an expansion of credit by banking institutions. According to the Banking School, even if convertibility was re-imposed, inflation would persist. The controversy reached a temporary conclusion in 1844, with the decision of the government to institutionalize the independence of the Issue Department of the Bank of England by means of a charter, which stipulated the bank must maintain convertibility (Arnon, 2010).

However, the controversy re-emerged in a new form with the disintegration of the gold standard in the interwar period. Central bankers and governments found themselves searching for new types of monetary anchors: if central banks did not maintain convertibility, what would restrict the issue of currency? Economists suggested that the central bank should follow a certain policy rule, such as targeting price stability (Simons, 1936). This was the historical context in which the rules versus discretion controversy was born: some argued that the central bank should follow rules irrespective of the economic circumstances, whereas others recommended that central banks should maintain a certain level of flexibility.

The rules versus discretion debate re-emerged in the 1970s when all the advanced economies faced high level of inflations. Economists of the New Neoclassical Synthesis School argued that inflation resulted from the lack of a monetary anchor and of central banks which did not have the capacity to resist the political pressure from governments to issue currency. The economists justified their analysis on the basis of the principle of rational expectations: if economic actors anticipate that the central bank will print money, they adjust prices in advance and an inflation spiral emerges (Alesina and Tabellini, 1987; Barro and Gordon, 1983;

Capie *et al*., 1994; Kydland and Prescott, 1977). The obvious conclusion to draw from this is that in order to enable the central bank to follow the policy rule, its independence must be institutionalized in its mandate (Cukierman, 1992).

The idea that a central bank must follow transparent rules and be independent of government is justified also on the basis of the legal principle of private property rights. Issuing money by the sovereign in order to finance state expenses implies a transfer of purchasing power from the citizens to the kingdom, or in other words, nationalization of private property. This process is called *seigniorage* or inflation tax (Fischer, 1982; Hetzel, 1997). By delegating the authority to print money to an independent central bank, which is instructed by decree to follow a monetary rules, the sovereign commits to respecting private property rights. North and Weingast, who formulated this argument, explained the establishment of the Bank of England in 1794 as a commitment mechanism that facilitated the Financial Revolution in England and the further development of the financial system (North and Weingast, 1989). The conventional political economic theory of central banking is therefore based on liberal institutional foundations and is consistent with the economic history of liberal market-based European economies.

The open question is whether rule-based central banking is congruent with the economic conditions in late-developing countries. In such countries, the primary role of economic institutions is not to maintain stability, but rather to transform the structure of the economy, in order to industrialize it and to increase long-term social welfare. Therefore, it can no longer be assumed that the advantages of the rule-based monetary policy would outweigh the advantages of monetary flexibility.

However, the distinction between central banking in advanced and late-developing countries, goes beyond the rule versus discretion debate. The interventionist instruments used by central banks in late-developing countries, were more intrusive than what Keynesian economists have in mind, when they refer to as "discretion."

Monetary policy instruments

To understand the roles of central banks in late-developing countries, it is necessary to dive deeper into the technical apparatuses, which central bankers use. As a point of departure, it would be convenient to distinguish between three types of instruments:

1 Interest rate policy instruments.
2 Open Market Operations.
3 Reserve ratio requirements.

During the gold standard period, central banks operated more or less according to what David Hume called the *price-specie-flow mechanism*. Hume argues that a trade surplus country—a country that exports more than it imports—accumulated foreign currency or gold, which resulted in an expansion of the domestic money supply. This leads to higher prices and wages and to a decline in the nation's international competitiveness. Lower competitiveness results in an economic slowdown and falling prices, which then bring the system back into equilibrium.[1] According to this model, the role of central banks is modest: they only "assist" the system to reach equilibrium through an interest rate policy which softens the adjustment process. The *discount rate* of the central bank—the interest rates central banks charge for their loans to commercial banks—affects the demand for money in the domestic financial market, and indirectly has flow-through effects at the level of economic activity, prices and wages. According to the "rules of the game" of the gold standard, when the balance of payments was negative and the gold reserves declined, the central bank increased the discount rate to slow down economic activity to lower prices and wages. Ultimately, the balance of payments would then improve and the higher interest rate would attract capital flows further helping to address the loss of gold reserves.

In addition to the interest rate policy, central banks can purchase and sell securities, an instrument also called *open market operations*, in order to affect the money supply. Purchasing securities in the secondary market, usually securities with short maturity periods, increases the money supply and leads to lower interest rates. Selling securities enables the central bank to absorb liquidity and hence to increase the interest rate in the financial markets.

The functioning of the conventional monetary instruments, therefore, depends on factors, which are not under the direct control of the central bank. In the period following World War II, the traditional monetary instruments—such as interest rate policy and open market operations—lost their effectiveness mainly due to the larger sizes of the nations' public sectors. The public sector does not respond to interest rate signaling as the private sector does and therefore interest rate adjustment was no longer an effective tool to impact the level of economic activity (Veit, 1957; Wood, 2005, pp. 225–227). Moreover, as public debts in the postwar period spiraled, any high interest rate policy would put considerable strain on public finances. Therefore, central banks were reluctant to increase the interest rate. Finally, commercial banks accumulated high levels of capital reserves and were no longer dependent on loans from central banks. This fact also reduced the responsiveness of financial markets to changes in the central bank rate (Fousek, 1957).

As the traditional monetary instrument became less effective, central banks started using reserve ratio requirements to restrict the money supply. This instrument aimed at controlling the supply of credit by commercial banks rather than the demand for credit from them. The basic logic of the reserve requirement policy instrument was based on the *money multiplier*. According to this principle, the money supply (M_1 and M_2) depends on the monetary base (M_0) multiplied by the money multiplier, which in turn depends on the reserve ratios: the higher the reserve ratio, the smaller the money multiplier and therefore this limits the money supply. This important mechanism will be explained and dealt with in more detail later on.

The power to instruct a private bank to keep a minimum level of reserves in its vault required special legislation because it involves a breach of the principle of private property rights. In the United States such legislation came into being with the enactment of the Banking Act (1935) in the context of the New Deal, which granted the Federal Reserve System extensive powers to control and regulate the supply of credit (Wood, 2005, p. 221). The introduction of a policy instrument to regulate the supply of credit provided central bankers, banks supervisors and governments with new tools to mobilize the banking sectors to not only regulate the volume of credit but also to intervene in its allocation.

Central banking in developing countries

The first wave of central bank inceptions in peripheral countries took place in the 1920s, and it was the result of an initiative of Montagu Norman, the Governor of the Bank of England, with the cooperation of Benjamin Strong, the Chairman of the Federal Reserve System, to restore global monetary stability. Strong put much effort into encouraging peripheral underdeveloped countries to establish central banks that followed the British model (Drake, 1989; Schuker, 2003). Even the use of the term "British model" implied that these banks were supposed to be independent, follow the rules of the gold standard and use only traditional monetary instruments.

The transplantation of the British model to the periphery was a failure. The problem was not so much that they were not independent enough but rather that their policy instruments were ineffective. As Richard Sayers explained, due to the fact that these countries lacked developed financial markets, there was no "transmission system" for central bank policy. Commercial banks did not pay attention to the central bank rate and they found alternative credit sources both domestically and from abroad. Therefore, as Sayers eloquently put it, "the central banker sat in splendid isolation, twiddling his thumbs" (1956, p. 5).

With the retreat of European powers from their colonies, the question regarding central banks in late-developing countries re-emerged. This time round, though, many, principally American, economists objected to the idea of transplanting the British model of central banking to late-developing countries. Sayers, one of the top experts in central banking at the time, acknowledged the failure of the British-style central banks in the 1920s and made the point that in late-developing countries, central banks should take a more active stance in promoting "the growth of a sound structure of commercial banks and other financial institutions" (ibid., p. 7). To this end, he added, it is important to allow "the central bank wider powers than the 'traditional' central banking techniques would allow." (ibid., p. 24). Sayers' approach became common among policy-makers in late-developing countries. His view, that central banks in late-developing countries must contribute to the industrialization of the economy also reached policy-makers and economists in Israel. In an article published in the *Economic Quarterly*, Max Halperin, an Israeli economist, argued that

> contrary to central banks in developed countries, which regard their main function to be the maintenance of monetary and economic stability and of reasonable levels of production and employment, in underdeveloped countries, especially since the Second World War, the main function of the central bank has been to ensure rapid economic development and to locate financing sources for the development of the economy—at least this is how the politicians saw it.
>
> (Halperin, 1958, p. 376)

During the 1950s, therefore, new set of ideas regarding central banking emerged, according to which developing countries required different types of central banking instruments. The economic rationale on which this new paradigm was based stated that in late-developing countries "market forces" lead to outcomes which are inconsistent with national interests and state preferences. In particular, underdeveloped banking systems produce expensive short-term credit and they allocate it to "non-productive" purposes. In more abstract and general terms, late-developing economies were characterized by a structural imbalance between savings and investment. The situation is typified by the fact that, on the one hand, the industrialization process created a high demand for long-term cheap credit; on the other hand, banks had a strong tendency to only provide short-term credit for low-risk purposes (Galbis, 1980; Park, 1980). Under these circumstances the traditional instruments would have condemned the developing country to a slow, painstaking growth process which would lock them into their developmental position for decades. Central banks, therefore, assisted governments in implementing the industrialization policies.

Not all economists adhered to the developmental interpretation of the economic situation in late-developing countries. Mainstream economists insisted that the financial problems of late-developing countries were not caused by their economic structure, but rather by the very instruments which government used to change this structure. The economists Edward Shaw, Roland Mackinnon and Maxwell Fry, who extensively studied the financial aspects of development, described the policies of most governments in late-developing countries as "financial repression" (Fry, 1988; McKinnon, 1973; Shaw, 1973). In their analysis they argued that the intervention of governments in the allocation of credit was designed to steer credit away from the private sector and into the public sector. As the public sector is not productive, the outcome is naturally a slower rate of development. In this chapter and in Chapter 6, it will be shown that the financial repression hypothesis does not take into account the option that central banks may intervene in the allocation of credit for selected productive purposes within the private sector. Therefore, whereas the analysis of Shaw, McKinnon and Fry may be applicable to certain cases, it is not applicable to all cases in which central bankers are involved in credit control.

The involvement of central banks in industrialization, however, does not make them necessarily politicized, in the sense that they allocate resources to powerful market and societal actors. Rather, central banks can assist governments to implement effective industrialization policies, only to the extent that they were quasi-independent with respect to domestic interest groups. This is an essential point in the political economy of central banking in late-developing countries: central banks were independent (or not), irrespective of their involvement in the allocation of credit. They could allocate credit according to political or economic criteria and improve the effectiveness of the government's developmental strategy.

This conceptual framework of central banking in late-developing countries is essential in order to understand the overriding incentive of the government of Israel to establish the Bank of Israel. It also explains the particular design of the bank as manifested in the central bank law and the peculiarities of the operation of the bank in its first years.

Monetary arrangements in Israel before the establishment of the Bank of Israel

Until the establishment of the State of Israel, the legal tender in Palestine was the Palestine pound, which was fixed to the British pound on a one-to-one exchange rate. Palestine was part of the pound sterling bloc, and therefore the currency was managed by the British Currency Board that maintained convertibility between the Palestine pound and the British currency. This implied that for every Palestine pound in circulation, the Board held one British pound in reserve which was invested in British bonds. This monetary arrangement provided the Palestine pound with stability, but exposed the Palestine economy to severe business cycles (Barkai, 2004; Kleiman, 1977).[2]

Two weeks before the official declaration of independence of the State of Israel, on June 1, 1948, the British Currency Board moved to London and continued its activities from there. To gain monetary flexibility, in August 1948, the newly appointed Israeli government signed a charter with the largest bank in Palestine, which was owned by the World Zionist Organization—the Anglo-Palestine Bank Company (later to become Bank Leumi). The bank was committed to establishing an "Issue Department" that would be responsible for issuing Israeli notes and coins.[3] The charter stated that the Issue Department would have a monopoly over issuing banknotes and coins but set very conservative rules concerning the terms under which the Issue Department was allowed to issue money.[4] It was instructed to hold a 100 percent reserve, 50 percent of which had be held in the form of "hard assets" (gold, foreign currency balances, and Palestine pound bills) and the rest as treasury bills and government bonds (Barkai, 2004, p. 48; Kleiman, 1977, pp. 44–47, 235).

It did not take long before the government realized that the conservative model was impractical and the government could not keep to it. In May 1949, the government amended the law and allowed the Issue Department to issue money in exchange for land deeds (*shitrei mekarkein*) which were declared as legitimate reserve assets.[5] Land deeds were non-commercial bonds issued by the government that used the national territory as collateral for money issuance

(Barkai, 2004, p. 48). For practical purposes, this arrangement removed any legal restrictions from the government on borrowing money from the Issue Department as the non-commercial land deeds did not represent actual redeemable debt. The original charter was signed with a validity period of three years, but it was extended several times until the government reached a decision to establish a genuine central bank toward the end of 1953. The official inauguration of the Bank of Israel took place in December 1954.

Why did it take the government six years to establish a central bank? Why did it decide eventually to establish a central bank in the first place? These questions can be dismissed as technical issues: the government was too busy with war waging all around and immigration absorption, it took time to do what every nation must do, establish a central bank. However, historical evidence suggests the timing of the decision to establish a central bank has a more substantial explanation.

Delays in the establishment of the central bank

During the first years after the declaration of independence, the government, headed by the dominant Labor Party, Mapai, did not have a strong incentive to establish an independent monetary authority: the prevailing arrangement allowed the government considerable monetary flexibility, which it needed to finance the high military expenses and the mass immigration project. Moreover, the dominant position of the government enabled it to impose monetary restraint when the government believed it was necessary, without an independent central bank. This was the case during the New Economic Policy of 1952. Therefore, until 1953, the government fended off any demands by the opposition to establish a formal central bank.

As early as 1949, the right-wing opposition parties had criticized the provisional monetary arrangements and demanded that the government establish a fully-fledged central bank. In a meeting of the Finance Committee, the chairman David Tzvi-Pinkas addressed a question to the minister of finance: "We must abolish not only the provisional form of the money but also the provisional arrangement with the Anglo-Palestine Bank. Does the Ministry of Finance intend to establish a government bank to issue money?" (Finance Committee, December 7, 1949, p. 12). Dr. Yochanan Bader, also a member of the Finance Committee, demanded the establishment of a monetary authority as soon as possible: "If we follow a path of guided currency … yet another thing is needed, the authority. An authority is needed that does not change its ways under external pressure, almost daily" (ibid., p. 4).

The issue of an independent central bank was raised again in parliamentary sessions, when the New Economic Policy (1952) was discussed. The New Economic Policy was designed to curb inflationary pressures. The government pledged to restrict the use of land deeds for the purpose of financing its expenses, but the right-wing opposition demanded a stronger commitment in the form of an independent central bank. In July 1952, the *Herut Party* submitted a Bill for the establishment of a national bank. The bill also included an item that institutionalized the membership of Israel in both preeminent international financial organizations, the IMF and the International Bank for Reconstruction and Development (IBRD). According to the bill, joining these organizations would "benefit the stability of the currency, the revival of international trade, and encourage imports and exports to the benefit of the other functions of the organizations." Moreover, it would "make it significantly easier to obtain foreign credit." Finally, the bill proposed the establishment of a central bank "with the exclusive authority to issue banknotes" (Knesset, July 9, 1952, pp. 2606–2607).

The Minister of Finance Eliezer Kaplan rejected these demands but did not provide a clear reason for doing so. "The matter depends on the situation in Israel and the situation abroad, and in my opinion right now is the worst time to discuss it," he argued (Finance Committee, December 7, 1949, p. 14). On another occasion he added: "I believe that we all agree that both in view of the political situation and of the economic situation, which has not sufficiently taken shape yet, the time has not come yet for a thorough reorganization" (Knesset, May 13, 1949, p. 682). During the discussion on the New Economic Policy in 1952, the new finance minister, Levi Eschkol, refused to make a decision: "the time is not ripe and the issue was not studied enough" (Knesset, July 9, 1952, p. 2601).

Contrary to the right-wing opposition party, Herut, the Progressive Party and the General Zionists, both center-right-wing liberal parties in the ruling coalition, supported the government's position. A member of the Progressive Party explained that "the global trend is to create large blocs, and even larger countries than us can live an independent national life without the luxury of independent currency" (Knesset, February 18, 1952, p. 1340). Even when the government started to formulate the central bank bill, certain members were still concerned by the idea. Yosef Serlin, a member of the General Zionists, insisted that "the experts whom I talked with believed that the time is not ripe" (Government, February 8, 1953, p. 8).

The right-wing parties legitimized their demands on economic grounds: an independent monetary authority would improve economic efficiency, guaranteeing price stability, and the financial stability would improve the confidence of economic actors in the government and would attract foreign investment. To summarize this situation, the right-wing parties perceived the future central bank of Israel along the lines of the British conservative model. However, they also had sectorial ground to demand an independent central bank: during the period under consideration the government allocated the lion's share of resources to the Histadrut sector—the political allies of the Mapai Party—while the private sector—the constituency of the right-wing parties—was not a substantial beneficiary of government control over the monetary authority.

For Mapai's part, the dominant party did not have any incentive to abrogate its monetary control to an independent authority. The Mapai government had the capacity to implement expansionary or contractionary monetary policies according to the prevailing economic and political circumstances. It had nothing to gain from an independent central bank. This naturally raise the question of what happened then to change the government's position.

Toward an Israeli central bank

The first committee for the establishment of a central bank was appointed in March 1951. It consisted of the heads of the two largest banks, three members of parliament and David Horowitz, the former Director General of the Ministry of Finance.[6] The committee was appointed despite resistance from the government to establish a central bank, probably as a means to postpone the issue coming to a head. Although recommendations were submitted to the government, the issue was not discussed in any meaningful way in government meetings.

Only in 1953 did Mapai's members, including ministers, voice the need for a central bank. At a government meeting in February 1953, the Finance Minister Levi Eshkol and the Agriculture Minister Peretz Naftali demanded a decision regarding the central bank: "We are faced with this decision, indeed, we have been facing this decision for a long time, and it is always delayed and delayed and dragged out and dragged out; at some point a decision must be taken" (Government, Feburary 8, 1953, p. 11). This meeting was the first time a consensus began to emerge within the upper ranks of the government that a central bank was urgently needed, and not only to appease the opposition. What made the government members change their mind? How can this seemingly sudden change of mind be explained? Furthermore, why was it the minister of agriculture who was the one pushing for the establishment of a central bank? It is argued below that the answers to these questions are related to the fact that during 1953 the government faced growing difficulty in controlling the allocation of credit to agriculture and other "productive" purposes. The minister of agriculture therefore expected the central bank to assist the government in solving this problem.

Since the beginning of the 1950s, the government had attempted to regulate the allocation of credit and for that purpose it tried to mobilize the commercial banks, but with very limited success. Despite the fact that the large banks—Bank Leumi and Bank Hapoalim—were owned by quasi-public organizations, the World Zionist Organization and the Histadrut, respectively, their management was independent enough to prioritize profit over the national interests. In the course of 1953, the minister of agriculture succeeded in getting several banks to allocate 20 percent of their credit to the agricultural sector. This was achieved through a cooperative effort between the government, the banks' supervisors and the commercial banks themselves. The government provided collateral to the banks and the banks; supervisors oversaw the implementation. The difficulties associated in arranging such cooperation persuaded the minister of agriculture that a central bank should be established to arrange and streamline this type of undertaking in the future: "I believe there is agreement that the Bank will be a tool for regulating credit," he said (Government, May 12, 1954, p. 14).

A week after the government meeting, it was decided that David Horowitz would be the first governor of the new Bank of Israel and that he should take all necessary actions to establish the institutional framework needed as soon as possible. There did, however, remain one final obstacle, namely, the link between the central bank and the IMF.

International financial institutions

The decision to establish a central bank was linked to Israel's membership at the IMF. Any country who wished to become an IMF member had to establish a central bank; but at the same time, without the technical back-up of the IMF, it was practically impossible for a small peripheral country to establish an effective central bank. Membership of the IMF was perceived by Israeli policymakers both as a reward and an obstacle. On the one hand, joining was expected to contribute to the confidence of foreign investors in the Israeli economy and to attract foreign capital as well as investment (Maxfield, 1997, Chap. 3). Moreover, membership in the fund was a pre-condition for applying for loans from the World Bank. The fund was also considered a prestigious and exclusive "club" of trusted nations. The annual conferences of the IMF became an important international forum in which key finance ministers and central bankers convened and discussed policy issues. These considerations were taken into account by the Israeli policy-makers and a few days after the government meeting in which the ministers gave their green light to a central bank, the Economic Committee of the parliament submitted its recommendation to take the necessary steps to join the IMF and the World Bank (Government, September 21, 1953: 18). David Horowitz was sent to negotiate the terms of membership and on his return he presented the outcome of those meetings both at a government meeting and to the Finance Committee. The key advantage of joining the IMF, explained Horowitz, was prestige: "Everywhere people ask us if we are members of the IMF. Besides the political value, if a country is not a member, this fact cast a shadow over it." Membership of the World Bank was important because it provided access to long-term credit: the World Bank "deals mostly with long-term credit—twenty, thirty years. At times even more than thirty years, for the development of countries that are not sufficiently developed. The bank obtains its resources from the developed countries." Horowitz explained that Israel would also like "to benefit from those large amounts that the World Bank lends to developing countries in need of development" (Finance Committee, November 4, 1953, p. 6).

However, on the other hand, membership of the IMF and World Bank raised concerns among policy-makers regarding their intervention in domestic affairs. Horowitz explained that, in principle, membership of the IMF required commitment to rather "orthodox arrangements in monetary matters" (Finance Committee, November 4, 1953). However, in his negotiations, Horowitz met with officials from the IMF, the World Bank, the US State Department and the British Ministry of Foreign Affairs, with whom he managed to reach an understanding regarding the Israeli case. First, it was promised that if Israel submitted an application, its membership would be approved before the next conference in September 1954. Horowitz was also promised that the IMF would use only "persuasive measures" to alter Israel domestic policy but that no direct pressure would be exerted on Israel to do so. Finally, the international financial institutions promised to grant Israel technical assistance at their own expense. In exchange for this, Israel was expected to contribute to the fund an amount of five million dollars, a quarter of which—or 10 percent of its reserves, whichever amount was lower—was to be in gold or US dollars. Upon membership, it was agreed that the IMF would send a delegation to evaluate the economic situation of the country (ibid.). These conditions were approved by the government and the last impediment for the establishment of the Bank of Israel was removed. The preparations for the establishment of this new key institution entered into their final phase: the approval of the central bank bill.

Conclusion

Central banks in late-developing countries behaved, and in some cases still do, differently from central banks in advanced market economies. This is not necessarily because central banks in late-developing countries are "politicized" or because they only serve as an "arm" of the government as the financial repression thesis argues (Fry, 1982; McKinnon, 1973; Shaw, 1973). In fact, *any* central bank is an arm of the government: after all, governments establish the central bank and finance it, and in that sense, any central bank is "politicized." However, when economists argue that a particular central bank is "politicized," they mean that it serves the short-term interests of specific power groups, rather than the long-term public interests. The key issue is that there is not always an agreement on what the "public interest" is. The debate regarding the operation of central banks in late-developing countries, is in fact a debate regarding the definition of the public interests.

The financial repression thesis assumes that the public interest that central banks must protect is the maintenance of the stability of the currency. This thesis, espoused usually by mainstream economists, assumes that the maintenance of the stability of the currency is a public good, the provision of which has no costs. Developmental economists, on the contrary, argue that a stable currency is perhaps a public good, but its provision, in the certain circumstances that prevailed in late-developing countries, has a cost in terms of the capacity of the state to industrialize the economy, promote exports and maybe other objectives, such as building military power, creating jobs combating inequality, etc. Therefore, they argue, in certain circumstances there is a justification to deviate from the orthodox model of central banking, and embrace the developmental model.

Acknowledging the policy ideas of developmental central banking is essential in order to tell the story of the Israeli central bank. If one dismisses the existence of these ideas, the only way in which one can explain the deviation of central banking practices in late-developing countries is based on the assumption that the designers of central banks were driven by short-term interests, rather than by "best practices." The situation in Israel, however, was different: in the 1950s, there was no agreement among economists what the best practices were.

Notes

1 This simple model does account for speculative capital flows, which may destabilize the system.
2 For monetary arrangements in the land of Israel before the establishment of the state, see also Gross and Metzer (1993); Metzer (1998, pp. 1978–1979); and Ottensooser (1955).
3 See Bank Notes Order, 1948, and Currency Order, 1948. *Minutes of the Provisional Council of Government*, June 16, 1948, vol. 1, pp. 4–22.
4 Bank Notes Bill, 1948 and Currency Bill, 1948, *Minutes of the Provisional Council of Government*, vol. 1, pp. 18–23.
5 Land Deeds Order, 1949, Bank Notes Order, 1949 (Knesset, May 13, 1949, p. 681). See also Kleiman (1977, p. 48, fn. 6).
6 "Preamble to the Bank of Israel Law," September 1952, State Archives 5595-C. See also Prager (1973, p. 38).

References

Alesina, A. and Tabellini, G., 1987. Rules and Discretion with Noncoordinated Monetary and Fiscal Policies. *Economic Inquiry* 25, 619–630.

Arnon, A., 2010. *Monetary Theory and Policy from Hume and Smith to Wicksell: Money, Credit, and the Economy.* Cambridge University Press, Cambridge.

Barkai, H., 2004. The Formation of the Monetary System. In: Liviatan, N. and Barkai, H. (Eds.), *The Bank of Israel.* The Bank of Israel, Jerusalem, pp. 37–183 (in Hebrew).

Barro, R.J. and Gordon, D.B., 1983. A Positive Theory of Monetary Policy in a Natural Rate Model. *Journal of Political Economy* 91, 58–610.

Capie, F., Goodhart, C., Fischer, S. and Schnadt, N. (Eds.), 1994. *The Future of Central Banking.* Cambridge University Press, Cambridge.

Cukierman, A., 1992. *Central Bank Strategy, Credibility, and Independence: Theory and Evidence.* The MIT Press, Cambridge, MA.

Drake, P.W., 1989. *The Money Doctor in the Andes: The Kemmerer Missions, 1923–1933.* Duke University Press, Durham, NC.

Eichengreen, B., 1992. *Golden Fetters: The Gold Standard and the Great Depression, 1919–1939.* Oxford University Press, New York.

Finance Committee. Various years. Minutes of Finance Committee, Knesset, Israel. Knesset Archive.

Fischer, S., 1982. Seigniorage and the Case for a National Money. *Journal of Political Economy* 90, 295–313.

Fousek, P.G., 1957. *Foreign Central Banking: The Instrument of Monetary Policy.* The Federal Reserve Bank of New York, New York.

Fry, M.J., 1982. Models of Financially Repressed Developing Economies. *World Development* 10, 731–750.

Fry, M.J., 1988. *Money, Interest, and Banking in Economic Development.* Johns Hopkins University Press, Baltimore, MD.

Galbis, V., 1980. Financial Intermediation and Economic Growth in Less Developed Countries: A Theoretical Approach. In: Coats, W.L. and Khatkhate, D.R. (Eds.), *Money and Monetary Policy in Less Developed Countries*. Pergamon Press, Oxford, pp. 71–84.

Gallarotti, G.M., 1995. *The Anatomy of an International Monetary Regime: The Classical Gold Standard, 1880–1914*. Oxford University Press, New York.

Goodhart, C.A.., Capie, F. and Schnadt, N., 1994. The development of central banking. In: Capie, F., Goodhart, C., Fischer, S. and Schnadt, N. (Eds.), *The Future of Central Banking*. Cambridge University Press, Cambridge.

Government. Various years. Minutes of Government Meetings. Israel State Archive.

Gross, N.T. and Metzer, J., 1993. Palestine in World War II: Some Economic Aspects. In: Mills, G.T. and Rockoff, H. (Eds.), *The Sinews of War: Essays on the Economic History of World War II*. Iowa State University Press, Ames, IA, pp. 59–82.

Halperin, A., 1958. Central Banking in Underdeveloped Countries. *Economic Quarterly* 20, 371–383 (in Hebrew).

Hetzel, R.L., 1997. The case for a monetary rule in a constitutional democracy. *Economic Quarterly* 83, 45–66.

Kleiman, E., 1977. From Mandate to State. In: Gross, N. *et al.* (Eds.), *A Banker for a New State: The History of Bank Leumi*. Masada, Tel Aviv.

Knesset. Various years. *Divrei Ha'knesset*. [Minutes of Knesset Sessions].

Krampf, A., 2012. Translation of Central Banking to Developing Countries in the Post-World War II Period: The Case of the Bank of Israel. In: Renn, J. (Ed.), *The Globalization of Knowledge in History*. Max Planck Research Library for the History and Development of Knowledge, Studies 1. Berlin: Edition Open Access., pp. 459–482.

Krampf, A., 2014. Between Private Property Rights and National Preferences: The Bank of Israel's Early Years. *Israel Affairs* 20, 104–124.

Kydland, F.E. and Prescott, E.C., 1977. Rules Rather than Discretion: The Inconsistency of Optimal Plans. *Journal of Political Economy* 85, 473–492.

Lindert, P.H., 1969. *Key Currencies and Gold, 1900–1913*. Princeton University, Princeton, NJ.

Maxfield, S., 1997. *Gatekeepers of Growth: The International Political Economy of Central Banking in Developing Countries*. Princeton University Press, Princeton NJ.

McKinnon, R.I., 1973. *Money and Capital in Economic Development*. Brookings Institution Press, Washington, DC.

McKinnon, R.I., 1984. *Financial Repression and Economic Development: The Inflation Tax, Monetary Control, and Reserve Requirements on Commercial Banks*. Institute of Economics, Academia Sinica, Nankang, Taipei, Taiwan, Republic of China.

Metzer, J., 1998. *The Divided Economy of Mandatory Palestine*. Cambridge University Press, Cambridge.

North, D.C. and Weingast, B.R., 1989. Constitutions and Commitment: The Evolution of Institutions Governing Public Choice in Seventeenth-Century England. *The Journal of Economic History* 49, 803–832.

Ottensooser, R.D., 1955. *The Palestine Pound and the Israel Pound: Transition from a Colonial to an Independent Currency*. E. Droz, Geneva.

Park, Y.C., 1980. The Ability of the Monetary Authority to Control the Stock of Money in LDCs. In: Coats, W.L. and Khatkhate, D.R. (Eds.), *Money and Monetary Policy in Less Developed Countries*. Pergamon Press, Oxford, pp. 329–333.

Prager, J., 1973. Power and Influence and the Bank of Israel. *Banking Quarterly* 49, 36–59 (in Hebrew).

Ruggie, J.G., 1982. International Regimes, Transactions, and Change: Embedded Liberalism in the Postwar Economic Order. *International Organization* 6, 379–415.

Sayers, R.S., 1956. *Central Banking in Developing Countries*. National Bank of Egypt, Cairo.

Schuker, S.A., 2003. Money Doctors between the Wars. In: Flandreau, M. (Ed.), *Money Doctors: The Experience of International Financial Advising*. Routledge, London, pp. 49–77.

Shaw, E.S., 1973. *Financial Deepening in Economic Development*. Oxford University Press, New York.

Simons, H.C., 1936. Rules versus Authorities in Monetary Policy. *The Journal of Political Economy* 44, 1–30.

Veit. O., 1957. Changes in Monetary Policy and their Consequences to Banking. In: *Relations Between the Central Banks and Commercial Banks* (The Lectures Delivered at the Tenth International Banking Summer School. Garmisch-Partenkirchen: 7–18.

Wood, J.H., 2005. *A History of Central Banking in Great Britain and the United States*. Studies in Macroeconomic History. Cambridge University Press, Cambridge.

6 The independence of the Bank of Israel

Mainstream economic theories attach great importance to a single institutional feature of central banks: their capacity to maintain price stability. This capacity became a defining feature of the independence of central banks. This aspect of central bank independence became essential in the 1970s and the 1980s, when advanced economies faced inflation shocks. Mainstream political economic theories of central banking assume that conventional central banks should use their institutional capacities—their independence—to target price stability. However, can this assumption be generalized? Is it the case that central banks at all times and in all places are supposed to use their institutional capacities to achieve this particular policy objective? Is it the case that any central bank, which pursues a different policy objective, is necessarily less independent than one that pursues price stability?

This chapter traces the discussions and debates among Israeli policy-makers, economists, politicians and bankers regarding the formulation of the Bank of Israel Law, with a focus on the issue of the independence of the bank and its managerial structure. The chapter argues that the Bank of Israel, as perceived by its designers, was not supposed to pursue price stability, because inflation was not considered a key policy problem, and the government was able to restrict money printing without a central bank. However, the government faced another problem that it could not solve by itself: the expansion of credit by the banking system, and its allocation to purposes which were not deemed essential by the government. It is argued here that this policy problem had a significant impact on the managerial structure of the Bank of Israel.

A board or a single governor?

The notion of central bank independence is a legal and formal concept which is manifested in a set of institutional arrangements. In the debates that preceded the approval of the Bank of Israel Law, three issues were discussed that directly or indirectly affected the independence of the bank. First, the question concerning the *managerial structure* of the bank: should the Bank be managed by a board of governors or by a single governor? Second, the question related to the *degree of flexibility and discretion* that the governor enjoys: to what extent should the law provide guidelines for the policies of the Bank? Third, the question regarding the *source of legitimacy* of the central bank: did the Bank's legitimacy draw on democracy, professionalism or sovereign-like authority? Each of these questions reflected on the position of the policy-makers regarding the independence of the Bank.

The first report concerning the establishment of a central bank was submitted to the government in September 1952 by a special committee headed by Ernst Lehman from the Ministry of Finance, after he consulted with American experts. Lehman recommended that the bank should be managed by a governor and two deputies, all three of whom would be appointed by the government (Prager, 1973). The policy of the bank, Lehman's report suggested, would be determined after consultation with an advisory council consisting of representatives of various economic sectors. A final proviso was recommended in that the policies of the bank would need final approval from the minister of finance (ibid., p. 39).

After the government decided to appoint Horowitz as the first governor, he was instructed to prepare the first draft of the bill. Horowitz inserted several changes to Lehman's draft which increased the powers of the governor with respect to the advisory council. Horowitz's draft increased the size of the advisory council but he left it devoid of any formal managerial power. In practice, Horowitz's draft turned the council into a purely symbolic body that had no practical impact on bank policy (Prager, 1975, p. 40, fn. 10). To compensate for this change, Horowitz added an advisory board, which was to consist of seven members appointed by the government and that would convene once a fortnight. Horowitz's draft achieved two key things. First, it provided the governor with the sole formal authority to make monetary decisions without having to seek the approval of any other person within the bank. The justification for this decision was that the bank must follow the government's instruction, rather than setting its own: "We must decide whether the bank must accept the authority of the government or if it is subordinated to a new body … which will become a second center of economic policy making in Israel," he explained (Horowitz, 1954, p. 13). He believed that the bank should be subordinated to the government. This position was based on the expectation that the bank would take part in the allocation of credit. The independence of the bank, he explained,

> does not concern merely 25 banks, but it concerns the entire country. This is why we protect so closely the authority of the government and of the state in these matters. These cannot be decreed by the Bank itself or by the governor, but by an executive institution, which depends on the legislative institutions.
> (Government, May 2, 1954, p. 6)

For similar reasons, Horowitz rejected the idea of an advisory body consisting of representatives from key economic sectors:

> In the government, the interests appear in a distilled form, as *ideological interests*. A Board … would represent actual *economic interests*—without

> these interests being illuminated by the interests of the state as a whole … so the matter is very dangerous for a national bank.
>
> (Finance Committee, July 13, 1954, p. 7. emphasis added)

Horowitz's somewhat vague distinction between "ideological interests" and "economic interests" can be interpreted by reference to Rousseau's distinction between the *will of all* (*volonté de tous*) and the *general will* (*volonté générale*). According to Horowitz, the government represents the general will, whereas a board of representatives would only represent the will of all.

This explains why it could be argued by government members that in Israel, "the government as a whole is more detached from this or that interest than is any board of governors." A board of governors, Horowitz assumed, would represent the economic interests of various sectors of the economy, and

> [I]f the question arises whether or not to print money, there is a danger that the position of this or that economic sector will decide, and it is possible that [a specific sector] is interested in printing money and having it distributed throughout the economy.
>
> (Government, May 12, 1954)

This position was supported by Mapai representatives as many assumed that "from the point of view of internal confidence … the confidence in the Bank is liable to weaken if the authority of the government is curtailed" (Finance Committee, July 29, 1954, p. 6).

From a liberal-democratic perspective, the claim that the government represents the "real" interest of the state, contrary to representatives of sectors, seems an empty rhetoric designed to legitimize the government's quest for more power. However, the alternative explanation is also plausible: the government was concerned that if the bank was managed by sectoral representatives, this would allow powerful actors to influence the bank's behavior. As will be argued later, the fact that the bank's board did not include a representative of the Histadrut was a critical fact that enabled the bank to confront the Histadrut and to contribute to the state's autonomy.

A central bank Law or Horowitz's law?

A prominent critic of Horowitz's proposal was the American-Jewish economist, Abba P. Lerner. Lerner was invited to take part in the Economic Advisory Staff (EAS) at the Prime Minister's Office, which was financed by the Technical Cooperation Program of the United Nations and was headed by Oscar Gass.[1]

Lerner was a Keynesian economist and a self-avowed social-democrat. One would expect that an economist with such views would be welcomed by Mapai, which was a Labor Party. However, this was not the case. Lerner believed that the final objective of socialism was democracy, personal freedom, equitable distribution of income, full employment and the optimal allocation of resources by markets

(Scitovsky, 1984, p. 1549). As part of these objectives, the rights and freedom of consumers were assigned significant weight. Free economic activity was a condition for the effectiveness of the price mechanism, "one of the valuable instruments of modern society" (ibid., p. 1549). Moreover, Lerner regarded monopolies as one of the great hazards of capitalism which impaired personal freedom and are harmful to the effective and optimal allocation of resources. The prevention of monopolies was, in his opinion, one of the main objectives of state intervention, in addition to such objectives as full employment and the equitable distribution of income. (Lerner, 1944, p. 3). This policy priority was not well received by Mapai.

In his capacity as an economic advisor, Lerner was asked to comment on Horowitz's draft for the Bank of Israel Bill. Despite the fact that Lerner received Horowitz's draft relatively late, he produced a long, detailed and highly critical report of no less than 26 pages, much longer than Horowitz's draft itself. The government tried to conceal Lerner's report from the members of parliament but somehow it was leaked to a member of the Herut Party, who complained in the Knesset:

> Why is it that the minister of finance, for example, did not make known to us the opinions of Dr. Gass and Dr. Lerner when they brought before the house a bill of such importance? … So that members of the house would not have to obtain the material through the back door?
>
> (Parliament, June 29, 1954, vol. 16, p. 2074)

It is not entirely clear why the drafters of the law submitted it for Lerner's inspection in the first place. One possibility is that the government had to submit the bill to Lerner's review because the Economic Advisory Staff, of which Lerner was a member, was financed in part by the Technical Cooperation Program of the United Nations, and they expected the Economic Advisory Staff to be involved.[2]

Lerner raised two issues regarding the structure of the bank's management. First, he believed the law did not endow the bank with enough independence to run monetary policy, and, second, he argued that the law endowed the governor with too many powers in areas which were not strictly speaking monetary. "An independent central bank enables a healthy division of labor. The central bank can concentrate on the regulation of volume of money issued, whereas the ministry of finance can concentrate on government spending, taxing and loans." Lerner pointed out that the law did not institutionalize such a division of labor: "the bank is not granted *any* independence in determining the volume of money, which is, after all, the main monetary policy instrument" (Lerner, 1954, pp. 11–12, emphasis in original). Lerner recommended that the authority to make policy should be delegated to a "small board" of five members rather than to a "single person." This arrangement, he explained "will provide the bank full control over monetary policy, with full independence with respect to the ministry of finance (ibid., p. 14).

Members of Knesset from the liberal-right factions—the Progressive Party, the General Zionists, and the religious party *Hapoel Hamizrahi*—supported Lerner's position. Knesset member, Eliyahu-Moshe Ganhovsky, of *Hapoel Hamizrahi*, argued that a board of governors would improve the effectiveness of the bank. The board should include "ministers, bankers, and public figures," he explained. "This is a unique and much more stable arrangement." Yeshayahu Foerder of the Progressive Party also supported a more decentralized managerial structure: "according to the current proposal, all the pressure will be exerted on the governor. The bank's capacity to resist pressure will be improved if the 'no' could be supported by a kind of 'monetary board' " (Finance Committee, July 13, 1954, pp. 7–9).

Foerder rejected the opinion that the government represented the national interest, whereas other bodies represent sectorial interests:

> I do not accept Horowitz's approach that the government presents a more ideological position, whereas in our debased life [sectors behave] according to their interests. People sit in the government as representatives of interests, and they take into account that they will have to be elected again.
>
> (Ibid., p. 8)

Ganchovsky argued that:

> A state bank is an important financial instrument, and it is in the interests of all of us to strengthen the confidence of the public in it. Therefore, it is important that its management will be strong, central and that it would serve the entire country and the entire economy.
>
> (Parliament, June 28, 1954, vol. 16, p. 2053)

It is not surprising that the liberal parties demanded a board of governors: for them, the establishment of a central bank was an opportunity to restrict the government's capacity to channel resources to its political allies in the Histadrut sector.

Representatives of the large banks also opposed Horowitz's draft and pushed for a board of governors. Dr. Aharon Bart, the Director of Bank Leumi, was invited to the Finance Committee to present the opinion of the banking system. Bart emphasized the importance of the reputation of the central bank in the modern international economy:

> The main asset of a central bank is the international confidence it enjoys. If Israel embraced a model that differs from the prevailing international convention, this might undermine the bank's reputation. I am not saying that we must follow exactly the path taken by other countries but I am saying definitely that we are not entitled … to create a revolutionary structure *ex nihilo*, so that anyone perusing our law will wonder about it and say: what type of creature is that?
>
> (Finance Committee, July 29, 1954, p. 4)

Although certainly a point of some conjecture, one may argue that Bart opted for a more independent central bank governed by a board rather than by a single governor because the large banks were concerned that the government would use the central bank to intervene in the banking system in a way that would jeopardize their interests. The more independent the central bank, the more difficult this would be for the government.

The centralization of powers in the hands of the governor raised the impression among many members of Knesset that the law was tailored for David Horowitz, who enjoyed the trust of the leaders of Mapai. A member of Knesset, Bezerano of the General Zionist Party, explained to the Finance Committee, it is not "about a central bank with an extensive level of independence, but rather it is about one person who receives this independence … the law delegates dictatorial powers to one person, and I detest anything that smells like dictatorship" (Finance Committee, July 13, 1954, p. 9). Dr. Bart supported this interpretation of the law: the question is of "economic dictatorship or of economic dictator; whether to delegate the power to a single person or to a group of persons that will be the management [of the bank]" (Finance Committee, July 29, 1954, p. 6). Lerner wrote: "It may be the case that the bill was formulated under the assumption that a certain personality will fulfil the role [of the governor]" (Lerner, 1954, p. 14). In the Finance Committee, one of the members asked the participants to ignore the fact that we "know who will fill this position" (Finance Committee, July 13, 1954, p. 9).

The personality of Horowitz was indeed an issue. In early 1953, a member of the General Zionists Party expressed the concern of his party over the candidacy of Horowitz: "we are not very happy with this candidate," he said but did not explain why (Government, February 8, 1953). Nevertheless, Mapai members insisted on the candidacy of Horowitz and Pinhas Lavon explained the position of the government:

> If the question before us was merely to select a banker qualified to manage a regular [commercial] bank, I would not recommend David Horowitz and I would have preferred perhaps, several other candidates.… But we are talking about a state bank, whose purpose is to cooperate [with the government] in shaping the economic and monetary policy in Israel … I do not know any other banker who can compete with him as a candidate for the management of such a bank, with these features and these roles.
>
> (Ibid.)

The Minister of Finance Levi Eshkol also supported Horowitz's nomination:

> There is no doubt regarding the personal authority and skillfulness of the candidate. There is no doubt that if you would ask someone from abroad, who had previous contacts with the Israeli economy and the Israeli financial world, he would not be able to find a better candidate.
>
> (Ibid.)

There is no question that the Mapai's leadership insisted on Horowitz's candidacy. One may argue that this is evidence of the politicization of the bank and of the expectations of Mapai's leaders that Horowitz would follow their instructions. However, it is more likely that Mapai's leaders sought a central banker who would be able to withstand pressure from the Histadrut sector. It must be kept in mind that Horowitz was the "architect" of the austerity policy of 1952 and he opposed Ben-Gurion publicly. Hence, Mapai's leader in the government endorsed him not because they believed he would serve the interests of Mapai, but because they believed he would contribute to the fortification of state autonomy.

Rules versus discretion

The question regarding the central bank's managerial structure was linked to the question regarding the managerial *flexibility* of the central bank. Horowitz and Mapai's leaders believed that central bank should have full flexibility and discretion. Therefore, Horowitz's draft endowed the bank with many powers and few rules. Lerner was highly critical of this approach. "Instead of providing general, defined, and clear rules of monetary policy making, the bill tends to endow the bank with arbitrary and extensive powers with no justification" (Lerner, 1954, p. 17). For example, Horowitz's draft included the establishment of an *Investment Committee*, which would be managed by the governor. The committee was supposed to consist of six members, four of whom would be appointed after consultation with "public and economic bodies and organizations," and two by the government (ibid., p. 15). The article concerning the Investment Committee was omitted from the final draft but its existence in the preliminary draft provides evidence of the motives of the government and David Horowitz.

In addition, Horowitz's draft provided the bank with the power to dictate the interest rate that commercial banks should charge depositors, the power to suspend and close banks, the power to set reserve ratios, the power to determine which assets will be considered liquid for reserve requirements, as well as the power to approve or deny a license to commercial banks (ibid., pp. 17–19). Lerner opposed the delegation of such extensive powers to the one person. Moreover, these powers, he argued, belong to the Banking Act (the supervision of banks' law). Lerner was not alone. The Commissioner of Legislation at the Ministry of Justice pointed out that the bill did not provide sufficiently clear guidelines for the governor's role. As for the article concerning the authority of the governor to issue and re-issue money for circulation, the Commissioner confessed: "I believe that the test must be objective rather than 'at the governor's discretion'." The Commissioner also recommended providing a "full legal definition" of liquid assets and "not leave it to the governor to decide," and he supported Lerner's view that the supervisory powers should be separated from the monetary authority: "the authority granted the governor in the section concerning bank supervision," he argued, "is too broad … I doubt that these directives should be part of the proposed law."[3]

The question of whether central banks should follow rules or be granted flexibility was not unique to the Israeli discourse and it was being discussed by central banking experts worldwide. During the gold standard period, and in fact until the end of World War II, the conventional view was that, ideally, central banks should follow rules. Under the Bretton Woods regime, central banks enjoyed more discretion, given the assumed trade-off between stability and growth. In late-developing countries, the flexibility of central banks was even broader. Richard Sayers, a British expert on central banking, argued, in his book, *Banking in the British Commonwealth* (1952), that "given successful management [of the central bank], the fewer fixed rules the law contains about the functioning of the central bank, the higher the likelihood that the bank will succeed [in achieving its objectives]" (quoted in Horowitz, 1954, p. 7). Horowitz quoted Sayers in his response to Abba Lerner's report, and he added that the "need for governmental approval in all matters involving high-level policy ensures that the use of this flexibility [shall be exercised] according to the state's interests" (ibid., p. 7).

The debates concerning the flexibility of the bank and its managerial structure were not independent of each other: a central bank with flexibility, required a board of governors, whereas a rule-following central bank, could have been managed by a smaller team of professionals. Horowitz's draft offered a combination of highly centralized managerial structure and highly flexible central bank mandate. This combination turned the bank—and Horowitz in person—into an "economic dictator," at least on paper. Whereas formally any decision of the bank required approval from the government, in practice, it was clear that the government did not have the means to oversee the decisions of the bank. "The arrangement proposed by the law is not serious," claimed Ernst Bart. "No person, however skilled, can work like this, so that for every serious decision he has to run, on one hand to the Advisory Board, and on the other hand to the government in order to obtain its approval" (Finance Committee, July 29, 1954, p. 3). Bedjerano supported this view, arguing that the ministers "are so overloaded with their work that they are not capable of delving into the details of the issues they are asked to approve" (Government, May 12, 1954, p. 9). Minister Pinchas Rosen raised the same point in the cabinet, saying that "the government will not decide in day-to-day matters on those which every bank's management must decide on. Matters of this sort can be left to the exclusive decision of the governor" (ibid., p. 7).

The analysis of these debates concerning the managerial structure of the bank and the flexibility of the management demonstrate that the government made much effort to provide the bank with as much power and flexibility as possible, and at the same time to concentrate these powers in the hands of the governor in order to made it easier for the government to oversee the behavior of the bank.

The Bank of Israel in comparative perspective

To assess the extent to which the government's choices were guided by global norms or by domestic considerations, this section compares the law of the Bank of Israel to the laws of the Bank of Ceylon and the Bank of South Korea. The Bank of Ceylon was chosen because its law served as the main model for the

Bank of Israel law (Bar-Yosef, 1981). The Bank of Korea law was selected because the drafter of this law was Arthur Bloomfield, who also advised the government of Israel.

The Bank of Korea was established in 1950 with the assistance of John Exter, who served as an economist at the Federal Reserve Bank of New York. Exter prepared for Ceylon a draft of its central bank law and then went on to serve as the governor of the bank until 1953 (Bank of Sri Lanka, 1990, p. 4). The Constitution of the Bank of Ceylon specifies that the bank is to be managed by a board of governors composed of three people: the governor, the secretary of the minister of finance, and a third person appointed by the governor based on the government's recommendation. The board "will be responsible for the management and the operation of the bank" (Exter, 1949 section 8, (1) and (2)). This is a structure that clearly emphasizes the importance placed on cooperation between the central bank and the government.

The law of the central bank of South Korea was drafted by Arthur Bloomfield and John Jensen. Bloomfield was a senior economist at the Federal Reserve Bank of New York. During the 1950s, he participated in several advisory missions to developing countries and he published numerous studies on the topic of central banking in late-developing economies (Bloomfield, 1959, 1957; Bloomfield and Jensen, 1951). At the end of the 1940s, Bloomfield and Jensen were invited by the government of South Korea to conduct research on the domestic banking system and to advise regarding the establishment of a central bank. The product of their visit was a report that included a draft proposal of a central bank law and a supervision of banking law.

According to the recommendations of Bloomfield and Jensen, the Bank of Korea would be managed by a board of governors composed of seven members: the minister of finance, the governor and five members appointed by the president with the approval of the government. Two members represented banking institutions, one from the Association of Merchants and Industrialists, one from the Ministry of Agriculture and Forestry and one from the Economic Council of the Planning Ministry (Bloomfield and Jensen, 1951, p. 84). Bloomfield explained the rationale behind this recommendation:

> We propose the establishment of a Monetary Board, representative of various broad interests in the national economy, to be placed in charge of the new central bank and of the formulation of the country's monetary, credit and exchange policies. A central bank is much too strategic and vital a factor in a country's financial and economic welfare to be guided by any one man or any one narrow group, no matter how well intentioned, and we firmly believe that the establishment of a Monetary Board will go a long way towards democratizing the Bank and its policies, reducing the possibility of unwarranted and arbitrary political pressures and interferences, and defining and allocating much more clearly than before responsibility for the Bank's operations and policies.
>
> (Ibid., p. 44)

Exter's and Bloomfield's recommendations for the composition of the board of governors are based on two different models: Exter's model outlines a structure placing heavy bias toward cooperation between the bank and the government; Bloomfield's model suggests that the board must be independent from the government, but not isolated from the various key economic sectors it will impact on.

The Israeli model was closer to that of Exter's: it was based on the assumption that the bank would have to cooperate with the government and that the government is the ultimate source of authority. However, even Exter's model provided more clout to the management of the central bank than was enjoyed by those running the Bank of Israel.

Hence, whereas the Bank of Israel law, as formulated by Horowitz, reflected a global trend in which central banks were not expected to operate independently of government preferences and the interests of economic sectors, in the case of Israel, the government went a long way to prevent a situation in which the management of the central bank could have too much influence and set its own policy agenda. For that purpose it approved a law which concentrated the managerial power of the bank in the hands of the governor.

Composition of the Advisory Board of the Bank of Israel

The Bank of Israel Law (1954) did not provide the Bank with a strong capacity to resist the government's requests for funding. It is argued here that the Bank was not designed for that purpose: rather, it was designed to confront two powerful actors in the Israeli political economy: the Histadrut sector and the existent banking system. The Bank was expected to shift resources away from the Histadrut to the private sector by tightening controls over the banking system. These two objectives were achieved by very different strategies. The first was achieved by a marginalization of the Histadrut sector from the policy-making circle. The second was achieved by a strategy that went in the opposite direction, namely, by maintaining a political economic exchange with the banking system which was granted certain privileges in exchange for its cooperation. This argument will be further elaborated upon in the following chapters.

The exclusion of the Histadrut and the link with the banking system are manifested in the composition of the Advisory Board. It has been claimed by some scholars that the Advisory Board of the Bank of Israel did not have any significant power, and that Horowitz, the governor, took all decisions by himself (Prager, 1973). However, so far no empirical study has been made to test this claim. This book presents evidence based on the minutes of the Advisory Board, and it shows how the composition of the Board affected the capacity of the Bank to confront powerful actors in the Israeli political economy.

The composition of the Advisory Board changed considerably over the years; however, during the first five years of the bank, from 1954 to 1959, it is possible to identify a pattern.

Two members of the Board were always representatives of the two large banks: Eliezer Siegfried Hoffein, Chairman of Bank Leumi, who was also Chairman of the Board, the second bank representative was Avraham Zbarski, Director of Bank Hapoalim and Chairman of the Saving and Loans Cooperatives Center [*Merkaz Kupot Hamilve*] of the Histadrut sector. The representatives of the large banks had superior experience in banking, and this fact endowed them with additional influence in the Board. A third member who was also related to the banking sector was Dr. Ernst Nebenzahl who had served as legal counsel for the Yeffet Bank during the 1933–1945 period and in 1956 was appointed to the Board of Governors at Bank Leumi.[4]

Besides the bankers, the Board included members of the Labor Movement: Giora Yoseftal was Mapai's Secretary from 1956 to 1959, and Kadish Luz who was a member of parliament on behalf of Mapai. The Jewish Agency was also represented in the Board by Yoseftal, who was also a member of the Jewish Agency's executive board from 1947 to 1952, and Dr. Nebenzahl was a director general of the Department for the Development of Jerusalem of the Jewish Agency.

A dominant figure in the deliberations of the Board was Shimon Bedjerano, an industrialist and one of the owners of the Assis food products factory. He was active in the General Zionists Federation and served as a member of parliament on behalf of the General Zionists Party. He was also a member of the Association of Industrialists and a member of the Board of Governors of Bank Leumi. The seventh member was Dr. Elyakum Ostashinski, who had trained as an agronomist and had served in several capacities in the agriculture sector: Director of the Agricultural Department in the Farmers' Association, Director of the Agricultural Department in the Citrus Marketing Board. He was also a member of the Board of Governors of Bank Leumi and of the Executive Committee of the General Zionists Party. We can therefore surmise that Bedjerano represented the industrial sector and Ostashinski the agricultural sector.

In brief then, there were always at least two bankers on the Board (Hoffien and Zbarsky), two members linked to Mapai (Yoseftal and Luz), two linked to the Jewish Agency, two members linked to the private sector and the General Zionist Party (Bedjerano and Ostashinski), and one member with ties with the Histadrut (Zbarsky).[5] In this composition of the Board, the Histadrut sector and the left-wing parties were under-represented. Zbarsky was the Director of the Bank Hapoalim, which was owned by the Workers Corporation, the Histadrut's holding company. But there was no representation of the Histadrut's industrial corporations or of the agricultural settlements of the Labor Movement.

Conclusion

Mainstream economists tend to undermine the significance of local institutional features and their impact on what is considered "best practices." However, this universalist perception of economic policy-making misses the fact that in late-developing economies policy-makers and economists faced very different policy problems from those faced by policy-makers and economists in advanced economies. Therefore, the fact that central banks in late-developing countries deviated from the conventional model does not inherently imply that these central banks were "politicized." Rather, policy-makers in the Global South followed an alternative non-liberal policy norm of central banking, which was advocated by a considerable number of reputable economists (Bloomfield, 1957; Brimmer, 1971; Chandler, 1962; Fousek, 1957; Sayers, 1956; Sen, 1956).

While the managerial structure of the Bank of Israel was part of a policy trend in the Global South, it was rather an extreme manifestation of this trend. This implies that the managerial structure of the Bank of Israel was also influenced by domestic factors. A key factor that influenced the choices of the policy-makers was the dominant position of the ruling party. Mapai did not face a significant threat from other parties, and therefore it dominated the Knesset and could pass any formal decision it deemed necessary. This meant that Mapai's leadership had little incentive to establish an independent central bank for the purpose of regulating the issuance of money.

Notes

1 "Arranging foreign currency payments for Oscar Gass," May 6, 1953, SA, 5509/14.
2 Ibid.
3 "To: The Legal Counsel of the Ministry of Finance, From: the Legislative Commissioner, The Ministry of Justice," 41211954, State Archives, 5416/18c.
4 Dr. Ernst Nebenzahl had a doctoral degree in law from Frankfurt University. In addition to the functions listed above, in 1947, he was appointed Chairman of the Board of Directors of Hollander and Partners, headquartered in Stockholm. In 1948, he was appointed Director of the Department for the Development of Jerusalem of the Jewish Agency and Director of the Jerusalem Economic Company. In 1954, with his appointment to the Advisory Board, he was named Chairman of the Postal Bank.
5 According to a survey conducted on the composition of the Board, until 1973, the Board always contained two bankers. After 1958, there were two representatives of industry, generally one representative of the agricultural sector, and at times two, and at least one politician, but no minister. At no time did anyone whose primary occupation was in the services sector (except for banking) serve on the Board. See Prager (1973, pp. 46–47).

References

Bank of Sri Lanka, 1990. *40th Anniversary Commemorative Volume of the Central Bank of Sri Lanka, 1950–1990*. The Bank of Sri Lanka, Colombo.

Bar-Yosef, I., 1981. The Central Bank of Ceylon Law as a Model for the Bank of Israel Law. *Economics Quarterly* 78, 15–31 (in Hebrew).

Bloomfield, A.I., 1957. Central Banking in Underdeveloped Countries. *The Journal of Finance* 12, 190–204.

Bloomfield, A.I., 1959. *Monetary Policy Under the International Gold Standard: 1880–1914*. Federal Reserve Bank of New York, New York.

Bloomfield, A.I. and Jensen, J.P., 1951. *Banking Reform in South Korea*. Federal Reserve Bank of New York, New York.

Brimmer, A.F., 1971. Central Banking and Economic Development: The Record of Innovation. *Journal of Money, Credit and Banking* 3, 780–792.

Chandler, L.V., 1962. *Central Banking and Economic Development*, University of Bombay, Bombay.

Exter, J., 1949. *Monetary Law: A Bill to Establish the Monetary System of Ceylon and the Central Bank*. Ceylon Government Press, Colombo.

Finance Committee. Various years. *Minutes of the Finance Committee*. Israel Knesset Archive.

Fousek, P.G., 1957. *Foreign Central Banking: The Instrument of Monetary Policy*. The Federal Reserve Bank of New York, New York.

Fry, M.J., 1988. *Money, Interest, and Banking in Economic Development*. Johns Hopkins University Press, Baltimore, MD.

Government. Various years. Minutes of Government Meeting. Israel State Archive.

Horowitz, D., 1954. Comments on the Memorandum of Mssrs Gass and Lerner from the Economic Advisory Staff on the Bank of Israel Law. May 2. Israel State Archive, 5617/13c.

Knesset. Various years. *Divrei Ha'knesset* [Minutes of Knesset Sessions].

Lerner, A.P., 1944. *The Economics of Control: Principles of Welfare Economics*. The Macmillan Co, New York.

Lerner, A.P., 1954. Memorandum, Economic Advisory Staff. April 27. Israel State Archive, 5617/13c.

Prager, J., 1973. Power and Influence and the Bank of Israel. *Banking Quarterly* 49, 36–59 (in Hebrew).

Prager, J., 1975. Central Bank Policy-Making in Israel: The Horowitz Governorship (1954–1971). *International Journal of Middle East Studies* 6, 46–69.

Sayers, R.S., 1956. *Central Banking in Developing Countries*. National Bank of Egypt, Cairo.

Scitovsky, T., 1984. Lerner's Contribution to Economics. *Journal of Economic Literature* 22, 1547–1571.

Sen, S.N., 1956. *Central Banking in Underdeveloped Money Markets*. Bookland Private Limited, Calcutta.

Shaw, E.S., 1973. *Financial Deepening in Economic Development*. Oxford University Press, New York.

7 Developmental central banking

The structure of a financial system, writes John Zysman, "affects the capacity of the national political executive to intervene in the industrial economy" (1984, p. 80). Therefore, he continues, "Unless it [the state] has direct influence in the allocation of credit by the financial system, it must either make the financial institutions its allies or confront them as political opponents to its interventionist strategies" (ibid., p. 77). Central banks and banks' supervision agencies are institutions, which possess the capacities to confront banks, as well as making them allies of governments. This claim, it is argued in this chapter, explains why the establishment of independent central banks and a powerful supervisory department was crucial for the implementation of industrialization policy in late-developing countries.

During the discussions and debates regarding the design of the Bank of Israel one of the key points of contention concerned the legal status of the bank supervision agency: should it be under the full control of the governor, or should it be endowed with a certain level of independence vis-à-vis the monetary authority? Whereas the government and David Horowitz opted for combining the monetary and the supervisory authorities, others were concerned by this choice.

This chapter explores the economic rationale that guided the choice of the government to eventually delegate all the supervisory powers to the governor of the central bank, as well as the economic rationale for the alternative approach of not doing so. In brief, the argument presented here will be that the designers of the Bank of Israel Law decided to combine the monetary and supervisory authorities in order to devise a powerful and effective institutional tool to confront the banking system and gain ironclad control over the banking system.

The decision to delegate the supervisory powers to the monetary authority was part of an international trend among late-developing economies, which used central banks and supervisory agencies for the purpose of economic development. This trend was not the product of a "politicization" of central banks—as central banks are already political institutions—but rather the product of the emergence of a new role for such banks, namely, developmental central banking.

Monetary policy-making and the supervision of the Bank

The monetary and the supervisory authorities have different objectives, but their functions overlap due to fact that they use common policy instruments. Therefore, in most cases, the two authorities are either combined or they cooperate closely together (Beck and Gros, 2012; Whelan, 2012). To understand why the two policy areas are functionally linked, it is necessary to take a technical detour.

The monetary authority, according to mainstream economics, seeks to affect the *money supply* (designated as M_1, M_2 or M_3), either directly or indirectly. The money supply depends on the monetary base (M_0), which consists of money issued by a central bank. The actual volume of the money supply is much larger than the monetary base due to the operation of the banking (and financial) system. The banking system creates means of payment through the process of receiving deposits and providing credit. The ratio between the money supply and the monetary base is defined as the *money multiplier*. The larger the money multiplier, the greater the money supply, even if the monetary base is constant. This naturally then implies that the central bank must have some control over the banking system if it wants to exert control over the money supply.

The multiplication of money by the banking system can be demonstrated as follows: let us assume a simple case that includes a depositor, a single bank and an investor (or any person who takes credit). The depositor deposits a sum of money in the bank (say, $100) and in exchange, she receives a debt bill or an IOU. If the bank is a respected institution, the IOU can still be used as a means of payment for other transactions. The bank does not keep in its vault all the deposited money but it uses a part of it (say, $80) to provide a loan to the investor. The rest ($20) is kept in the vault as a *reserve*. In that case, the reserve ratio is 20 percent. The investor holds now $80, which can be used for any purpose, in addition to the $100 held by the depositor. Hence, after the two transactions the "public" hold $180: $100 of which = the monetary base, and $80 = created by the bank. In this case the money multiplier is 1.8. If the bank lowers the reserve ratio, more money goes back to the market and the money multiplier increases.[1] This simple model implies that the reserve ratios of private banks affect the supply of money, and therefore the level of economic activity.

What are the factors that shape the consideration of the commercial banks, regarding the reserve ratio they hold? There are three types of considerations:

1 *Profitability of banks*: Banks' profits come from two sources: selling services (commission) and the spread between the interest rates they charge for credit and the interest rate they pay for deposits. Hence, the lower the reserve ratios, the more loans banks can provide, the higher is their expected profit (assuming the commission is constant).
2 *Financial stability*: the higher the reserve ratio, the more steady is the bank. When a bank lowers its reserve ratio, its exposure to the risk of illiquidity

increases. Ideally, each bank would set its own reserve ratio independently to reflect the individual institution's risk of illiquidity. In practice, central banks tend to underestimate risks due to moral hazard consideration—they expect to be bailed out—so they key lower levels of reserve than needed. Therefore, the supervisory agency may impose a certain level of reserve on private banks.

3 *Impact on the supply of money*: as reserve ratios affect the supply of money, it is also in the interest of the central bank to dictate the commercial bank reserve ratios. It must be stated that economists do not agree on the extent to which the money supply is manageable through the reserve ratios. However, for our purposes, suffice it to say that the practice of targeting the money supply through a reserve ratio policy was common during the post-World War II period. However, today most economists agree that in the majority of cases, this instrument is ineffective in controlling the supply of money.

The reserve ratio, then, is determined by three considerations: profit, financial stability and monetary considerations. The relative weight of each consideration changes over time and across countries. Until the middle of the nineteenth century, commercial banks in England determined reserve ratios according to their own discretion, which was based on profitability and stability considerations. As a result of frequent bank runs and periodical crises, the Bank of England gradually took upon itself the responsibility of being a Lender of Last Resort. This informal role of the central bank provided it with the power and legitimacy to intervene in setting minimal reserve requirements. Therefore, the Bank of England began acting as an informal sector-wide bank supervisor (Goodhart, 1988, p. 5; Sayers, 1950, pp. 29–41).

Following the Great Depression in the 1930s, central bankers had more legitimacy to intervene in the management of commercial banks despite the fact that this intervention was inconsistent with the principle of private property rights. The new trend was justified not only on the grounds that it was necessary in order to protect depositors and to maintain the stability of individual banking institutions, but also on the grounds that the behavior of the banking system has collective consequences. Hence, a government, through the central bank and the bank's supervisor, has the legitimacy to regulate the banking system.

The trend originated in the United States during the World War I, when large amounts of gold flowed into the country and created inflationary pressures. The Federal Reserve System lost its capacity to influence the supply of credit because commercial banks had alternative sources of credit. In 1931, a Federal Committee on Bank Reserves stated:

> [The] most important function served by member bank reserve requirements is the control of credit.... It is the function of reserve requirements to restrain such overexpansion by making it necessary for banks to provide for additional reserves before they expand their credit.
>
> (Quoted in Goodfriend and Hargraves, 1983, p. 5)

This method of controlling the supply of credit was also discussed by Keynes in his *Treatise of Money* (1930) and by the Macmillan Committee (1931) in Britain (Sayers, 1956, pp. 20–22).

The essential point to note here is that in the 1930s, due to a change in the economic and political environment, central banks started to rely more heavily on the reserve requirements as a policy tool than on the "traditional" interest rate policy and open market operations. Therefore, much closer cooperation was needed between the monetary and the supervisory authorities.

Central banking and banks' supervision in late-developing countries

The need to combine the monetary and supervisory authorities was more significant in late-developing countries than in the more developed nations. To understand why, it is necessary to account for the unique features of financial systems in late-developing countries. Such economies are typically characterized by two financial features: low supply of long-term credit and high demand for long-term credit. Mainstream economics describes it as an imbalance between saving and investment. The "imbalance" is created due to low saving rates and by a preference of private banks to provide short-term rather than long-term credit in underdeveloped financial systems (Bloomfield, 1957; Fousek, 1957; Khatkhate and Villanueva, 1980; Sen, 1956). The under-supply of credit creates a problem at the national level as governments in late-developing countries have a strong preference to promote industrialization, which requires large-scale, cheap and long-term credit. Developmental economists, therefore, argue that in late-developing countries, there is a structural disequilibrium between savings and investment. Without intervention by the state in the allocation of credit, the economy is doomed to a painfully long and slow process of industrialization, which is likely to lock it into a low position in the hierarchical structure of the world trade system as well as yielding lower levels of social welfare.

The conventional solution of mainstream economists is to liberalize the financial system, let interest rates rise until saving and investment reach an equilibrium, a solution which would result in slow development, unemployment and, in some cases, social crisis. The preferred choice of most late-developing countries was to intervene in the financial system in order to allocate the scarce available credit to designated purposes which contributed to long-term growth, job creation, industrialization and other economic activities deemed necessary from the state's perspective.[2] In order to do that effectively, governments needed to have special tools and capacities such as provided by a developmental central bank.

Satyendra Nath Sen, an Indian economist, who has extensively studied banking and central banking in late-developing countries, argued that central banks in such countries received powers "much broader than central banks have had at any time in the past" (Sen, 1952) and he continued:

> The concentration of all these powers in the hands of the central bank is therefore a move in the right direction. It would avoid the possible conflicts of policy that might develop if these functions were entrusted to [two] independent bodies. The danger that if the central bank is granted the power to inspect banks, it might attempt to exercise these power in pursuit of its particular monetary policy and neglect consideration of the solvency of the banks is more apparent than real. Nobody is more interested than the central bank in ensuring the solvency of banks, and a monetary policy which may result in undermining the solvency of the banks is not likely to be ever adopted by a central bank. All these methods have important monetary consequences and should therefore be undertaken by the bank, which is the best institution available for taking all aspects into consideration.
>
> (Ibid.)

This global trend also shaped the choices of the Israeli policy-makers.

Supervision of the banks before the establishment of the central bank

The legal basis for banking supervision in Israel drew on the legal infrastructure laid down during the British Mandate. With the onset of the British Mandate, the government enacted the Banking Act of 1921, which included minimal regulatory directives that concerned the opening of new banks. After the bank run in 1935, the British government imposed minimal reserve requirements. From 1936, banks were instructed to keep reserves ranging between 30–40 percent in order to protect depositors. The reserve requirements were simple and enforcement was based on persuasion. In 1941, the Banking Act was updated but no significant change was made in its content.

When the State of Israel was established, the supervision of banks was handled by a small department at the Ministry of Finance, whose powers were defined by the Banking Act (1941). The Banking Act followed the traditional British style of bank supervision and it gave the bank supervisor very limited powers to intervene in the business of private banks. Its main concerns were twofold, namely, to protect depositors and promote the stability of individual banking institutions. After the establishment of Israel, the Israeli government adopted the British Banking Law and the Banks Supervision department became part of the of Ministry Finance (Bar-Yosef, 1961).

As inflation pressure ensued, in November 1950, the government made the first attempt to use its powers as a banking supervisor in order to restrict the money supply. The government preferred to use this instrument rather than raise the interest rate, due to socio-economic considerations. The Bank Supervisor issued a decree requiring commercial banks to hold a 45 percent liquidity reserve on all deposits. In addition, the government started to distinguish between "productive" and "unproductive" or "consumer" credit, and it put pressure on banks to refrain from providing credit for "speculative" purposes and to prioritize credit for "productive purposes" (Bar-Yosef, 1955, p. 420).

The government's attempt failed, however, due to the fact that during the same period the volume of deposits grew and therefore commercial banks could continue to increase the supply of credit without breaking the reserve requirements. In response to this, in March 1951, the government issued a new reserve requirement according to which commercial banks had to hold 50 percent of old deposits in reserve and 75 percent of new ones. The government also tightened its control on the allocation of credit, and banks were instructed to avoid credit provision for the purpose of purchasing gold, securities and housing. Nevertheless, inflationary pressures persisted and in April 1953 the reserve requirement was raised to 90 percent on new deposits (ibid.).

The inability of the government to restrict the growth of credit led to a confrontation between the government and the banking system, which reached a climax in 1953, when the two organizations blamed each other for ever rising inflation levels. David Horowitz, as the Director General of the Ministry of Finance, represented the government on the Banking Advisory Council, composed of the directors of the large banks. Horowitz expressed the government's concern:

> In recent months we notice signs of inflation … this is caused by the fact that, due to the rising amount of deposits, banks and credit associations granted credit without breaching their reserve requirements. We are on a dangerous path.
>
> (Banking Council, August 23, 1953)

The bankers dismissed Horowitz's accusations and put the blame back on the government. "The government itself uses a significant amount of credit," claimed Hoffien, the director of Bank Leumi. The banks, he explained, only react to a growing demand for credit:

> We are a country of development and dynamics.… The development produces new and great demands. The factories whose establishment we encouraged, and which completed their construction and their equipment, and began operations will not be able to operate unless they receive credit from the banks.
>
> (Banking Council, January 26, 1954)

This conflict between the government and banking system can be summarized as follows: the government sought to restrict the overall volume of credit in order to curb inflation, whereas at the same time it sought to enable investors to receive cheap credit for "productive" purposes. The banks sought profit, and therefore they were happy to provide credit to anyone who asked for credit, be that for "productive" or "unproductive" purposes. Up until the establishment of the central bank, the government did not have any instrument to control the credit that was channeled to the private sector. This was exactly what the Bank of Israel was supposed to achieve.

Discrimination

The government accelerated the process of the establishment of the central bank in 1953, when it faced difficulties in forcing the commercial banks both to restrict credit and to allocate it to "productive" purposes. The minister of finance and the minister of agriculture envisaged the central bank as an instrument that would accomplish what the government could not. For that purpose, the government delegated to the governor not only the authority to implement monetary policy, but also extensive powers of bank supervision.

The concentration of power in the hands of the governor raised criticisms from economists and politicians alike. Abba P. Lerner, who served on the Economic Advisory Staff at the Prime Minister's Office, was one of the fiercest opponents of the merging of the monetary and supervisory authorities. He was concerned by the fact that the supervisory powers would give the governor the capacity to use discriminatory policy instruments for purposes these powers were not designed for. In his long and detailed report Lerner was unambiguous about his position regarding the status of the supervisory authority: it "would be most desirable" if the two authorities were to be separated, to "reduce to a minimum the dangers from confusing the functions of providing honest and reliable banking services to the community with the functions of the management of monetary policy" (Lerner, 1954, pp. 17–18). Lerner did not mince his words when expressing his disapproval: the choice of the government to combine the monetary and the supervisory authorities reflected, he wrote, "the general tendency in Israel for everybody to want to control everything instead of sticking to his particular job." Moreover, he predicted that the central bank would act in an "arbitrary and indeed in a discriminatory and tyrannical manner towards banks with which it is for any reason displeased" (ibid., pp. 16–21).

Lerner provided several examples to demonstrate how the governor would be able to use his power in discriminatory ways. The draft granted the governor the power "to order banking institutions to hold liquid assets at a certain rate and of a given composition" (BoI Law, 1954 section 49). The law did not provide any guidelines, let alone concrete rules that the governor was expected to follow. Moreover, the draft did not include any directive that instructed the bank to apply its policies uniformly and homogeneously on all banks.

A comparison with the statutes of the Central Bank of Korea of the Bank of Ceylon demonstrates that in both cases the mandates of the banks explicitly indicated that the bank must treat all banks equally. The Bank of Korea Law stated that the "the ratios shall be applied *uniformly* to all banking institutions" (Bloomfield and Jensen, 1951a, p. 89, my emphasis). The Central Bank Law of Ceylon specified that the "reserves required to be held by any commercial bank shall be proportional to the volume of its deposit liabilities" (Exter, 1949, p. 38, section o92 (2)).

The issue of the *uniformity* or rules was not merely a theoretical or technical issue. After the establishment of the Bank, the question of discrimination came up at several meetings of the Advisory Board. In one case, the board considered allowing a new branch of Bank Hapoalim in Nazareth to raise its credit ceiling beyond the standard credit ceiling imposed on other branches of the bank. The governor suggested that "given the special circumstances and without creating a precedence, we will allow Bank Hapoalim to raise the credit ceiling" (BoI Board, December 21, 1954, p. 4). The suggestion was accepted by the board members.

In another case, which had wider implications, the Advisory Board discussed the question of how to distribute between the banks the "right" to participate in the rediscounting arrangements initiated by the Bank of Israel.[3] The rediscounting of bills was a method used by the Bank of Israel to channel credit at a below-market interest rate to selected businesses. The Bank of Israel lent the money to the commercial banks and the commercial banks then lent the money to the selected business in exchange for securities. The banks, therefore, profited from the interest differential without having to take any risk. Eliezer Hoofien, the Chairman of the Board and Chairman of the Executive Board of Bank Leumi, insisted that the smaller banks should not take part in rediscounting operations. "There are several banks that can be trusted. In this case, the Bank of Israel has no choice but to discriminate to some degree between the banks." The clear implication here being that there are several banks that cannot be trusted. The governor accepted the view that "it may be preferable to operate the rediscounting loans using a few banks," but he was concerned that "this might raise the concern that we do not treat all banks equally" (BoI Board, n.d., November 11, 1955, p. 5). On another occasion when the issue of the "discrimination" was raised, Eliezer Hoofien stated the consensus in the board: "Although there is a measure of discrimination toward the entire banking system, it is the result of unique conditions, and I do not accept the 'discrimination' rationale" (BoI Board, n.d., May 3, 1955, p. 4).

Lerner also opposed the decision to delegate to the governor the power to license new banks. Horowitz's draft, as well as the final bill, did not specify any criteria on the basis of which that decision would be made: "This is again a matter for the Banking Code but constitutes so complete a departure from the rule of Law in regulating the banking business as to constitute rather the very negation of a Banking Code" (Lerner, 1954, p. 21). In the case of Korea, the power to grant licenses to banking institution was a part of the Banking Code, which specified a detailed procedure of decision-making: first, the application for opening a new banking institution had to be submitted to the supervisor, which evaluated it according to three criteria: (1) the expected contribution of the bank to the public interest; (2) the initial capital at the disposal of the applicant; and (3) the integrity of the applicant. The recommendation was then transferred to the Board of Directors of the central bank, which could approve or reject the license application(Bloomfield and Jensen, 1951b, Art. 12).

Why, then, did the Israeli government resist what seemed to be a reasonable approach to provide the supervisory authority rules and guidelines? Lerner provided an explanation that gives some insight into the motivation of the government to provide the governor with extensive discretionary policy space. He believed that the designers of the law expected the central bank governor to use his discretionary supervisory powers to reduce the number of banking institutions for the purpose of reducing the interest rate. In Israel, he argued, there are many small banking institutions that compete among themselves over deposits and savings. To attract these deposits and savings, small banks offer customers higher (creditory) interest rates than their larger competitors, and to finance the incurred expenses they had to increase the (debitory) interest rates they charge on loans. This situation was detrimental from the perspective of the state which sought lower interest rates to boost development.[4] Lerner's prediction was that the Bank of Israel would use its supervisory powers to restrict competition among banks to lower lending interest rates:

> The proposal to give the governor arbitrary power over the licensing of banks seems to be based on the premise that there are enough banks and the existence of more banks would be harmful because they might compete for deposits, paying higher interest rates, and they might then not be able to keep to the low interest rates that the Central Bank would like to maintain. This is a possible way of relating the provision for licensing banks to the conduct of monetary policy.
>
> (Lerner, 1954, pp. 21–22)

However, Lerner rejected this strategy in very harsh words. It was not only a "futile use of blackmail and of police power to prevent the symptoms of illiquidity from showing" (ibid., pp. 17–18), but also inconsistent with liberal values: "This is not the kind of monetary policy for which free economies have found it desirable to develop Central Banks independent of Treasuries" (ibid., p. 22).

Protection of customers

Another reason why Lerner objected the idea of merging the monetary and the supervisory authorities was his concern that the customers' interests would be sacrificed on the altar of macro-economic aims. "The purpose of these ordinances," he wrote about the sections that concerned banking regulation, "is to protect the customers from unfair bank conduct. If such ordinance must exist at all, they must be part of the Banking Code" (ibid., pp. 17–18). Lerner was not the only person who believed that the law did not sufficiently protect depositors. Peretz Bernstein of the General Zionists Party argued that "the objective of the Banking Law should be the protection of the depositor.... Nothing else should be included in the Banking Code" (Government, May 12, 1954).

The issue of market regulation and competition was close to the heart of Lerner. In his (1944) book, *Economy of Control* he pointed out three objectives of economic regulation: (1) maintaining full production and full employment through efficient allocation of resources; (2) maintaining a reasonable level of equality by redistribution of income; and (3) the elimination of poverty and the elimination of monopolies as well as the social waste that they cause (Lerner, 1944, p. 3). In more conventional terms, Lerner discusses in his book macro-economic policy, social policy and antitrust policies. In the case of Israel, the objective of anti-trust policies was very low in the government's priorities. The economic strategy of Israel was not based on a competitive market economy and monopolies were judged on the basis of their contribution to national development rather than on the basis of the damage they caused to competition.

Lerner's speculation regarding the considerations that guided the government's choices are consistent with the conclusion of recent studies. Jacob Paroush has recently shown that until the 1980s the Bank of Israel sacrificed customer protection in order to achieve monetary goals as the banking system served as an "agent of the government both for raising savings from the public and for granting credit (selective credit and credit from special deposits)" (Paroush, 2007). During this period, which Paroush calls the "period of direct supervision" (as opposed to the period of regularization), the centralization of the banking system increased along with the monopolistic power of the three largest banks, resulting in a decline in service to the customer. According to Paroush, the centralization of the banking system was the direct result of the policy of the Bank of Israel which denied entry to new players because

> otherwise the high return on equity in the Israeli banking system, relative to the other branches of the economy, would have attracted new investors. The incentive of the central banks to centralize the banking system was the lower cost of supervision. The cost of supervision is lower when the number of banks is smaller.
>
> (Ibid.)

A comparative perspective

The Bank of Israel Law (1954) reflects the decision of the government to merge the monetary and supervisory authorities, and to avoid institutional or functional differentiation between the two. The Banking Act of 1941 stated:

> The High Commissioner is entitled to appoint an officer from among the officers of the Palestine Government to serve as supervisor of banks. This officer will hold the powers of general supervision and of auditing of the management of banking business in Palestine.
>
> (Banking Act, 1941 Section 5(a))

The law did not specify the criteria to appoint a supervisor or to replace or dismiss one. After the establishment of the state, the Banking Act of 1941 was adopted by the government as-is and the power to appoint a supervisor was transferred to the government. Under the Bank of Israel Law, the powers of the banks supervisor were delegated to the governor. Article 69 states that "the government is entitled to transfer to the governor any power of its powers granted by the Banking Act of 1941" (BoI Law, 1954, Article 69).

The Bank of Israel Law (1954) does not make any reference to a supervisor or to a supervision department. Based on this formulation, the legal responsibility for supervision fell entirely to the governor. This situation was changed only in 1969, with an amendment to the Banking Act, in which it was stated that "the governor is entitled to appoint a banks supervisor" and that the "governor is entitled to assume any power that is granted to the supervisor."[5] Thus, until 1969, the statutory status of the banks supervisor was not legalized. Yaacob Paroush pointed out almost 40 years later that "the Governor of the Bank of Israel carries the regulatory responsibility over the banks" (2007, p. 128). To estimate whether the decision of the government was driven by domestic factors or international influences, the Bank of Israel Law can be compared to laws governing other central banks in the Global South. A comparison of the Bank of Israel Law to the central banks' mandates of South Korea and Ceylon demonstrates that the features of the Bank of Israel were part of a global trend, but they were a rather extreme manifestation of this trend. That is, whereas most central banks in late-developing countries received extensive powers and broad discretionary policy space, the discretion of the Bank of Israel was broader than that of other central banks.

In contrast to the Israeli law, the bill drafted by Bloomfield for the South Korean bank stated that the supervisor of banks could be appointed or dismissed by the President of the Republic, based on the recommendation of the Board of Directors of the bank (Bloomfield and Jensen, 1951a, p. 87, Article 28). After his appointment, the supervisor is subordinated to the Board of Directors. Hence, there are two main differences between the South Korean and the Israeli laws: first, in South Korea, the supervisor is appointed and can be dismissed by the president, a procedure which grants the supervisor autonomy vis-à-vis the governor. Second, the supervisor is subordinated to the board and not to the governor.

The Central Bank Law of Ceylon also endowed the supervisor with a legal status. The law states explicitly the duty to appoint a supervisor while defining the position's powers and scope of responsibility (Exter, 1949, Section 28). Moreover, the law states explicitly the division of labor between the governor and the supervisor (ibid., Article 29[4][a]). The law does not state explicitly how the supervisor is appointed, but states that he reports to the Board of Directors (ibid., section 30), which indicates that it was probably the Board of Directors that appointed the supervisor.[6] The structure of the Central Bank Law of Ceylon grants less independence to the supervisor than the South Korean law does, but more than what the Israeli law grants to the supervisor of banks. The Bank of Ceylon law includes detailed directives that ensure that the supervisor acts in accordance with the procedures specified by the law and that his authority is not usurped by the governor or by the board.

The comparison of the Bank of Israel law to the laws of the central banks of Ceylon and South Korea indicates that the decision of the Israeli government to transfer supervisory powers to the governor cannot be explained only as part of an international trend. There were also local factors, that shaped the decision of the government, that were exceptional in comparison to other central banks, which were established in the same period in late-developing countries.

Ideas, power and law

The issue of the relationship between the monetary and supervisory authorities was a key topic in the debates concerning the design of the Israeli central bank, and it was in fact more divisive than the question of the independence of the central bank. To understand why this issue was cardinal and how the choice of the government to combine the two authorities affected Israel's political economic strategy, it is useful to discuss three aspects of the debate: the economic, the political and the legal.

From the economic aspect, the choice to combine the monetary and the supervisory authorities rested on a new developmental economic rationale that emerged during the 1950s and the 1960s. During the 1950s, new ideas regarding central banking in late-developing economies appeared. One may even go as far as to say that there was a new type of policy norm for central banking that was diffused among the newly independent countries in the Global South (Krampf, 2012, 2014). These ideas emerged from the Federal Reserve during and after the Great Depression, and from there they were diffused and developed in the Global South (Krampf, 2013). Liberal and orthodox economists rejected the economic rationale that justified the used of developmental central banking practices (Fry, 1988; Fry *et al.*, 1996; McKinnon, 1973; Shaw, 1973). Liberal and orthodox academic economists explained the divergence between central banking practices in the Global North and the Global South by arguing that it was the result of politicization processes and the incapacity of societies in late-developing countries to establish effective institutions. However, developmental economists, as well as central bankers with hands-on experience, recognized the economic rationale of developmental central banking (Bhatt, 1971; Bloomfield, 1957; Brimmer, 1971; Chandler, 1962; Coats and Khatkhate, 1980; Fousek, 1957; Kim, 1965; Sayers, 1952; Sen, 1952). There were two key structural features of late-developing countries that justified the use of heterodox central banking methods. First, under-developed financial systems did not produce sufficient credit and banks preferred to allocate credit to short-term purposes rather than to long-term industrial and riskier endeavors. Therefore, in late-developing countries, employing the traditional "free market economy" approach would involve a very slow process of industrialization. This brings us to the second feature of late-developing countries: a strong preference for rapid industrialization. To spur industrialization, the government had to amass the limited resources available in the economy and inject them into specific production areas which it deemed essential for long-term growth. For that purpose, governments needed highly effective institutional infrastructure, and in most cases they used a central bank and a supervisory authority. These two institutions possessed the practical and theoretical knowledge, experience, prestige and legitimacy to accomplish this as well as being semi-independent vis-à-vis powerful domestic actors.[7]

The new roles that developmental central banks fulfilled in the Global South affected also the political position of central banks. The orthodox theory of central banking prescribes that central banks should be independent from the government because the government is seen to be exposed to pressure from powerful market and societal actors which the bank must be protected against. The central bank, therefore, must be independent from the government in order to protect the interest of the public and maintain a stable currency. Developmental central banks operated in an institutional environment in which the state was porous and the central bank was supposed to assist the government in confronting powerful domestic actors in order to serve the long-term public interests, as perceived by the political leadership. Therefore, the claims that developmental central banks were "weak" and that they "simply" served as an "arm of the government" overlooks the fact that central banks in the Global South followed a different rationale than those of the Global North. A broad consideration of Global South central banks shows that they were actually powerful institutions that contributed to the consolidation of their states.

In the case of Israel, the Bank of Israel contributed to the capacity of the state to weaken its dependence on its key political ally, the Histadrut. The link between the government and the Histadrut sector was one of the government's main assets during the 1940s and the early 1950s.[8] The Histadrut, as well as its holding company, the Workers Corporation, assisted the government in achieving rapid industrialization, full employment and job creation. As the director of the Workers Corporation proclaimed, the Histadrut "complements the government's policy" in "rationing and supervision" (Economic Committee LM, April 1, 1954, p. 6). During the 1950s, and more forcefully in the 1960s, a new coalition of state actors emerged, which included the Ministry of Finance, the Ministry of Trade and Industry and the Bank of Israel and was further supported by the Ministry of Foreign Affairs as well as numerous academic economists. This new coalition shared the view that it was in the interest of the state to abandon the full employment policy and to shift to an export-oriented development strategy. In this context, the link between the government and the Histadrut sector, in its old form, had become more of a liability than an asset. The Bank of Israel, by tightening the control over the banking system, enabled the state to divert credit from the Histadrut sector to the private sector. Chapter 8 will demonstrate in greater detail exactly how this was done.

The delegation of the supervisory powers to the central bank—which were actually powers to allocate credit—affected also the legal basis of the central bank: is the delegation of the power to allocate resources to a non-elected body consistent with the governing principles of liberal democracies? In liberal democracies there is a division of labor between the fiscal and the monetary authorities. The fiscal authority—the government—has the legitimate right to tax, spend and redistribute resources. The legitimacy of the fiscal authority to breach private property rights stems from the fact it is an elected body, which implies that it acts on behalf of the people. The monetary authority is not an elected body but an agent of the parliament. The central bank has a mandate to perform a clearly defined and rule-based task which does not have a direct distributive outcome, such as maintaining price stability.[9]

In late-developing countries, for the reasons described above, the government delegates to the central bank tasks which require discretion, redistribution and discrimination. Therefore, developmental central banks are inherently non-liberal institutions. Their performance, even when they contribute to social welfare, is inconsistent with liberal democratic governing principles.

This explains why liberal members of the Israeli parliament objected to the delegation of powers to the central bank to allocate credit. A member of the General Zionists Party warned that there was "a danger, especially in a small country such as ours that credit will be allocated not to particular sectors but to particular factories." Therefore, if measures to control the allocation of credit are necessary, "it does not belong in the central bank law." The minister of trade and industry, also a member of the General Zionists, argued that "we must specify in greater detail what needs to be in the Banking Law. In my opinion, the allocation of credit does not belong there … it is a matter for the government" (Government, May 12, 1954, pp. 6–10). Dr. Bart from Bank Leumi also objected the "positive" credit control—a case in which the central bank dictates where credit must be supplied—because, he argued, it was inconsistent with the "sanctity of private property rights" (ibid., p. 3).[10] Nevertheless, minister of finance Levi Ekshol and minister of agriculture Peretz Naftali insisted on the "positive" credit control. "It seems to me," declared Naftali, "that we all agree that the central bank will be an instrument for credit control" (ibid., p. 14).

Conclusion

The debates regarding the formulation of the Bank of Israel Law led to the conclusion that the Bank of Israel Law had three key features: (1) it possessed a low level of independence vis-à-vis the government with respect to its control of monetary issues; (2) it possessed extensive power and discretion in the policy area of bank regulation; and (3) formally, the decision-making powers were delegated to the governor rather than to a board.

These features could be explained either by the "financial repression" thesis, which argues that the bank was established to assist the government extract credit from the banking system and in order to enable it get loans from the central bank, or by the argument made in this book, that the bank was establish to ameliorate the state autonomy and to enable it to control the allocation of credit to productive purposes, on the basis of a combination of the two.

The financial repression thesis, however, is inconsistent with the fact that during the 1950s and the 1960s there were many economists who legitimized the unique structure of central banks in late-developing countries. It may be argued, of course, that the developmental economists were wrong in their analysis, and that in fact the developmental model of central banks was less effective in terms of their contribution to the social welfare than conventional central banks would have been. However, the question discussed here does not concern the effectiveness of the central banks, but the considerations that led to their establishment. The chapter showed that this also included economic considerations based on developmental assumptions.

Moreover, the financial repression thesis is inconsistent with the fact that the government did not nominate any representative of the Histadrut to the Advisory Board of the Bank of Israel. This implies that the government intended to depoliticize the bank, in the sense that it prevented the most powerful non-state actor in Israel at the time, the Histadrut, from affecting the policy-making process of the central bank.

The account of the establishment of the Bank of Israel provides another piece of the puzzle explaining Israel's road to a market economy. It shows, however, that the road did not always follow the liberal path. The Bank of Israel was endowed with instruments that enabled the government to discriminate between banks and it had an inherent disposition to sacrifice the property rights of individuals—the bank customers—to attain macro-economic objectives which were consistent with state preferences.

Notes

1 On the history of the money multiplier, see Humphrey (198) and O'Brien (1984).
2 A more detailed explanation appears in Chapter 8.
3 According to Article 42 of the Bank of Israel Law (1954): "For the purpose of regulating the volume, cost and application of bank credit, the Bank may provide money to any banking corporation either by discounting bills, promissory notes or other negotiable instruments or by loans secured to its satisfaction."
4 Lerner did not refer to an alternative scenario, in which competition between banking institution reduces the interest rate: if banks compete over the provision of loans, competition would reduce the interest. However, in Israel the demand for credit was much higher than the supply, and therefore banks competed over savers rather than over investors. Chapter 8 discusses the actual situation in Israel, and it shows that Lerner's analysis was accurate.
5 Banking Act, 1941, Section 5, Amendments from the years 1969, 1981, 1997.
6 For example, if the supervisor reaches the conclusion that a banking institution is in danger of insolvency, he is required to submit a report to the Board of Directors, which can then use its authority against the banking institution. In these cases, the banking institution can go to court to prevent these measures.
7 This does not imply that central banks in late-developing countries could have been used for purposes which do not increase welfare. The argument is that developmental central banks in the Global South could have been independent or politicized like orthodox central banks.
8 For details, see Chapter 4.

9 It may also be argued that the policy of an orthodox central bank that pursued price stability has a distributive outcome.

10 Dr. Bart's position was presented to the government by the minister of finance, Levi Eshkol:

> We combined the Bank of Israel Law and the Banking Law. Dr. Bart explained his objection to this approach … he said that the government wants the right to tell the banks to lend to agriculture 25% of their loans rather than 20%. He asked: where is the sanctity of private capital?
>
> (Government, March 12, 1954)

References

Banking Act, 1941. *The Official Gazette* No. 1118, p. 614.

Banking Council. Various years. Minutes of the Banking Council.

Bar-Yosef, I., 1955. Qualitative Credit Control. *Economic Quarterly* 8, 415–422 (in Hebrew).

Bar-Yosef, I., 1961. Qualitative Credit Control. *The Economic Quarterly* 31, 252–264 (in Hebrew).

Beck, T. and Gros, D., 2012. *Monetary Policy and Banking Supervision: Coordination Instead of Separation.* CEPS Policy Brief No. 286, December 12.

Bhatt, V.V., 1971. Saving and Flow of Funds Analysis: A Tool for Financial Planning in India. *Review of Income and Wealth* 17, 61–80.

Bloomfield, A.I., 1957. Central Banking in Underdeveloped Countries. *The Journal of Finance* 12, 190–204.

Bloomfield, A.I. and Jensen, J.P., 1951a. *Banking Reform in South Korea.* Federal Reserve Bank of New York, New York.

Bloomfield, A.I. and Jensen, J.P., 1951b. General Banking Code. In: *Banking Reform in South Korea.* Federal Reserve Bank of New York, New York.

BoI Board, Various years. Minutes of the Bank of Israel Advisory Board.

BoI Law, 1954. Bank of Israel Law, 1954.

Brimmer, A.F., 1971. Central Banking and Economic Development: The Record of Innovation. *Journal of Money, Credit and Banking* 3, 780–792.

Chandler, L.V., 1962. *Central Banking and Economic Development.* University of Bombay, Bombay.

Coats, W.L. and Khatkhate, D.R. (Eds.), 1980. *Money and Monetary Policy in Less Developed Countries.* Pergamon Press, Oxford.

Economic Committee LM,,. Economic Committee of the Labor Movement. *Labor Party Archive.*

Exter, J., 1949. *Monetary Law: A Bill to Establish the Monetary System of Ceylon and the Central Bank.* Ceylon Government Press, Colombo.

Fousek, P.G., 1957. *Foreign Central Banking: The Instrument of Monetary Policy.* The Federal Reserve Bank of New York, New York.

Fry, M.J., 1988. *Money, Interest, and Banking in Economic Development.* Johns Hopkins University Press, Baltimore, MD.

Fry, M.J., Goodhart, C.A.. and Almeida, A., 1996. *Central Banking in Developing Countries: Objectives, Activities and Independence.* Routledge, London.

Goodfriend, M. and Hargraves, M., 1983. *A Historical Assessment of the Rationales and Functions of Reserve Requirements.* Federal Reserve Bank of Richmond Working Paper Series 83–1. Richmond, VA.

Goodhart, C.A.E., 1988. *The Evolution Of Central Banks*. MIT Press, Cambridge, MA.

Government. Various years. Minutes of Government Meeting. Israel State Archive.

Humphrey, T.M., 1987. The theory of multiple expansion of deposits: what it is and whence it came. *Economic Review* 73 (2), 3–11.

Khatkhate, D.R. and Villanueva, D.P., 1980. Operation of Selective Credit Policies in Less Developed Countries: Certain Critical Issues. In: Coats, W.L. and Khatkhate, D.R. (Eds.), *Money and Monetary Policy in Less Developed Countries*. Pergamon Press, Oxford, pp. 589–603.

Kim, B.K., 1965. *Central Banking Experiment in a Developing Economy: Case Study of Korea*. Korean Research Center, Seoul.

Krampf, A., 2012. Translation of Central Banking to Developing Countries in the Post-World War II Period: The Case of the Bank of Israel. In: Renn, J. (Ed.), *The Globalization of Knowledge in History. Max Planck Research Library for the History and Development of Knowledge*, Studies 1. Berlin: Edition Open Access., pp. 459–482.

Krampf, A., 2013. The Life Cycles of Competing Policy Norms: Localizing European and Developmental Central Banking Ideas, KFG Working Paper No. 9. KFG "Transforming Power of Europe," Berlin.

Krampf, A., 2014. Between Private Property Rights and National Preferences: The Bank of Israel's Early Years. *Israel Affairs* 20, 104–124.

Lerner, A.P., 1944. *The Economics of Control: Principles of Welfare Economics*. The Macmillan Co, New York.

Lerner, A.P., 1954. Memorandum, Economic Advisory Staff. April 27. Israel State Archive, 5617/13c.

McKinnon, R.I., 1973. *Money and Capital in Economic Development*. Brookings Institution Press, Washington, DC.

O'Brien, D.P., 1984. Monetary Economics. In: Creedy, J. and O'Brien, D.P. (Eds.), *Economic Analysis in Historical Perspective, Butterworths Advanced Economics Texts*. Butterworths, London, pp. 3–45.

Paroush, J., 2007. Banking Supervision in Israel, in H. Barkai and N. Liviatan (Eds.), *The Bank of Israel: Selected Topics in Israel's Monetary Policy*. Oxford University Press, New York, pp. 130–170.

Sayers, R.S., 1950. *Modern Banking*. Clarendon Press, Oxford.

Sayers, R.S., 1952. *Banking in the British Commonwealth*. Clarendon Press, Oxford.

Sayers, R.S., 1956. *Central Banking in Developing Countries*. National Bank of Egypt, Cairo.

Sen, S.N., 1956. *Central Banking in Undeveloped Money Markets*. Bookland Ltd, Calcutta.

Shaw, E.S., 1973. *Financial Deepening in Economic Development*. Oxford University Press, New York.

Whelan, K., 2012. *Should Monetary Policy Be Separated from Banking Supervision?* Directorate General for International Policies, European Parliament, Brussels.

Zysman, J., 1984. *Governments, Markets, and Growth: Financial Systems and the Politics of Industrial Change*. Cornell University Press, Ithaca, NY.

8 A financial revolution in Israel

During the 1950s the Israeli banking system went through a rapid and drastic structural change. Within a period of two years, between 1954 and 1956, the decentralized banking system, consisting of more than 100 geographically spread small banking institutions—both banks and credit associations—was transformed into a highly centralized banking system dominated by a small number of credit institutions, each with a large number of branches. The numbers demonstrate this process succinctly: between 1950 and 1954, the number of credit institutions in Israel was still growing and went from 108 to 118. The trend changed in the mid-1950s and by 1960 the number of credit institutions had fallen to 53. At the same time, the number of branches rocketed from just below 100 in 1950 to over 600 by 1960 (see Figure 8.1). The transformation of

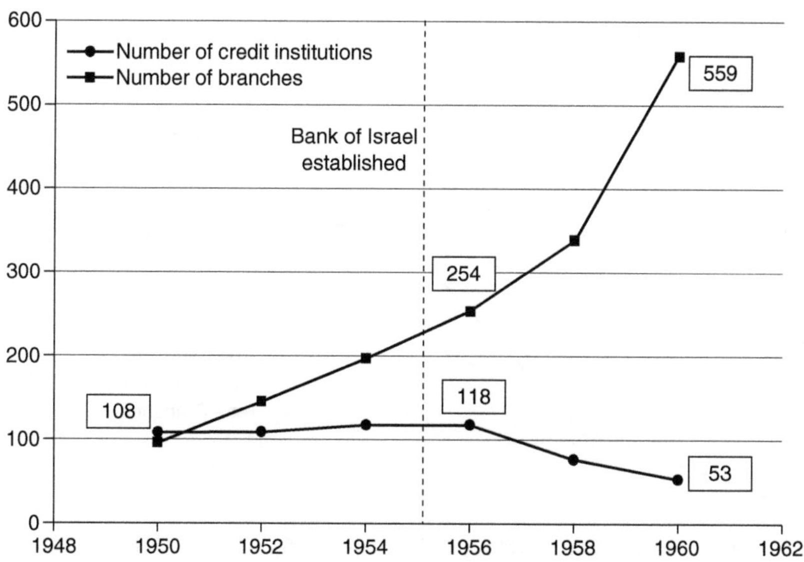

Figure 8.1 Number of banking institutions and branches, 1950–1960.

Sources: Krampf (2015, p. 186, Figure 3). Data: Het (1970, p. 58, Table 8).

the banking system was manifest in other indices of centralization as well. Whereas in 1951 the three largest banks owned 23.5 percent of the nation's banking premises (headquarters and branches), in 1956, they owned 31 percent and by 1961 no less than 55 percent. Other indices of centralization—the number of employees in the banking sector employed by the three largest banks, their share of deposits and their share of banking income—each paint a similar picture: clearly, between 1956 and 1961, the banking system in Israel went through a rapid process of centralization (Figure 8.2).

What were the factors that led to this dramatic change? The first explanation that comes readily to mind is that the process was a "natural" result of market forces: as the principle of *economies of scale* predicts, competition among banks is likely to lead to the collapse of small institutions or to their acquisition by the large ones. However, the economy of scale thesis cannot explain the timing of the process: during the British Mandate and up until the establishment of the Bank of Israel, the regulatory regime was lax and small banking institutions thrived. The centralization process started only after the Bank of Israel and the government changed the regulatory rules. The correlation between the establishment of the Bank of Israel and the onset of the structural changes within the banking sector suggests that the two events were causally linked.

This chapter puts forward two questions. The first question is what were the factors that transformed the Israeli banking system between 1954 and 1958? In that regard, the chapter argues that Bank of Israel was the single most significant factor in that process. On the basis of a detailed examination of the minutes of the Bank of Israel Advisory Board sessions, it is possible to trace how each policy

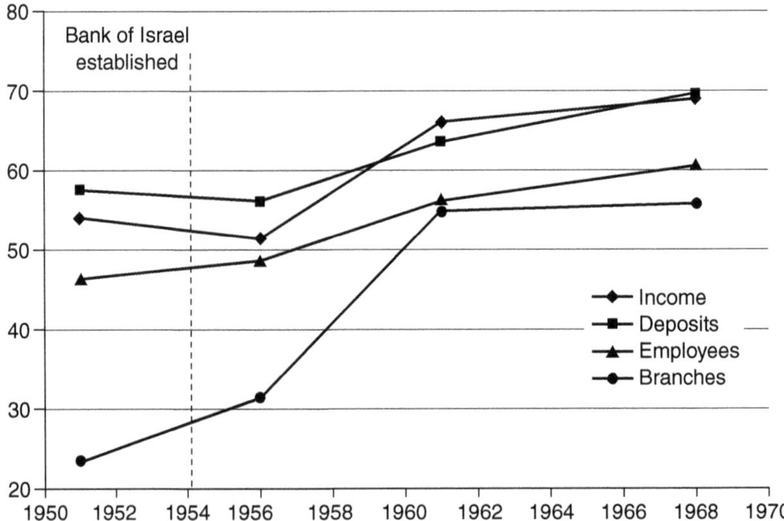

Figure 8.2 Centralization indices: share of the three largest banks (%).

Sources: Krampf (2015, p. 188, Figure 4). Data: Het (1966, p. 47, Table 11).

choice made by the Bank of Israel narrowed the alternatives of the smaller banking institutions until they had no choice but to integrate with the larger banks.

The second question is why did the Bank of Israel follow this path? This chapter argues that the centralization of the banking system was part of a political economic exchange between the central bank and the largest of the private banks: the central bank provided these banks with privileges in exchange for their cooperation with the government's selective credit policies. It is proposed here that this was a second-best choice from Horowitz's perspective as he would have liked to control the allocation of credit while maintaining a decentralized and competitive banking system. However, he realized that the two objectives were mutually exclusive within the institutional and political constraints under which he operated.

The chapter traces the operation of the Bank of Israel during its first five years of operation and examines whether the expectations of policy makers, that the bank would assist the government to allocate credit, were fulfilled. It concludes the argument put forward in the previous chapters, by demonstrating how the expectations of the designers of the bank were fulfilled. It cannot be suggested that the designers of the bank had foreseen each and every strategy the Bank of Israel would employ. As the historical record shows, it was a much more murky and sketchy series of events than that. However, in the final analysis, the Bank of Israel did fulfill expectations that it would ameliorate the capacity of the state to control the allocation of credit.

Financial repression versus selective credit control

According to liberal market-oriented economic theories, the role of the financial system is to intermediate between savers and investors: economic units with a surplus of resources and economic units that require those resources. Accordingly, financial systems perform efficiently when economic units are free to lend and to receive loans for an interest rate that is determined by the supply and demand of credit. Under these conditions, financial markets reach "equilibrium" when aggregate saving equal aggregate investment. The role of the central bank, in such conditions, is only to affect the aggregate demand for money by affecting the interest rate.

Late-developing countries were characterized by a persistent disequilibrium as the demand for credit surpassed the supply of credit, and the question was how to respond to this gap. Liberal market-oriented economists contended that the gap between savings and investment was caused by the repression of the financial system by the state (Fry, 1988; McKinnon, 1973; Shaw, 1973). Financial repression is defined as a policy in which the government employs its sovereignty to acquire cheap credit from a selected number of banks in exchange for privileges that are extended to these banks. The loans are then used to finance government expenditure which is not conducive to growth (Fry, 1982, p. 732). Financial repression is resulted by a division of the financial system into a "regulated" sub-system characterized by a low interest rate and an "unregulated" sub-system characterized by high interest rate for the private sector (see Figure 8.3). Employing this strategy of financial repression then clearly leads to a slow-down of economic development (Hanson and Rocha, 1986).

Therefore, liberal economists recommended that governments in late-developing countries liberalize their financial systems, allow floating interest rates and let market forces determine the supply and demand for credit (Fry, 1988; McKinnon, 1973; Shaw, 1973). The downside of the liberalization solution was a very slow industrialization process: given the low domestic supply of credit, a liberalized financial system would produce insufficient credit to finance a rapid industrialization process. Therefore, from the perspective of policy-makers in the Global South, the liberal policy recommendation was inconsistent with state preferences.

Developmental economists and central bankers in late-developing countries, on the other hand, argued that the gap between savings and investment in late-developing countries was not the product of ineffective state intervention, but of the unique circumstances of late development: the under-supply of developmental credit by the local financial system and the high demand for such credit to spur industrialization (Choi, 1993; Gerschenkron, 1962). To redress the gap, developmental economists recommended intervention by the state in the financial system to allocate the limited credit to productive uses, while maintaining low interest rates (Bhatia and Khatkhate, 1975; Brimmer, 1971; Khatkhate and Villanueva, 1980), an approach referred to as *selective credit control.*

Effective selective credit control requires a high level of institutional infrastructure, know-how, reliable bureaucracy and enforcement capacity. This is

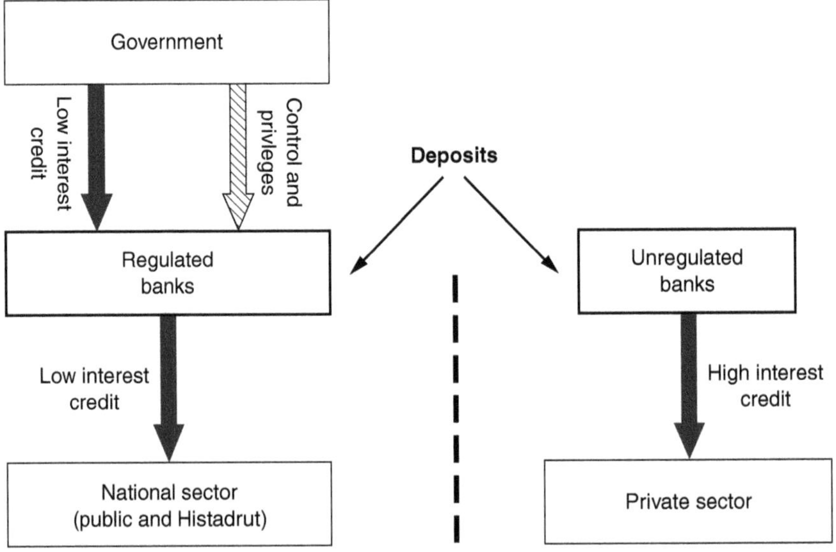

Figure 8.3 Financial repression.

Source: Krampf (2015, p. 190, Figure 5).

why developmental central banks contributed to new states' capacity to implement selective credit control effectively. The developmental central bank, with its extensive supervisory powers, had the necessary tools to control the banking system by shaping its incentive structure and credit policy. The control exerted by a central bank over a banking system had two distinct advantages in comparison to the financial repression model. First, the regulated credit was channeled by an institution that was less exposed to pressure from market and societal actors than the government was, and, second, the central bank had the capacity to impose its control over the whole banking system, thereby avoiding a division of the financial system into "regulated" and "unregulated" sub-systems (see Figure 8.4).

The literature, therefore, offers two models that explain the interaction between the government (and the central bank) and the banking system in developing economies: the financial repression model and the selective credit control model. Each of the two models provides a different understanding of the policy problems and the policy recommendations associated with the governing financial systems in under-developed countries.

This chapter will use the two models to explain the transition of the Israeli banking system during the 1950s. Prior to the establishment of the Bank of Israel, the interaction between the government and the banking system is best portrayed by the financial repression model: the government could regulate only part of the banking system. It regulated the large banks by providing them certain privileges. The "controlled" credit was allocated mainly to the public

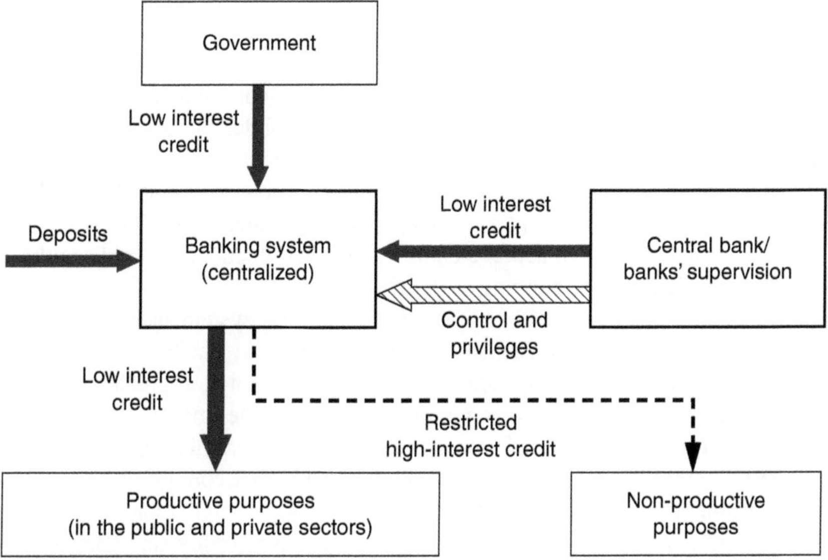

Figure 8.4 Selective credit control.

Source: Krampf (2015, p. 191, Figure 6).

sector, which included the government and the Histadrut sector. The banking institutions that were not "regulated" provided expensive credit for any purpose. After the Bank of Israel was established, it enabled the government to tighten its control over the banking system and to control a larger portion of the available credit for both the national and the private sectors.

However, any structural change involves winners who promote the change, and losers who resist it. In most cases, to effect the change, the effective opposition of the losers has to be overcome if they are sufficiently powerful to block the change. The obvious questions from here then are who were the winners and the losers associated with the transformation of the Israeli banking system, and how was the opposition of the powerful losers overcome?

Financial repression and the Histadrut sector

When the Israeli state was established, the banking system was highly decentralized and numerous credit institutions had spread throughout the country. Indeed, the government had a certain level of control over the large banks—Bank Leumi, for example, which was owned by the Jewish Agency and Bank Hapoalim, which was owned by the Workers Corporation—but even these banks were managed by independent boards of directors that were not always attuned to the requests of the politicians. Moreover, the legal infrastructure of the state was not compatible with the need to regulate the banking system, and, therefore, the state bureaucracy simply did not have the know-how necessary in order to deal with professional bankers and their highly skilled employees.

Another factor that restricted the government's capacity to control the banking system was geopolitical. In the 1950s, the government of Israel made the choice to join the "Free World," which embraced the market economy. While the government nationalized public utilities, as was common in other market economies, it did not dare to nationalize the banks. Under the geopolitical conditions prevailing after the onset of the Cold War, nationalization of banks could have created the impression that Israel was joining the Communist bloc, which was not in the government's interest to do. The government, therefore, faced the following problem: how to achieve control over the allocation of credit without formally nationalizing the banking system?

Prior to the establishment of the state, the banking system in Palestine was mildly regulated. Under the British Banking Act of 1941 banks were regulated only to maintain their stability, and there was no attempt to regulate banks for the purpose of achieving macro-economic goals. When the state was established, by default, this tradition continued. In 1951, the government made the first attempt to restrict bank credit in the context of the New Economic Policy when the government raised the required reserve ratios and instructed banks to refrain from providing credit for the purchase of gold, securities or housing (Bar-Yosef, 1953, p. 189).

The government's attempts to restrict credit growth led to a confrontation with the bankers, who denied their responsibility for the rising inflation rates that were being experienced. David Horowitz, the Director General of the Ministry of Finance, represented the government in the Banking Advisory Council, which consisted of the managers of key commercial banks.[1] The bankers strongly objected to the accusations and they threw the blame back on the government. Aharon Bart, the General Director of Bank Leumi, proclaimed that he absolutely opposed any attempt to accuse the banks, as if they were on trial. The banks, he argued, "did whatever they could to deal with situations caused by other forces. I do not believe that in this period anyone gave credit arbitrarily to make profit" (Banking Council, January 26, 1954).

The problem of the government was not only to control the *volume* of credit but also the *price* of credit, that is, the *interest rate*. When the state was established, it inherited the Ottoman interest rate law, which dictated that lenders who charged higher interest rate than 9 percent, were not entitled to legal protection if the debtor defaulted. The Ottoman interest rate law was kept during the British Mandate and became a state law after the establishment of the state of Israel.

The Ottoman interest rate law, therefore, set a 9 percent limit on legitimate interest rates, but the law did not prohibit an interest rate higher than 9 percent in cases where the lender was willing to take upon itself the risk that the debtor would default. The result was that the banking system was split between the banks that kept to the Ottoman law and those that did not. The large banks, which maintained a close working relationship with the government, kept the 9 percent ceiling on interest rates. The smaller banks and the credit associations, on the other hand, provided credit at interest rates that were much higher than the Ottoman ceiling. The large banks were rewarded for good behavior with various types of privileges. For example, they were given the task of managing the government's deposits. In 1952, 21 percent of total deposits held by large banks originated from government sources, whereas only 2.6 percent of the deposits in small banks originated from the government, and only 2.1 percent of the deposits in the credit associations.[2] The result of this situation was that the large banks "voluntarily" kept the 9 percent limit that was encouraged by Ottoman law, whereas the small credit institutions remained free to act and charge as they wished (Economic Committee LM, January 19, 1955: 15). The division of the banking system between "regulated" and "unregulated" banks is consistent with the model of financial repression described above (Figure 8.3).

The inability of the government to enforce a uniform interest rate on all credit institutions created two further problems. From the perspective of the government, given that its preference was to maximize growth and job creation within the limits of prevailing resources, the problem was that the smaller institution allocated credit to any purpose, mainly to consumption, and therefore they did not contribute to industrialization. From the perspective of the large banks, the problem was that they competed with the small institutions on unequal terms that favored the small institutions: the high demand for credit in the private sector enabled the small banking institutions to charge higher interest rates for their loans, a fact which enabled them to attract savers by offering higher rates for their deposits which explains why until 1956 the small institutions flourished.

When the Bank of Israel was established, this issue was among the first to be raised by the directors of the two large banks represented in the Advisory Board. "There are organizations that finance the expansion of consumption in large amounts," warned Zbarsky, the Director General of Bank Hapoalim:

> There are provident funds that grant large loans, at times at usurious interest rates, and many of them lend large amounts to their members for non-productive purposes. It is necessary to find ways to make the directives for the restriction of credit comprehensive, and to apply them to all.
>
> (BoI Board, December 21, 1954: 2)

Hoofien, the Chairman of the Board of Bank Leumi and the Chairman of the Advisory Board, threatened that "the assumption that the banks that abide by the law will continue to observe a maximum interest rate of 9 percent while no measures are taken against the other banks has no ground." The large banks "have waited for years and they will wait no more, and after they warn the government and the Bank of Israel they will raise their interest" (BoI Board. March 7, 1955: 3).

The governor, David Horowitz sympathized with the bankers' complaints, but admitted that the Bank of Israel did not have the instruments to deal with the problem. The Bank of Israel, he explained, suffers from "lack of administrative capacity and an adequate apparatus" (BoI Board, December 13 1955, p. 2). One of the ways proposed to address this problem was to float the interest rate, or at least raise the maximum rate permitted by the law. Such a move, the Advisory Board believed, would reduce the gap between interest rates in the regulated and unregulated financial sectors and would allow more competition between the two banking sub-systems. However, it was clear to Horowitz that the government would not approve this solution (ibid., 24 January 1956, p. 2).

The government's inability to control the allocation of credit affected its ties with the Histadrut sector. So long as the government could not gain control over the banking system it was dependent on the Histadrut for channeling credit to productive purposes. The Workers Corporation, the holding company of the Histadrut—the Labor Union of the Jewish Workers in Israel—owned a large number of companies in all the important economic sectors: agriculture, transportation, retail and housing and construction. The size of the Workers Corporation—around one-fifth of the Israeli economy in terms of production and employment—as well as its hierarchical and centralized managerial structure, made it an asset for the government, in terms of its capacity to govern the economy. By channeling credit to the Workers Corporation, the government could ensure that a large proportion of it would be invested in economic activities that were consistent with the state preferences.[3] As Ze'ev On, the Secretary General of the Workers Corporation, explained, the Histadrut complemented the government: "We can be an assisting factor, like in any other area, like in rationing and [price] control, all the operations that the government must do through law, we can contribute to progress and cooperation more than any other sector" (Economic Committee LM, April 1, 1954: 6).

Cooperation through conflict

The dependence of the government on the Histadrut sector had its drawbacks: the Workers Corporation specialized in labor-intensive industries. It served the government so long as the primary aim was to create jobs and expand production for domestic use. Once the government prioritized exports, it had to transfer resources to capital-intensive industries with higher productivity, and the dependence on the Workers Corporation restricted the government's capacity to do so. Hence, the government had to nurture its previously neglected links with the private sector, for which it needed to develop a capacity to control the allocation of credit in the private sector.

The question not yet addressed is how the Bank of Israel achieved these aims and why it was more effective in achieving these aims than the government could have been alone. The answer to this question is found in the minutes of the Advisory Board. Whereas the Board consisted of representatives of different sectors,[4] in practice, most of the debates involved disagreements between two foci of power: the first was the governor (and the supervisor of banks, when he participated in the meetings) and the other was the representatives of the two largest banks: Eliezer Hoofien, who was the Chairman of the Board of Directors of Bank Leumi and Avraham Zbarsky, the General Director of Bank Hapoalim. Any decision of the Advisory Board, therefore, had to be acceptable to both the governor and to Hoofien and Zbarsky.

Formally, the governor had full authority to set the policy of the bank and he was not obliged to follow the recommendations of the Advisory Board.[5] In practice, however, the Advisory Board functioned as a de facto board of governors: within the period covered by the research for this publication, the governor took no decision without the approval of the Advisory Board.

Whereas formally the status of Hoofien and Zbarsky, the representatives of two largest banks, was equal to that of other members, in practice, the representatives of the two largest banks played a key role in shaping the policy of the Bank of Israel.

In many instances it appears as if their capacity to shape the decisions of the board outweighed that of the governor. What then granted these two bankers such influence on the board? First, they clearly had more banking experience than any of the other members, including the governor: the bankers were the only members of the board who had hands-on and long-standing experience in banking, and therefore their opinion and recommendations could not simply be brushed aside by the other members. Moreover, the unwritten rule in the board that all decisions must be approved unanimously meant that each member in effect had veto power. Indeed, from the establishment of the Bank of Israel until the end of 1959, the governor never used his prerogative to impose his will through his vested authority on the board. In addition, and in contrast to other members of the board, the interests of the two largest banks were highly congruent and they could coordinate their position regarding policy issues discussed by the board. This provided them with the capacity to present a united front and shape the opinions of other individual members in the board. The representatives of the large banks could also offer other members in the board lucrative jobs in order to steer the decisions of the board in a direction that benefited the banks they managed. Finally, and perhaps the most significant asset of the bankers in the board, was the fact that the governor needed their cooperation in order to achieve the objectives of the Bank.

The governor's key source of power was obvious: the law. The law endowed the governor with the power to regulate the banking system. The governor had at his disposal a massive bureaucratic apparatus, by which he could affect the profitability of the banking system as well as the distribution of profits among the banks. The governor could use his power to increase or decrease the profitability of the banking system as whole, or the profitability of the large banks in particular. The balance of power between the governor and bankers created strong incentives for both sides to cooperate and reach a common strategy that would, on the one hand, safeguard the profitability of the large banks, and, on the other hand, enable the governor to realize the objectives of the Bank.

There were two key issues over which the governor and the bankers disputed: credit allocation and the competitiveness of the banking system. Initially, the governor wanted to achieve both goals: effective credit control and maintain a competitive banking system. The bankers—as representatives of the large banks—expected privileges in exchange for their cooperation with the government's selective credit control strategy which undermined competitiveness. Eventually, both sides came to an arrangement: cooperation in exchange for privileges. However, there was no agreement as to the exact "price" the central bank had to pay in exchange for the cooperation of the banks. The interaction between the governor and the bankers can therefore be described as *cooperation through conflict*. Both sides had a strong incentive to cooperate, but at the same time conflict persisted regarding the substance of the privileges the central banks had to provide to buy cooperation.

This dynamic was the underlying factor that shaped key aspects of the transformation of the banking system in Israel, notably, the governor sacrificed the small banking institutions in exchange for securing the large banks' cooperation.

Rediscounting bills

With the above in mind, one should not imagine the governor and the bankers sitting in a closed dark room reaching devious agreements. It can safely be presumed that in December 1954, when the Bank of Israel was launched, no one in the bank or the government planned to rapidly centralize the banking system of Israel. The process unfolded gradually and step by step. At each step the governor and the bankers negotiated how to address certain technical problems and each solution shifted the regulatory rules incrementally. In hindsight, this series of choices can be interpreted as a transition in the financial regulatory regime which led to a deep transformation of the banking system; just how this series of choices unfolded will be traced in the following sections.

Rediscounting bills is a common and traditional monetary instrument used by central banks. The procedure of rediscounting consists of the purchasing and selling of private companies' bills by the central bank in the secondary market. Central banks used this instrument in order to affect the short-term interest rate or to influence the demand for money—or at least to attempt to do so. By selling and/or purchasing bills at a certain price, the Bank determines the rate by which commercial banks can receive credit or the interest rate which they can get for their reserves.[6] In developing countries, financial markets were either all but non-existent or underdeveloped and therefore central banks could not use this type of instrument. Moreover, in most developing countries, and certainly as was the case in Israel, the interest rate was under the control of the government, meaning that the rediscounting of bills was used very differently.

In Israel, rediscounting of bills was used as a selective credit instrument. The central bank purchased "a limited amount of bills of agricultural and industrial businesses whose products increase exports, replace essential imports, or make some other essential contribution to the national economy" (Bank of Israel, 1955, p. 186; see also Het, 1966, p. 95). That is, when the Bank of Israel sought to provide cheap credit to a particular firm, it purchased its debt and provided cash money in exchange. However, the central bank performed this operation through the mediation of commercial banks. A commercial bank received credit from the Bank of Israel and transferred it to a company in exchange for a company's bill, which was then transferred to the Bank of Israel. The commercial bank made a profit from the difference between the central bank interest rate of 6 percent and the interest rate paid by the firm of 8.5 percent. Therefore, rediscounting bills provided commercial banks with risk-free profit.

The question was how to distribute the right to perform this operation among the commercial banks. Horowitz's initial position was that "it must be done through the banking institutions based on some objective criteria, for example, according to a certain ratio of the deposits they maintain with the central bank or according to their total credit balances" (BoI Board, January 11, 1955, p. 3). Hoofien, the representative of Bank Leumi, argued that national interests dictated that large banks be granted a greater share of the rediscounting business than their relative size. "In an operation of this type, what must be taken into account is not what is good for the banks but what is good for the economy." He justified his position by the fact that "There is also a question of trust in the matter of allocating credit, and there are a few banks that can be trusted." In this case, he argued, "The Bank of Israel has no choice but to discriminate to some extent between banks, the same way that the government does in selecting qualified traders in foreign currency or in granting loans from its deposits" (ibid., p. 5). Horowitz expressed his concern regarding

> [the] possible allegation that we do not treat banks equally. It would be very difficult for us to exclude a few banks. This is especially difficult as we demand from all banks the allocation of 20% of their loans to agriculture.
>
> (Ibid., p. 6)

An advisor from the International Bank for Reconstruction and Development (IBRD), who visited the Bank, supported Hoofien's position that only a limited number of banks should be used for the purpose of rediscounting. He explained that "some of them [the banks] will receive very small amounts and it will be impossible to effectively supervise their use" (BoI Board, January 18, 1955, p. 2).

To reach a decision, a sub-committee was established, which recommended that the operation of rediscounting bills would be carried out by 22 of the 118 banks that then existed, which implied that less than 20 percent of the banks would participate in the operation. In practice, of the 22 banks, only a few had business relations with customers who were entitled to use the operation. Eventually, the vast majority of rediscount transactions were carried out by one of the five larger banks—Bank Leumi, Bank Hapoalim, Discount Bank, Bank Igud, and the Industrial Bank—with 60 percent of the transactions carried out by the three largest of these (BoI Board, November 29, 1955). The Chairman of the Advisory Board described the relationship between the Bank of Israel and the banks as based on "goodwill." The central bank, he continued, made the commercial banks "trustees of sorts of the Bank of Israel" (BoI Board, January 18, 1955, pp. 3–4). Horowitz described the division of labor between the Bank of Israel and the commercial banks in more technical terms:

> We check the value of the loan from the point of view of the national economy. The commercial banks check the security of the loan [from a business perspective], because a commercial bank knows a lot more than the Bank of Israel about the manner in which a loan is used.
>
> (BoI Board, November 29, 1955, pp, 2, 4)

Protecting the banks from competitors

Another policy issue that was discussed in the Advisory Board was that of the licensing of new banks. The law provided the governor with extensive powers in this area and in principle he had full discretion to approve the establishment of a new bank or to reject it. The law did not even set any rules or criteria that restricted the governor's discretion. Nevertheless, the Bank of Israel was very conservative regarding the licensing of new credit institutions despite the dramatic fall in the number of banks during the 1950s. Throughout the years 1954–1970, the Bank of Israel issued licenses for the establishment of only four new banks (not including investment banks): the Bank Lemelacha (1954), the Bank for Foreign Trade (1956), the Arab-Israeli Bank (1960), and Bank Igud (1965).

The conservative approach of the Bank of Israel consolidated gradually, after the governor embraced the position of the bankers in the Board. The first request for the opening of a new bank reached the Board in February 1955, two months after the establishment of the Bank of Israel, from the Association of Foreign Investors. The governor asked the Board to approve the request because, he explained, in recent years the number of banks had decreased as a result of mergers between small and large banking institutions. Horowitz pointed out that

> a certain number of banks achieved a monopolistic status, and there is an ongoing process of centralization in the banking system, as some of the large banks have recently purchased several small banks so that in fact the number of banks has decreased.

Therefore, the governor contended that the request should be granted, but suggested "limiting the granting of such licenses to cases in which the entrepreneurs can contribute something to the resources of the economy by raising foreign capital, and to cases in which the group of entrepreneurs is a serious one" (BoI Board, February 22, 1955, p. 4). He was firm in his opinion and argued that "it has never been decided that we do not grant new licences to banks … and I do not see sufficient reason to refuse." He was supported by the representative of the General Zionists on the Board, Shimon Bedjerano, who claimed: "I cannot justify refusing the license. The argument of 'What is the special benefit we will derive from it?' will be valid for all requests for a banking license" (ibid., p. 10).

The heads of the large banks used all their influence to try to prevent the approval of the license. Hoofien from Bank Leumi argued that there were already too many banks. "We all know that there is harsh competition between them and there is no monopoly.… We could exist for years to come without additional banks." Hoofien rejected out of hand the claim that his position had anything to do with him trying to promote the interests of Bank Leumi;

> The argument that I am seeking a monopoly for the existing banks makes no impression on me. In our small country there are 25 banks, and I say it without being ashamed: that is enough. There is no need for an additional bank.

Zbarsky, the Director General of Bank Hapoalim, followed this line and argued that the opening of a new bank contradicts the "stated policy of non-expansion of credit and non-conversion of currency." He added that in his opinion, granting licenses to applicants would lower the ethical level of the banking industry. "I'm afraid that we have resigned ourselves to the opinion that the banking profession does not require a level of integrity that is beyond all doubt" (ibid., pp. 4, 9).

Whereas in the first months after the inception of the Bank, the governor put an emphasis on the importance of competition and the decentralized structure of the banking system, within two or three years his position had drifted and he eventually accepted the principle that no new banking institution were needed. Right up until 1959 the Board rejected requests from such applicants as local municipalities and Sollel Boné. At the beginning of 1959, Horowitz noted before members of the Board that "various local groups, including public organizations, approached me with requests for licenses for banking operations. I refused all these organizations." This position was supported by all members of the Board, which agreed that

> For now the rule in force is the one that was decreed in the past, whereby the governor will consult the Board before issuing any new licenses, and the policy is not to issue such licenses except in special cases.

Two explanations were presented in support of this policy: "at the moment new banks cannot contribute anything of real value to the economy," and "small banks are objectively not viable" (BoI Board, January 20, 1959, pp. 1–2).

The change in the position of the governor cannot be explained on the basis of change of circumstances. In 1955, when Horowitz insisted that new banks should be licensed, the number of banking institutions was 118. By 1958, when he opposed the licensing of new institutions, their number had fallen to 77. Two years later, their number dropped to 53 (see Figure 8.1). Therefore, the change in the governor's view can only be explained as being a part of the new regulatory financial regime that had been consolidated in which the Bank guaranteed the interests of the large banks in exchange for their cooperation.

Competition between the big banks

During the second half of the 1950s, the Israeli banking system underwent also an intensive process of branch opening. Whereas in 1956 there were 254 bank branches operating in Israel, four years later, the number of branches had reached 559, an increase of 220 percent (Het, 1966, p. 47, Table 11). (See Figure 8.1.) The government, the governor, and the supervisor of banks considered the over-expansion of branch networks as a negative phenomenon that did not contribute to the efficiency of the banking system or to economic development. From the perspective of the governor, there was "no difference between the opening of new branches and the opening of a new bank." The rapid branching process also drew criticism from the government and the parliament. The Financial Committee of the Parliament voiced criticism against the multiplication of branches, especially in large cities (BoI Board, January 24, 1956).

The criticism against this process drew a trenchant response from the bankers. Hoofien accused the Finance Committee of a "lack of knowledge of the facts and lack of economic understanding." New branches are essential, he insisted:

> The main office is packed to the hilt. Both the clerks and the public suffer intensely from the great congestion. The noise is horrible, and there is no possibility of quiet personal contact between the clerk and the customer.... The clerks are nervous, and working under these conditions shortens their lives and damages their health.

Blocking the expansion process, argued the bankers, would hurt not only the banks and their customers, but also the national interest as these branches

> are the main instruments for the distribution of securities and for the dissemination of the notion of savings. At a time when we are making so many efforts to encourage savings, should we destroy the instrument that encourages savings, or encumber it?
>
> (Ibid.)

Hoofien pointed out other wasteful projects being built at the time, such as cinemas. "Is that more useful than bank branches?" He pointed accusingly at the wastefulness of the Histadrut and of the MoF, whom he claimed erected for themselves buildings more expensive than the bank branches.

Hoofien also responded to the accusation regarding the competition between Bank Hapoalim and Bank Leumi:

> Would the government, the Bank of Israel, and the public approve if the largest banks, say, Bank Leumi, Bank Hapoalim, and Discount Bank were to merge? ... They should be allowed to exist and to open branches.... There is no wastefulness at all in this.

The position of the bankers was endorsed by other Board members—some of them in the meantime having become professionally associated with one of the large banks. The representative of the General Zionists, Shimon Bedjerano, who was a nominated board member in Bank Leumi, rejected the authority of the Finance Committee to interfere in this policy area: "It is not the job of the Finance Committee to manage the banking system" (BoI Board, January 24, 1956). The governor and the supervisor of banks continued to voice their opposition to the branch openings arguing that "the central bank cannot be responsible for the profitability of the bank when it is not asked about the opening of branches" (BoI Board, February 17, 1959, p. 4). Nevertheless, the banks' rapid expansion of their branch networks continued.

The Credit Association's Fees Act

An important regulatory change that also affected the distribution of income among the banks and the structure of the banking system took place shortly before the formal inception of the Bank of Israel. At the end of 1954, the government introduced the Fees Act (Cooperative Credit Associations), which abolished the special status of credit associations as cooperatives, a status that had granted them certain tax exemptions. The new law decreed that all credit institutions—banks and cooperative credit associations—were liable to pay the same tax rates. Moreover, the new law imposed regressive tax brackets on credit institutions, that is to say, those smaller institutions had to pay higher fees in proportion to their size. There is no evidence that either Horowitz or the Bank of Israel were involved in the formulation of the law, but the timing suggests that there was a link between the Fees Act and the launching of the Bank.

A memorandum published by the Ministry of Finance in October 1955 stated that "a substantial number of cooperative credit associations exist in Israel that operate in a way that is similar to banks. But whereas the banks pay an annual fee ... no such obligation is placed on the cooperative credit associations" (Fees Act, 1954). Most parliamentary members agreed at the time that few of the cooperative credit associations were expanding and their size had stalled at that of small banks, hence they should be taxed as banks. However, they opposed the implementation of regressive tax brackets as these implied that the purpose of the Fees Act was to abolish the small banking institutions.

According to the bill, a credit association with equity of up to 100,000 IL in membership fees was supposed to pay a fee that represented 30 percent of its equity, while a bank whose equity was slightly over one million IL was expected to pay a fee representing 8 percent of its equity (Knesset, May 31, 1955, p. 1776). Yeshayahu Foerder, of the Liberal Progressive Party, argued that "It appears to me that we should not demand more from the cooperatives than what we demand from the banks" (Knesset, June 23, 1957, p. 1688). Aharon Zisling, a member of Mapam, a social-democrat party, argued that credit associations were created to provide financial services on a small scale to the community members, and therefore their status was not the same as a bank. Moshe Sneh, of the Communist Party, Maki, explained to the parliament what the real motive was behind the bill: the existence of a credit association was not consistent with the government's objective to reduce access to credit to small manufacturers and businesses, and to channel it to the large firms that were perceived as making higher contributions to the national interests (Knesset, May 23, 1955, p. 1686).

Despite the widespread concerns and opposition, the Fees Act was approved without amendments. The new law negatively affected the operations of small banking institutions and it contributed significantly to the rapid centralization of the banking system in Israel.

The reserve requirement reform

Perhaps the most critical—and also the most controversial—decision taken by the Board during its first five years of operation concerned the reserves requirement reform. To understand why this issue became so controversial, it is necessary to delve deeper to the technical aspects of monetary policy-making at the time.[7] When the Bank of Israel started its operation, its main policy instruments were based on the restrictions it imposed on private banks lending (Barkai, 2004, p. 91). It employed two types of restrictions: *reserves requirements* (or in *liquidity requirements*) that were uniform for all commercial banks but varied by the type of deposits and *volume requirements* or *credit ceilings* that differed from bank to bank (Bank of Israel, 1955, pp. 180–181). The combination of reserve requirements and credit ceilings created an anomalous situation in which some credit institutions that were more successful in attracting deposits and savings reached their credit ceiling, and they accumulated higher reserve ratios than they otherwise would have been. Other credit institutions that were less successful in attracting deposits and savings held lower reserve ratios as stipulated by the law. Prior to the establishment of the Bank of Israel, the smaller institutions were more successful in attracting savings and deposits than the larger banks and therefore they held higher ratios of reserve. In 1957, the average reserve ratio among the credit associations was 57 percent whereas among banks it was only 36 percent (BoI Board, April 9, 1957, p. 3). The smaller institutions were more successful in attracting funds not because they were more efficient, but because they did not observe the Ottoman interest rate law, which restricted the interest rate to a 9 percent ceiling. Their income from high interest rate credit operations enabled them to offer higher rates for savers.

The gap between the reserves ratios of the two types of institutions resulted in the managers of the cooperative credit association complaining about their excessive reserve ratios. Eliahu Margalit, the Director of the Credit Association in Rehovot, described the situation as follows:

> For two years now we have been working under conditions of restriction of the volume of credit and a high percentage of liquidity [or reserve ratio].... Nevertheless, in these two years 1,200 new members joined us, and this again places a burden on the volume [of credit]. In view of the government's demand to give priority to productive industries, we face difficulties in meeting the needs of individual members.
>
> (Quoted in Gross and Grinberg, 1994, p. 371)

In 1956, the governor and the supervisor of banks sought to simplify the reserve requirement system and to eliminate the per-bank credit ceiling. The existing provisions, the governor explained, were "cumbersome and inflexible ... and from an administrative point of view the calculations based on these provisions are very complicated" (BoI Board, August 7, 1956, p. 3). The plan was to use a uniform reserve requirement system for all credit institutions and to keep the overall volume of credit constant. This implied that the small credit institutions would be able to extend more credit and thus reduce their actual reserve ratio, and that the larger institutions would have to freeze credit until their reserve ratios reached the level determined by the Bank of Israel.

This would, of course, result in a dislocation of income from the large banks to the small banks, and this outcome was not acceptable to the large banks. The proposal unsurprisingly raised fierce debates in the Board's meetings. The bankers in the Board, as well as the other members, most of whom by now were professionally associated with the large banks, determinedly resisted the plan. "The proposal will radically change the structure of the banking system, and I think that this is a very serious flaw," argued Bedjerano (BoI Board, November 11, 1956, p. 2). The outcome of the new arrangement, he warned, would be that "the share of the banks will shrink and that of the credit association will grow.... Trade and industry will appeal to the credit association [for credit], which is not desirable for the economy" (BoI Board, April 9, 1957, pp. 3–4). Osteschinsky warned that the reform is "liable to destabilize the banking [system] and hurt respectable banks" (BoI Board, November 11, 1956, p. 2), and it would encourage credit associations that "do not play a vital role in the economy" (BoI Board, April 9, 1957, pp. 3–4). Zbarsky argued that credit associations had long ago lost their role in the economy because "there is no difference between the characteristics of a bank and a credit association." What seemed to add weight to Zbarsky's comment in particular was the fact that it was during this period that the banks started to open new branches all over the country, therefore there was allegedly no specific need for credit associations anymore (ibid., pp. 3–4).

The debates regarding the reserve requirements reform stretched over months. The Advisory Board meetings were tense, as one can read from the protocols. In a moment of crisis the governor explicitly accused the Board members of putting the interest of the institutions they represented before the interests of the public: "It is essential," he asserted, "that the Board does take into account the interests of various groups and allows us to use the reserve ratios as an effective instrument for allocating credit" (BoI Board, June 18, 1957, p. 1). "I am sorry to say," noted one of the members, "that this is the first time that I did not have a good feeling at the Board meeting" (ibid., p. 1).

At the time the issue of the reserve requirements was being discussed, the bankers had strengthened their influence in the Board by appointing three of the Board members—Bedjerano, Ostashinski and Nebenzahl—to the Board of Directors of Bank Leumi. Except for the governor, only two members were now not directly associated with one of the two large banks: Giora Yoseftal and Kadish Loz, who were too busy in the Knesset and the government to make a dedicated stand in the Board.

Shimon Bedjerano put forward the suggestion to set higher reserve requirements for credit associations than for banks (BoI Board, April 9, 1957, p. 3). "We must take into consideration," he argued, "the justified claims of the large institutions and repair the current deficiencies" (ibid., pp. 3–4). The governor and the supervisor of banks tried to stick to their position. "The weak point of the Israeli economy is its rigidity. We must encourage free competition and not interfere with it" (BoI Board, September 11, 1956, p. 2). Moreover, the Governor realized that Bedjerano's proposal would ultimately lead to the elimination of the credit associations and he did not want that. "In recent years," he explained, "the policies of the government and of the Bank of Israel have undermined their [the credit associations'] profits." The proposal to set a higher rate of liquidity for the credit associations would raise yet additional obstacles for them concurrent with the existing ones. "If we set higher liquidity rates for them than for the banks, we are fining them for a situation that was created by our regulation alone and contrary to the demands of the associations" (BoI Board, April 9, 1957, p. 3). The supervisor of banks pointed out that in fact the credit associations fulfill all the directives of the Bank: "Today, credit associations finance, in accordance with our directives, important agricultural and industrial projects, and as a result we are able to allocate more credit to these sectors." But they do not enjoy the benefits which the large banks enjoy, "such as transactions in foreign currency," for example (ibid., p. 4).

The representatives of the large banks, however, did not yield and over the course of 1958 the governor and the supervisor of banks had to make concessions to the banks. They proposed that banks could substitute reserves in foreign currency for reserves in domestic currency. The amended proposal stated that "every bank would have the option to choose to include foreign currency into their liquid assets … or not to include it" (ibid., p. 4). The banks had to choose between 70 percent liquidity including foreign currency or 60 percent liquidity without foreign currency (BoI Board, July 16, 1957, p. 2).

Formally, this option was available to all banks, but in practice only the large banks could take advantage of it because only they were legally entitled to handle foreign currency transactions. Moreover, most of the foreign currency deposits of the government were held in a small number of large banks. During the second half of the 1950s, the volume of foreign currency deposits expanded enormously due to the reparation payments from the West German government. Whereas, in 1957, foreign currency deposits were only 3.9 percent of the banks' total deposits, by 1961, this had risen to 18.4 percent (Het, 1966, p. 128, Table 36). Furthermore, the deposits were not distributed equally among the banks: 86 percent of the foreign residents' accounts (Patach) were handled by the five largest banks and 80 percent of the fixed term deposits (Pazaq) were handled by the three largest banks (ibid., p. 129). Therefore, only the large banks were free to choose between denominating their reserve in domestic or foreign currency.

The governor made an additional concession by entirely releasing the deposits of public organizations from any reserve requirement (BoI Board, July 16, 1957, p. 2). Whereas the government sometimes claimed to attempt to distribute its deposits among the commercial banks according to their size, the small credit institutions did not handle public deposits at all. According to Meir Het, "Whether this was a deliberate policy or whether because of administrative reasons it was not convenient to distribute the deposits to such a greater extent, it is clear that important assistance was withheld from the small associations" (1966, pp. 136–137).

The two concessions, however, did not satisfy the large banks. The governor then agreed that "no bank will reduce its volume of credit in practice, and the implementation of the directives will be linked to the degree to which deposits will increase at each bank." This meant that if the new calculation revealed that a given bank maintained a reserve ratio that was lower than necessary, it would not be required to increase its reserves immediately. Half of the new deposits the bank received would be used to increase the reserve ratio and the other half could be used by the bank to grant credit (BoI Board, July 16, 1957, p. 3). In addition, the governor promised to allow banks to provide "certain types of loans" beyond the credit directives (Bank of Israel, 1957, p. 195). This concession meant that the actual percentage of liquidity became lower than that which the central bank specified in its directives.

This series of concessions, made by the central bank to the commercial banks should be conceived as the "regulatory price" the central bank (and the government) had to pay in order to "buy" the cooperation of the large banks with the government's selective credit control. With each decision taken, more resources were re-directed away from the small banking institutions, and toward the larger ones, which served to increase both their economic power as well as the dependency of the Bank of Israel on them.

Abolishing the credit associations

By 1956 most of the credit associations that survived were associated with the Workers Corporation and were part of the Histadrut sector. One may assume that Bank Hapoalim could have used its political influence to force the managers of the cooperative credit associations to merge with it. This was not the case. The credit associations were legally independent economic units and they were managed by democratically elected directors. Therefore, neither the Bank of Israel, nor Bank Hapoalim or even the Workers Corporation—all of whom had an interest in promoting a merger with Bank Hapoalim—had the legal authority to impose such a decision on them. Additional means were needed to push the credit associations into merging.

The person who was in the position to push the credit associations into a decision to merge with Bank Hapoalim was Avraham Zbarsky. Zbarsky was the single most powerful person in the financial system of the Histadrut sector: he managed Bank Hapotalim, he was a member of the Bank of Israel Board and he was also the Chairman of the Center of the Cooperative Credit Association. From this position he could persuade as well as make credible threats to the managers of the credit associations.

In the meeting of the Center, Zbarsky explained to the managers that the Israeli banking system was becoming more centralized, and therefore the financial system of the "workers' sector" must also become more centralized. "The credit associations must grasp the importance of the advantage that Bank Hapoalim must gain," he explained (Credit Association, August 26, 1954). The representatives of the left faction in the management of the Workers Corporation opposed this move, because they perceived it as a further infringement of the interests of the small agricultural settlements and a continuation of the centralization trend of the Israeli economy. Berl Reptor, the representative of Mapam in the Secretariat of the Workers Corporation, argued that what was at stake was not only the fate of the credit associations but also a transition of the Israeli economy from "one form of financial economy to another" (Workers Corporation, December 20, 1956, p. 27).

The managers of the various credit associations acknowledged the problem but they opposed the solution offered by Zbarsky. Instead of merging with Bank Hapoalim they opted to establish several regional banks. Eliyhu Margalit, the manager of the credit association in Rehovot, proposed the creation of "7 or 8 regional associations" (Credit Association, August 26, 1954). However, besides the credit associations, none of the other actors involved—the Bank of Israel, Bank Hapoalim or the Workers Corporation—had any interest in this solution.

In the summer of 1957, the governor informed the Advisory Board that there was a "serious crisis situation" in the credit associations sector. The governor reported on five cases of "irregularities" and corruption within the managements of the credit associations, some of which had been handed over to the police (BoI Board, November 5, 1957, p. 4). The governor admitted that "the apparatus at our disposal is not sufficient" to cope with these cases (BoI Board, July 23,

1957, p. 6). Giora Yoseftal responded that "the entire credit association sector has been shaken, and it is necessary to find a way to do away with it for the benefit of the public" (BoI Board, October 8, 1957, p. 5) The Supervisor of Banks Israel Bar-Yosef also saw in the credit associations a "source of serious concern" and contended that from his point of view there was no difference between a credit association and a bank, and therefore the associations are not entitled to any kind of concessions (BoI Board, July 23, 1957, p. 7). Horowitz summarized the opinion of the Board that "there is a contradiction between the trend of expanding the portion of credit offered for productive purposes in agriculture and industry, and the trend of encouraging the associations to provide credit to their members, which is consumer credit" (BoI Board, November 5, 1957).

The intervention of the police in the affairs of the credit associations was the final nail in their coffin. Within less than a year they were all merged with Bank Hapoalim.

The effectiveness of the selective credit control

Abolishing the credit associations was the last step in the formation of the new regulatory financial regime in Israel. Once it was achieved, the Israeli state gained more effective control over the banking system. The banking system became more concentrated and the Bank of Israel had the means to shape the incentive structure of the large banks, and therefore to affect their behavior. This invites the question, then, to what extent did the Bank of Israel achieve its aim to create developmental credit?

Development credit is characterized by three features: (1) *allocation*: developmental credit is allocated to economic sectors which are consistent with state preferences, however these are defined. In most late-developing countries agriculture and manufacturing were perceived as "productive" in contrast to credit allocated to consumption. The construction sector was a gray area; (2) *time structure*: the longer the term of loans, the more the credit is considered "developmental"; and (3) *price*: developmental credit must be as cheap as possible, so investment becomes more profitable. To what extent, then, did the new financial regulatory regime in Israel produce developmental credit?

Figure 8.5 presents the share of credit allocated to productive sectors—agriculture and manufacturing—to non-productive purposes and to construction. The data shows that the share of credit allocated to productive sectors rose from 30 percent in 1951 to 55 percent in 1955 and remained at that level until 1961. The relative expansion of productive credit took place at a period during which the volume of credit expanded seven times in nominal terms. During this period the volume of credit allocated to productive sectors expanded 12-fold, and the credit allocated to non-productive purposes expanded four-fold (Figure 8.6), all of which strongly indicate the effectiveness of the financial regime.

Another indicator of the Bank of Israel's effectiveness is the change of the temporal structure of credit. From 1952 to 1961, the share of long-term loans in the total volume of loans grew from 18 percent to 25 percent and the share

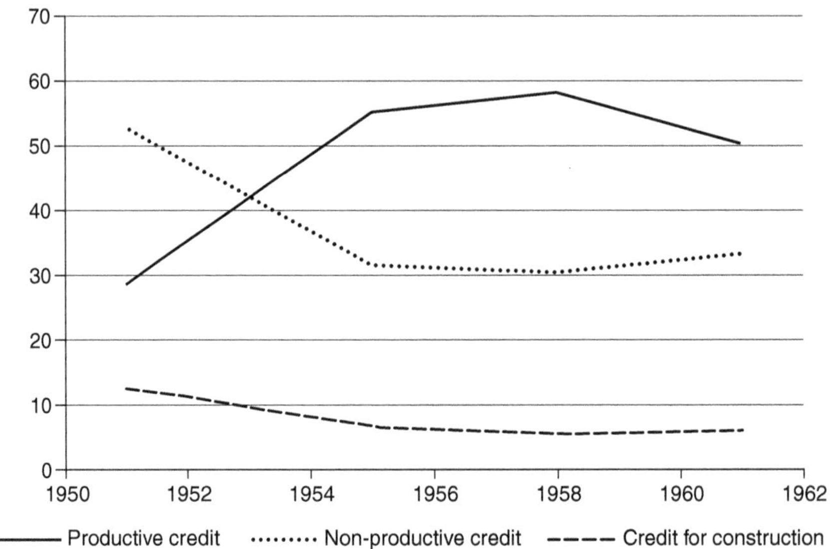

Figure 8.5 Distribution of credit between productive and non-productive sectors, 1951–1961 (%).

Sources: Krampf (2015, p. 211, Figure 7). Data: Het (1966, p. 1966, Table 66).

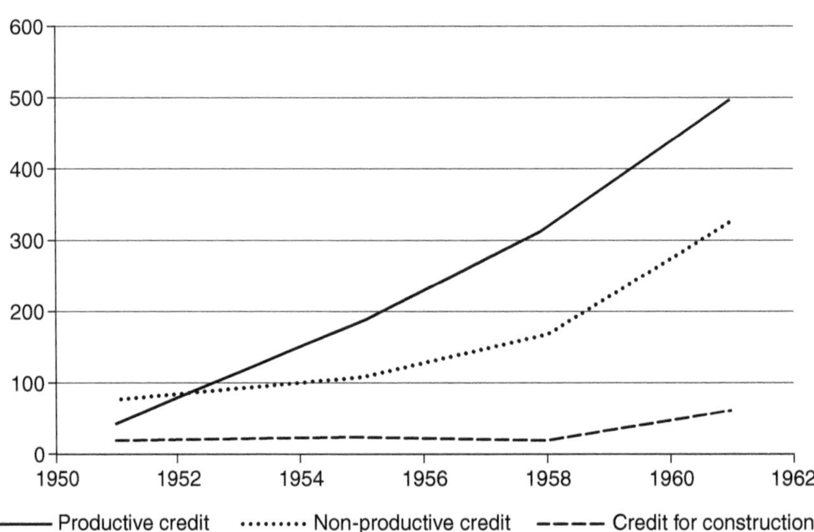

Figure 8.6 Allocation of credit to productive and non-productive sectors, 1951–1961 (millions of Israeli Liras).

Sources: Krampf (2015, p. 211, Figure 8). Data: Het (1966, p. 1966. Table 66).

of short-term loans fell from 37 percent to 27 percent (Het, 1966, pp. 187–188, Tables 67 and 68). Finally, the effectiveness of the Bank of Israel's strategy was also reflected in the *spread* between the interest rate that banks charged for loans and the rate they offered for savings and deposits. This issue requires a brief explanation: according to conventional economic theories, the spread between interest rate on loans and savings (and deposits) is a proxy for the efficiency of the banking system and its competitiveness: a wider spread indicates a lack of competitiveness and that the banks are reaping unjustified profits (economic rent); a narrower spread is an indication that banks are competing efficiently among themselves for depositors and borrowers. A competitive banking system is perhaps a sufficient condition for a low spread, but not a necessary condition: low spread may be achieved through effective regulation, as was the case of the Bank of Israel. The Bank of Israel was successful in narrowing the spread: from 1956 to 1958, the rate differential between loans and long-term deposits fell from above 6 percent to below 4 percent (Figure 8.7).

This finding confirms the claim that the interaction between banks and the Israeli authorities after the establishment of the Bank of Israel cannot be explained on the basis of the model of financial repression. Rather, the Bank of Israel managed to create a financial regime in which banks reduced the spread and therefore they contributed to national development.

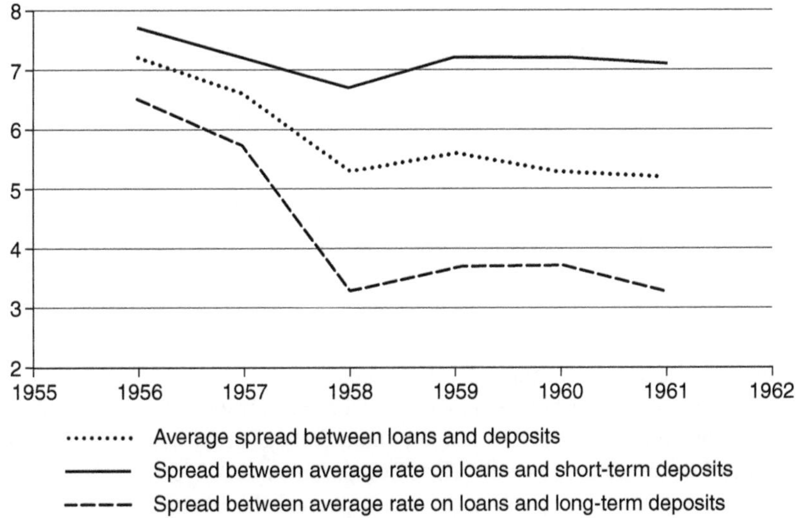

Figure 8.7 Interest rates spread, 1956–1961.

Sources: Krampf (2015, p. 212, Figure 9). Data: Bank of Israel (1963, p. 40, Table 20).

The capture of the Bank of Israel by the commercial banks

However, there was the flip side to this coin. The success of the Bank of Israel in controlling credit had a cost: the central bank had to provide the big banks with privileges, securing their profitability and restricting competition in exchange for their cooperation.

The commercial banks had two sources of income: income generated by the spread between interest they charged on loans and the interest they paid on deposited funds, and income generated by fees they charged for services they provide customers. Prior to the establishment of the Bank of Israel, the banking system was decentralized and quite competitive. Therefore, the share generated by fees was relatively low in comparison to income generated by the interest rate spread. When the large banks came to dominate the banking system, the share of income generated by fees grew markedly. In 1950, 80 percent of the banks' profit were generated from their financial assets, that is, from operations associated with their role as financial intermediaries and from the spread between the lending rates and deposit rates. The rest, 20 percent of their income, was derived from commissions they charged for their services. In 1954, the percentage of income from financial assets fell to 68 percent, and in 1958 to 63 percent (Het, 1966, p. 213, Table 83). Hence, within eight years, the banks had almost doubled the income they generated from fees on services. The increase of income generated by fees was a direct result of the centralization of the banking system as two or three large banks came to dominate the banking system and customers lost competitive choices.

Since 1955, the profitability of the banking system had stagnated with the bankers placing the blame on the Bank of Israel's policies, and for which they expected to be compensated. Yeshayahu Foerder, who by that time was a member of Bank Leumi's board, argued that "we must remember that the banks are an important device and we must protect them" (BoI Board, June 24 1958, p. 2). The Bank of Israel "should feel the same degree of responsibility toward the banking system as toward any other sector of the economy." Whereas, on the one hand, Foerder pointed out that the Bank of Israel had an obligation to the banking system because it cooperated with the Bank, he also indicated that the banks were private institutions and therefore it was their "duty and right" to "make a profit" (BoI Board, January 6, 1959, pp. 2–3). The bankers in the Board complained that "over 50% of credit is directed" and that under these conditions the managements of the banks had no discretion. "This creates hard feelings at the banks and affects the attitude of the customers as well" (BoI Board, January 20, 1959, pp. 2–3).

The governor and the supervisor of banks pushed the blame back onto the banks' managements. Profitability had dropped, they argued, due to unjustified and irresponsible expansion of banks' spending. The expansion of the banks was described as a "waste" caused by "wild competition" between the large banks. To support the claim, the supervisor of banks presented data showing that the number of employees in the banking system had grown over the course of 1957 by 1000 and reached 5580, and this expansion, he argued, had no economic justification (BoI Board, June 24, 1959, p. 2). The claims of the supervisor of banks are consistent with the study of Meir Het, which shows that, from 1952 right through until the end of the 1950s, the number of employees in the banking sector rose by approximately 1000 each year (Het, 1966, p. 226). The governor also contended that "the salaries of the banks' employees are inflated, the working hours are too low and that with the increase in the number of branches contribute to rising expenses" (BoI Board, January 6, 1959, p. 2).

The competition between the large banks led to another problem that had macro-economic implications, according to the governor: the banks competed over customers by offering high interest rates on deposits and savings. As interest rates on deposits and savings increased, the spread diminished and the profitability of the banks naturally fell.

One possible solution was to reach an accord between the large banks:

> The banks must reach an arrangement between themselves to prevent excessive interest on credit, because this draws money to banks that are not solid and results in breaking the law. In the same way, it is possible to prevent the opening of unnecessary branches in areas in which there is no need for such branches.
>
> (BoI Board, January 20, 1959, p. 4)

This proposal revived an old idea of Hoofien, who had suggested four years earlier that the "Bank of Israel initiate an agreement between the banking institutions that would fix the credit interest rate" (BoI Board, March 7, 1955, p. 4). Whereas in the past the governor had dismissed the idea, this time he actively encouraged it, and said: "It is indeed desirable that the banks reach an agreement between themselves in this matter, and we are prepared to help" (BoI Board, March 3, 1959, p. 2). There is no written documentation that such an agreement materialized, but we also cannot rule out the possibility that the banks reached an informal agreement and coordinated their interest rate policies.

The Board also sought alternative sources of income for the banks. In August 1958, the governor announced that the Bank of Israel would raise the interest rate it paid on the banks' deposits at the central bank by 0.25 percent:

> Given the worsening of the situation with respect to the profitability of the banks, I believe it is justified to increase the interest on banks' reserves deposited at the Bank of Israel.... This appears to me to be preferable to any other means of improving the condition of the banks.[8]

The *Annual Report for 1958* stated:

> The increases were intended to adjust the interest rates paid by the Bank of Israel to the interest rates of the banking institutions, on one hand, and to improve the profitability of the banking institutions given the legal limitations imposed on interest rates on the other.[9]

In practice, the average interest paid by the Bank of Israel to the banks was raised by more than a quarter of a percent. But the increase was not distributed homogeneously among the banks. Calculations based on official data shows that, whereas in 1958 the interest rate payments by the Bank of Israel to the large banks represented 2.4 percent of their overall reserves at the central bank, three years later, in 1961, the central bank paid 4 percent. Smaller institutions were worse off: in 1958, the average interest rate paid to banks other than the four largest banks was 1.7 percent and in 1961 it had increased to 2.1 percent (see Table 8.1).

The data indicates that toward the end of the 1950s, the Bank of Israel had assumed increased responsibility for the profitability of the banking system in comparison to the early 1950s and that it literally paid money to private banking institutions in order to maintain their profit margins. These payments were added to the income reaped by the large banks through fees on banking services. This trend was more pronounced in the case of the large banks than in the case of the small banks. The added responsibility of the Bank of Israel for the profitability of the banks was part of the cost of the banks' cooperation with the selective credit policy.

Conclusion

This chapter posed two questions. The first was: what were the factors that can explain the transformation of the banking system in Israel during the 1950s, and which led to its transition into a highly centralized banking system? The chapter argues that the key factor was the policies of the Bank of Israel during its first four years of operation. The second question was: why did the Bank of Israel implement such a policy? The chapter argued that centralization was a cost the bank was ready to accept in order to control the allocation of credit. The governor extended privileges to the large banks and guaranteed their profitability, in exchange for their cooperation.

Table 8.1 Interest rates and payments paid to commercial banks by the Bank of Israel, 1958–1961

		1958	*1959*	*1960*	*1961*
Bank balances held by the Bank of Israel (million IL)	The four large banks[1]	134.6	169.2	233.7	291.3
	Other banks[2]	40.8	53.5	75.3	98.9
Interest payments paid by the central bank (million IL)	The four large banks[3]	3.2	4.8	8.4	11.7
	Other banks[4]	0.7	1.0	1.6	2.1
Bank of Israel interest on deposits (%)	The four large banks[5]	2.4	2.8	3.6	4.0
	Other banks[6]	1.7	1.9	2.2	2.1

Source: (Bank of Israel, 1966 Appendix, Tables 2, 3, 11, 12).

Notes

5 Calculated from 1 and 2.

6 Calculated from 2 and 4.

This chapter completes the picture described in Chapter 4, regarding the transition from the paradigm of rapid development to the paradigm of economic independence. Whereas the paradigm of rapid development was implemented by the institutional triangle that included the government, the Histadrut and the Workers Corporation, the objective of economic independence—an export-led growth strategy—was implemented by a new institutional network that included the economic ministries, the Bank of Israel and the private sector. The government needed to have a capacity to channel credit to productive economic units in the private sector. For that purpose, it needed to mobilize the banking system, and the Bank of Israel enabled the government to do that, without formally nationalizing the banking system. The ability to control the banking system was a necessary step, in the process of market-building. The chapter showed that the process of market-building was achieved by using illiberal policy instruments, which included discrimination between market actors.

Moreover, the policies of the Bank of Israel, during the second half of the 1950s, had a deep impact on Israel's institutional path. The centralized structure of the banking system has become one of the key feature of the Israeli economy.

Notes

1 See Chapter 7 for details.
2 Large banks are defined here as those whose assets are above 20 million IL, and the sum of their deposits are above 10 million LI. (Het, 1966, p. 134, Table 39).
3 See Chapter 4 for details.
4 See Chapter 6 for details.
5 See Chapters 6 and 7 for details.
6 This description is based on the experience of the 1950s (Fousek, 1957, pp. 13–30; see, Sayers (1950, pp. 49–50). In recent times central banks call this policy instrument "Open Market Operations."
7 For a detailed explanation of the monetary implications of the reserve ratio, see Chapter 7.
8 Horowitz proposed increasing the interest by 0.25 percent so that it fluctuated between 2.5 percent and 4.2 percent. (BoI Board, August 26, 1958, p. 2).
9 The increase in the interest came into effect on September 1, 1958. Interest on checking account deposits was increased from 2.5 percent to 2.75 percent, on 3-month deposits from 3 percent to 3.25 percent, on 6-month deposits from 3.75 percent to 4 percent, on 9-month deposits from 4 percent to 4.25 percent.(Bank of Israel, 1958, p. 279).

References

Bank of Israel, 1955. *Annual Report*. Bank of Israel, Jerusalem.
Bank of Israel, 1957. *Annual Report*. Bank of Israel, Jerusalem.
Bank of Israel, 1958. *Annual Report*. Bank of Israel, Jerusalem.
Bank of Israel, 1963. *Annual Report*. Bank of Israel, Jerusalem.
Bank of Israel. 1966. *Annual Report*. Bank of Israel, Jerusalem.

Banking Council. Minutes of the Banking Council, Israel State Archive, 5617/2-Gimel.

Barkai, H., 2004. The Formation of the Monetary System. In: Leviatan, N. and Barkai, H. (Eds.), *The Bank of Israel*. The Bank of Israel, Jerusalem, pp. 37–183 (in Hebrew).

Bar-Yosef, I., 1953. Credit Policy in Israel. *The Economic Quarterly* 1–2, 187–196 (in Hebrew).

Bhatia, R.J. and Khatkhate, D.R., 1975. *Financial Intermediation, Savings Mobilization, and Entrepreneurial Development: The African Experience*, Staff Papers—International Monetary Fund 22, 132–158.

BoI Board. Various years. Minutes of the Bank of Israel Advisory Board.

Brimmer, A.F., 1971. Central Banking and Economic Development: The Record of Innovation. *Journal of Money, Credit and Banking* 3, 780–792.

Choi, B.-S., 1993. Financial Policy and Big Business in Korea: The Peril of Financial Regulation. In: Haggard, S., Lee, C.H. and Maxfield, S. (Eds.), *The Politics of Finance in Developing Countries*. Cornell University Press, Ithaca, NY, pp. 23–54.

Credit Association. Various years. Minutes of the Center of Credit Association, *Labor Movement Archive*, IV-4–204–66, IV-4–204–65.

Economic Committee LM. Various years. Minutes of the Economic Committee of the Labor Movement. Labor Party Archive.

Fees Act, 1954. *Proposed Memorandum for the Fees Act (Cooperative Credit Associations)*, October, Israel State Archives 5415/8C.

Fousek, P.G., 1957. *Foreign Central Banking: The Instrument of Monetary Policy*. The Federal Reserve Bank of New York, New York.

Fry, M.J., 1982. Models of Financially Repressed Developing Economies. *World Development* 10, 731–750.

Fry, M.J., 1988. *Money, Interest, and Banking in Economic Development*. Johns Hopkins University Press, Baltimore, MD.

Gerschenkron, A., 1962. Economic Backwardness in Historical Perspective. In: Gerschenkron, A., *Economic Backwardness in Historical Perspective*. Belknap Press of Harvard University Press, Cambridge, MA, pp. 5–30.

Gross, N.T., 1977. *A Banker for a New State: The History of Bank Leumi*. Masada, Tel Aviv (in Hebrew).

Gross, N.T. and Grinberg, I., 1994. *Bank Hapoalim: The First Fifty Years*. Am Oved, Tel Aviv (in Hebrew).

Hanson, J.A. and Rocha, R.R., 1986. *High Interest Rates, Spreads, and the Costs of Intermediation: Two Studies*. World Bank, Washington, DC.

Het, M., 1966. *Banking Institutions in Israel*. Falk Center for Economic Research in Israel, Jerusalem (in Hebrew).

Het, M. 1970. Several Economic and Legal Tests of Imperfect Competition in Israeli Financial Markets. Doctoral thesis, the Hebrew University, Jerusalem.

Khatkhate, D.R. and Villanueva, D.P., 1980. Operation of Selective Credit Policies in Less Developed Countries: Certain Critical Issues. In: Coats, W.L. and Khatkhate, D.R. (Eds.), *Money and Monetary Policy in Less Developed Countries*. Pergamon Press, Oxford, pp. 589–603.

Knesset. Various years. *Divrei Ha'knesset* [Minutes of Parliament Sessions].

Maman, D. and Rosenhek, Z., 2011. *The Israeli Central Bank: Political Economy, Global Logics and Local Actors*. Taylor & Francis, London.

McKinnon, R.I., 1973. *Money and Capital in Economic Development*. Brookings Institution Press, Washington, DC.

Sarnat, M., 1977. Transition to a Modern Financial System. In: Gross, N., Halevi, N., Kleiman, E. and Sarnat, M. (Eds.), *A Banker for a New State: The History of Bank Leumi.* Masada, Tel Aviv.

Sayers, R.S., 1950. *Modern Banking.* Clarendon Press, Oxford.

Shaw, E.S., 1973. *Financial Deepening in Economic Development.* Oxford University Press, New York.

Workers Corporation. Various years. Minutes of the Secretariat of the Workers Corporation, Labor Movement Archive, IV-4–204–1506.

Part III

The path to neoliberalism

9 The Stabilization Plan

On the morning of Sunday, June 30, 1985, the government convened for a secret meeting that lasted until the following morning. At the end of the meeting, after a brief break, Prime Minister Shimon Peres and the Minister of Finance Yitzhak Moda'i rushed to the Knesset to announce the Emergency Economic Stabilization Plan. The plan, which was designed as a response to the economic crisis, triggered institutional changes that deeply transformed the Israeli economy. This change was portrayed as a transition from the age of "intervention" or "socialism" to the age of liberalization and globalization.

Professional economists hailed the transition of the Israeli economy, and within several years numerous books and articles by Israeli economists had been published, the common theme of which was that the Israeli government had finally overcome vested interests and populism and was able to adopt an economic strategy more in tune with mainstream market-oriented economic theories (Aharoni, 1991; Ben-Basaț, 2002; Ben-Porath, 1986; Kleiman, 1997; Plessner, 1994; Razin, forthcoming; Zilberfarb, 2005). Sociologists and political economists saw the transition in a different light. The transition to neoliberalism, they argued, was the product of an ideological shift, driven by ideas originating in the United States, which reflected the rising power of private businesses (Filc, 2006; Maman and Rosenhek, 2011; Ram, 2013; Svirski, 2006).

There are also studies that focus on the Stabilization Plan itself, rather than on its long-term consequences. This category includes Michael Bruno's and Stanley Fischer's writings, in which they provide their own account of the choices they made, as well as those made by the government. Obviously, they highlight the economic aspects of the plan, and they perceive the policy-making process as a problem-solving process rather than a political process of social learning (Bruno, 1985, 1987; Fischer, 1995). Ronen Mandelkern and Michael Shalev (Mandelkern and Shalev, 2010) along with Ricky Shiv (Shiv, 2013) as well as Daniel Schiffman, Warren Yound and Yaron Zelekha (Schiffman *et al.*, forthcoming), also trace the role of economists in shaping the plan from different perspectives.

The Stabilization Plan was undoubtedly a transformative event in the economic history of Israel and it is very likely that it triggered a series of institutional changes that can be portrayed as "liberalization." Moreover, one cannot deny the significant role played by economists in shaping the plan, in respect to previous years. However, one should be cautious not to read into the plan the liberalization policies and rhetoric that became common in the following years. The plan, it will be argued here, did not liberalize the Israeli economy nor was intended to. Rather, this chapter will argue that the plan should be perceived as a re-mobilization of the Israeli economy. It was a process of an adjustment of the state preferences and the means of governing the economy to fit the post-Bretton Woods era. However, whereas the economic means changed, the government still prioritized export-led economic strategy. This preference explains many of the choices made by the government. Moreover, the chapter will challenge the claim that the plan was designed by economists and was imposed on Israel by the United States. Instead, it will present a more nuanced argument, which underlines the policy trade-off the government faced and its policy choices.

The chapter will trace the process that led the decision of the government to implement the Stabilization Plan, from 1977 to 1986, with the aim of identifying the way policy-makers perceived the state preferences and how these preferences shaped the policy choices of the government. There are four key relevant state preferences that will be considered: (1) the state's inclination to maintain its fiscal autonomy and discretion; (2) the state inclination to build and sustain its military power; (3) the preference to promote exports; and, finally, (4) the state's interest in maintaining a high standard of living and a generous welfare system. It will be argued that the state faced a trade-off and was not able to realize all these preferences simultaneously.

To put the Stabilization Plan into a historical context, the chapter will examine the period from the "political revolution" in May 1977 when Likud dominated the election up to the beginning of 1986 when the Stabilization Plan was announced as being successful. Not only was this period economically unstable, but during these eight years Israeli governments searched for a new policy strategy that would suit the new globalized world economy. To begin this consideration, Simha Erlich's failed attempt to liberalize the Israeli economy has been selected as a starting point and it ends with the Stabilization Plan that was successful from many perspectives, but not from the liberal viewpoint.

The 1970s: happy days or a lost decade?

From a socio-economic perspective, the 1970s were a prosperous decade for most Israeli citizens. Israel was no longer a small state struggling for its existence in a hostile region. The country had the world hegemon as its closest friend and was now a regional superpower with a modern military force that, in boxing terms, was able to "punch above its weight." The standard of living rose significantly and social disparities were starting to narrow. Nevertheless, Israeli economists depict the period from 1973 to 1984 as "the lost decade" due to the fact that growth was sluggish and inflation was on the rise.[1] In technical terms, it was a period in which a fiscal crisis quietly began to take root. A fiscal crisis is defined as

> a period of heightened budgetary distress, resulting in the sovereign taking exceptional measures. A country may experience fiscal distress, when large imbalances emerge between inflows (revenues and financing) and outflows (primary expenditures and debt service). These imbalances may lead to a fiscal crisis if the country does not (is not able to) sufficiently adjust its fiscal position—i.e., it may face an acute funding distress and need for exceptional and disruptive actions.
>
> (Farah-Yacoub *et al.*, 2017, p. 7)

Whereas in 1968 government spending accounted for 41 percent of GDP, by 1976, it had increased to 70 percent (Table 9.1). The lion's share of the rising expenditure was allocated to the defense budget. On the eve of the Six-Day War,[2] military spending was 10 percent of GDP. Immediately after the Yom Kippur War,[3] military spending peaked at almost 30 percent and then it fluctuated around the 20 percent mark until the Stabilization Plan (Table 9.1). In absolute terms, in 1977, the defense budget was seven times larger than in 1966 (Lifshitz, 2000: 156, Table 1; p. 177, Table 7). The growth of the defense budget was the result of both material conditions and perceived threats. After the Six-Day War, the army had to defend much longer borders and it became responsible for governing the occupied territories and the Palestinian population. Moreover, the experience of the Yom Kippur War, which put the very existence of the Israeli state at risk, contributed to the view that no cost was too high to maintain Israel national security (Ne'eman, 1984).

Despite the relatively low growth rate and the high level of military spending, during the 1970s, Israeli citizens enjoyed a relatively high level of social welfare on average and in comparison to the previous two decades. Average numbers do not tell the whole story and often conceal important details and anomalies. However, they tell an essential overall part of the story: in 1970, GDP per capita—a standard measure for the average standard living—was three times higher than in 1950.[4] Workers received more for their labor: in 1982, real wages were 1.5 higher than in 1968.[5] The rising real wage level was facilitated by the institutional power of the Histadrut, the Labor Union, and by the legal arrangement of wage indexation (Kleiman, 1986). Moreover, inequality decreased and income was more evenly distributed between low and high earners. This was partly achieved due to changes in the labor market, and partly due to a more generous welfare system that was created during the 1970s (Gal, 1994a, 1997; Rosenhek, 2002). Whereas until 1965, the welfare payments consisted of 4 percent of the GDP, by 1980, it had reached 14 percent of GDP (Table 9.1).

Businesses, mainly exporting ones, also enjoyed generous subsidies from the government through selective credit control and the Encouragement of Capital Investment Law. In 1965, subsidies to private businesses stood at 1.8 percent of GDP, by 1980, government subsidies to businesses had reached 8.3 percent, about a quarter of which was allocated to exporters (Table 9.1). The growing subsidies to business contributed to a trend of consolidation among large business groups that started in 1967 (Maman, 2002). The economic and political

Table 9.1 Selected economic indicators, 1965–2014

	GDP growth[1]	Public spending[2]	Inflation (CPI)[3]	External debt[4]	Current account deficit[5]	Central Bank foreign exchange reserves[6]	Military public spending[7]	Welfare payments[8]	Direct Subsidies and credit to domestic producers[9]	Direct Subsidies and credit to exporters[10]
	%	% GDP	%	% GDP	$ million	$ million	% GDP	% GDP	% GDP	% GDP
1965	5.1	29	7.1	21.0	–202	643	8.9	3.3	1.5	0.3
1966	–0.5	32	7.8	24.0	–160	621	9.9	4.0	1.6	0.8
1967	–1.9	41	0.2	24.0	–15	714	17.1	5.0	1.5	1.3
1968	21.2	41	1.9	31.2	–218	662	17.3	6.2	2.0	1.7
1969	13.9	42	3.9	36.8	–421	412	18.9	6.3	1.8	1.7
1970	10.1	48	10.1	41.6	–612	483	24.2	6.6	1.7	2.3
1971	12.0	48	13.4	48.0	–35	758	21.9	7.1	1.7	3.2
1972	11.9	44	12.4	41.6	–55	1287	19.1	7.6	1.7	2.7
1973	4.3	59	26.4	39.0	–425	1979	28.9	9.3	2.2	2.7
1974	3.7	59	39.7	43.2	–1601	1258	26.9	11.6	2.0	3.6
1975	1.7	69	39.3	52.0	–2246	1289	30.3	12.4	5.6	3.6
1976	2.4	70	31.3	60.0	–990	1458	26.1	13.9	8.0	4.3
1977	2.8	67	34.6	59.2	–481	1571	21.0	14.5	7.2	5.2
1978	7.3	64	51.0	64.8	–971	2783	22.7	14.3	6.5	1.3
1979	5.7	64	78.0	60.8	–918	3234	18.7	14.0	7.4	1.9
1980	–1.0	70	131.0	55.2	–878	3526	21.6	9.8	4.7	2.1
1981	5.6	73	117.0	56.0	–1360	3814	23.1	8.7	8.1	2.3
1982	2.4	70	132.0	64.8	–2257	4317	19.7	8.2	6.1	2.4
1983	4.1	64	191.0	64.0	–2373	3780	16.9	7.4	5.2	2.5
1984	1.0	69	445.0	75.2	–1578	3255	19.4	8.3	5.8	2.8
1985	2.7	65	185.0	80.0	988	3795	19.0	8.2	4.8	1.7
1986	5.0	60	19.6	62.4	1277	4705	14.2	8.5	3.2	1.2
1987	7.9	57	16.1	52.8	–1407	5924	17.1	8.2	3.1	1.2
1988	1.8	56	16.4	42.4	–838	4091	14.5	9.0	3.0	1.2
1989	1.6	56	20.7	38.4	208	5330	12.3	9.4	2.3	1.2
1990	6.6	55	17.6	32.8	163	5763	12.6	8.9	1.8	0.9
1991	6.7	53	18.0	28.8	–1278	7027	12.0	10.0	1.7	0.6

1992	9.9	54	9.4	29.6	–875	6362	10.7	11.4	1.9	0.5
1993	7.0	54	11.2	30.1	–2480	6741	10.9	10.9	1.7	0.3
1994	9.5	51	14.5	27.8	–3447	6896	9.3	9.4	1.6	0.2
1995	9.9	49	8.1	24.0	–4700	8309	8.0	9.5	1.1	0.1
1996	7.0	50	10.6	24.3	–5020	11575	8.2	9.9	1.1	0.1
1997	4.4	50	7.0	23.2	–3131	20,333	8.0	10.0	0.9	0.0
1998	5.0	49	8.6	23.5	–815	22,674	7.8	9.8	0.8	0.1
1999	3.8	48	1.3	26.0	–1676	22,515	7.7	10.0	0.7	0.1
2000	11.0	46	0.0	23.8	–1865	23,281	7.2	9.5	0.7	0.1
2001	–0.8	44	1.4	20.8	–1775	23,379	7.5	10.5	0.8	0.1
2002	–1.5	46	6.5	22.2	–1103	24,083	8.4	10.5	0.7	0.0
2003	1.4	47	–1.9	23.2	967	26,314	7.9	10.3	0.8	0.0
2004	6.7	47	1.2	23.3	2630	27,095	7.2	9.4	0.7	0.0
2005	4.9	44	2.4	22.9	4891	28,259	7.1	9.0	0.7	0.0
2006	6.9	42	–0.1	22.8	7293	29,055	7.3	8.9	1.1	0.0
2007	6.9	42	3.4	19.8	5800	28,460	6.6	8.7	0.8	0.0
2008	3.8	41	3.8	16.3	3085	42,513	6.4	8.7	0.8	0.0
2009	1.5	40	3.9	14.1	8077	61,545	6.1	9.7	0.6	0.0
2010	6.8	40	2.7	13.6	8140	70,913	5.9	9.1	0.5	0.0
2011	4.4	39	2.2	11.9	6831	75,154	5.6	8.8	0.5	0.0
2012	3.0	39	1.6	11.9	4251	75,906	5.6	9.1	0.7	0.0
2013	3.4	39	1.8	10.6	8474	80,589	5.5	9.0	0.7	0.0
2014	2.7	40	–0.2	9.6	11234	86,101	5.6	8.9	0.7	0.0

Notes

1 Source: Central Bureau of Statistics.

2 Source: 1960–1979: Calculated from Central Bureau of Statistics data; Years 1980–2014: Bank of Israel Statistical Bulletin 2014.

3 Source: Bank of Israel.

4 Source: Bank of Israel.

5 Sources: Central Bureau of Statistics.

6 Source: Bank of Israel.

7 Source: Central Bureau of Statistics.

8 1965–1979: payments include compulsory loans and imputed civilian and defense pensions. Source: Bank of Israel. Annual Report 2015, Table 6.A.11.

9 Source: Bank of Israel.

10 Source: Bank of Israel.

power of these groups enabled them to put pressure on the Treasury to further expand subsidies (Bichler and Nitzan, 2001; Shalev, 1998).

The government also financed the creation of a large military-industrial sector, which grew rapidly after the Six-Day War. The military-industrial sector tripled in terms of employees between 1966 and 1985 and military export expanded 76-fold during the same period.[6] Hence, the military became a powerful interest group, not only in terms of its size, but also in terms of its strategic position and perceived importance by policy-makers and the public.

The fiscal crisis, therefore, was not only an economic crisis but also a political crisis. The crisis has been explained as state exhaustion: the disintegration of the state's capacity to resist power groups' demand to allocate resources in their favor (Maman and Rosenhek, 2012; Shalev, 1992) or as populism (Razin, forthcoming). But it can also be explained as *state over-extension*: the state was not able to prioritize its objectives, and it tried to achieve objectives, which were beyond its financial capacities. In the 1970s, the government sought to build and sustain its military power, to sustain its external economic position and to finance a welfare state. This resulted in a large budget financed by foreign financial support, loans and monetary expansion.

Creeping problems

Two policy problems were creeping during the 1970s. The first problem had a strong visibility and it was experienced in everyday life and therefore it attracted most attention: inflation.

Before elaborating further on the issue of inflation, it must be kept in mind that, in the 1970s, inflation was not considered as dangerous phenomenon as it has been since the 1980s. Most advanced countries suffered from inflation levels of between 10–20 percent and inflation levels among developed countries were even higher.[7] Inflation was perceived as but one among several other issues policy-makers should be worried about.

In Israel, inflation rose incrementally throught the 1970s and until 1985: it peaked to around 40 percent annually in 1973 due to the oil shock and the expenses of the Yom Kippur War. Then, the failed attempt of Simha Erlich to liberalize capital control (more about it below) was followed by another step upwards to around 70 percent. The second oil shock of 1979 pushed inflation to around 120 percent and finally, in 1983, the government made an attempt to narrow the balance of payments deficit through a devaluation of the lira, which resulted in another inflation boost to more than 400 percent annually (Bruno, 1997); see also, Table 9.1.)

Over the years, several explanations have been offered as to the hyperinflation in Israel but no consensus has emerged (Liviatan and Piterman, 1986).[8] The debate split the community of economists into two epistemic camps, which were often identified by the academic affiliation of their members: the Tel Aviv professors, who advocated an orthodox interpretation of the crisis and a small group of professors from the Hebrew University in Jerusalem and from the Bank of Israel, who advocated a heterodox interpretation based on institutional theories.

The Tel Aviv professors argued that the main cause of inflation was the high level of public spending and the large budget deficit, which reached 14.5 percent in 1984 (Razin, 1985; Razin *et al.*, 1985). This interpretation—the fundamentalist interpretation—assigned the causes of the crisis to deficient fiscal policy, which resulted from the incapacity of the state to confront powerful societal and market actors.[9] The fundamentalist camp included mainly economists from the Tel Aviv University such as Assaf Razin and Elhanan Helpman, and therefore, in the media they were called "the Tel Aviv Professors," but their views were also supported by the American economist Herbert Stein and by his political patron, the Secretary of State, George Shultz. The fundamentalist thesis did not have supporters within the policy-making circles for obvious reasons: this interpretation implied that *any* effective response to the crisis would entail a massive cut in public spending.

As the crisis deepened, a smaller group of economists, consisting of Nissan Liviatan and Sylivia Piterman from the Bank of Israel, Michael Bruno and Stanley Fischer—offered an alternative causal explanation of the crisis, based on the notion of "inflation inertia": due to certain institutional factors, they argued, the Israeli economy was locked in a quasi-equilibrium of high inflation. The institutional features included wage indexations and expectations of further devaluation of the currency (Bruno and Fischer, 1984; Liviatan and Piterman, 1986). The debate between the Tel Aviv and the Jerusalem group of economists was intense and it continued even after the government approved Bruno's plan (Eshet, 1986).

Along with the problem of inflation, the government had to deal with another problem, which was less visible in everyday life, but was actually more critical: Israel's external economic position. A country's external economic position is defined here in terms of three variables: (1) the current account balance; (2) external debt; and (3) foreign currency reserves. These three variables are linked: a deficit in the current account requires the government to borrow more abroad, hence increasing its external debt or alternatively to use its foreign currency reserves to cover the shortfall.

The deterioration of Israel's external position was manifested in the steady expansion of its foreign debt: from a level of 21 percent of GDP in 1965, it had reached 80 percent by 1985. During the same period, foreign currency reserves dwindled from an equivalent of 6 import months to a level equivalent to about 2.5 import months in 1975. After a period of recovery, reserves deteriorated again to 2.5 import months by 1984 (BoI Annual Report, various years; see also Table 9.1.) The deficit in the current account fluctuated periodically and each time it worsened—in 1970, 1975 and 1983—the government responded by devaluing the currency and providing increased subsidies. When the current account improved, the response was unsurprisingly followed by a period of higher levels of inflation.

Handling such a high level of debt has economic costs—namely, the interest payments—but also political costs. The deterioration of a country's external economic position diminishes its capacity to make autonomous choices vis-à-vis political pressure from its creditors, and it puts the country at increased risk of a debt crisis or even a default. For a country that faces continuous national security threats, the risk of losing its capacity to make autonomous choices poses an existential risk.

National security interest and the United States

For a small country in a permanent state of war preparedness, every policy issue is also a national security policy issue. No significant policy decision is made in Israel, without considering its implication on national security. This was also the case when the government had to make a decision regarding the Stabilization Plan.

After the 1967 Arab–Israeli War, successive Israeli governments increased military spending significantly. The occupation of the West Bank, the Gaza Strip, the Sinai Peninsula and the Golan Heights expanded the workload and area of operations of the army. Not only did it now have to defend longer borders, but it also had the responsibility to implement Israel's Military Governorate in the occupied territories.

The Yom Kippur War, despite the fact that it ended with an Israeli military victory, was perceived as a traumatic experience that justified further military spending. During the 1970s and up until 1985, Israel had enjoyed a steady flow of civil and military financial aid from the United States, the total sum of which grew from a few million dollars annually during the 1960s, to above $3 billion annually by 1985 (Sharp, 2016). The United States has never spelled out specific conditions for this aid, but as we shall see below, informal conditions were applied.

After Israel's invasion of South Lebanon in Operation Peace for Galilee (1982), which soon turned into a war, voices within and outside the military establishment started to question the justification of Israel's high military spending: is it that the defense budget finances necessary security needs, or that it creates incentives for unnecessary wars? The demand to reconsider the defense budget intensified as a growing number of economists pointed out that there was a trade-off between Israel's prevailing national security strategy and the need to address its economic problems. The economics professor, Eitan Berglas of Tel Aviv University, who was also involved in the design of the Stabilization Plan, argued that the government had not yet found "an economic solution that would enable it to maintain simultaneously high military spending, price stability and a reasonable size of trade deficit" (Berglas, 1984, p. 65). Yaacov Arnon, former Director General of the Ministry of Finance, was more straightforward, arguing that Israel had lost the balance between carrying its security burden and maintaining a strong economy and a healthy society. This imbalance, he argued, "impairs all fields of life in the country." He concluded that only "a peace with the Palestinian people, would be able to bring equilibrium and secure the real independence of Israel" (Arnon, 1984, p. 160). Amnon Neubach, former Deputy

Director of the Budgets Department and Peres' advisor, explained: "The military burden has reached the point in which it very well may be that the country cannot carry it anymore" (1984, p. 184).

Hence, there was growing concern among experts and technocrats that the Israeli security model was not sustainable due to its socio-economic toll. One must keep in mind, however, that military spending also contributed indirectly to the achievement of socio-economic objectives. A decade of high military spending created a military-industrial sector that employed a quarter of all industrial workers in Israel and produced over US$1 billion in exports (Mintz, 1985, p. 623). Hence, taking an axe to the defense budget had security, economic and political expected costs.

The debate concerning Israel's military needs among academics took a political twist when these ideas penetrated the policy-making circles. As early as 1978, Peres had expressed his belief that the Middle East was in a process of transition from a state of war and an arms race to a state of cooperation and economic development. Therefore, he called for "building an infrastructure for economic cooperation between us and the Jordanians and the inhabitants of Judea and Samaria" (Peres, 1978, p. 12). Peres believed that the Middle East would be stabilized eventually through economic cooperation and by ties between business sectors of the countries in the region (Keren, 1994). The Likud Party signing a peace treaty with Egypt in March, 1979, was a milestone in what could have been interpreted as a realization of Peres' vision. Amnon Neubach argues that when the government made the decision on the Stabilization Plan, Peres perceived it as an element in Israel's "new profile," which was presented a few years later in his book on the *New Middle East* (Peres, 1993; see also, Ben Porat, 2005).[10]

In the unity government that was put together in September 1984, Peres, the prime minister, and Rabin, the defense minister, were in conflict over that issue. For Peres, a reduction in military spending was consistent with his broader vision of the New Middle East. Rabin, the former Chief of Staff, was more of a pragmatist and a realist. Despite the fact that he did not participate directly in the Yom Kippur War, the national trauma associated with the war was ingrained in his political DNA and he was genuinely concerned by the impact of the budget cuts on Israel's military preparedness. Michael Bruno writes in his notes that at the meeting of June 30, when the government approved the Stabilization Plan, Rabin "smoked like a steam engine" and "walked nervously in back and forth" (Bruno, 1985). Eventually, Rabin conceded after he and Peres agreed to share the ministerial responsibility for this decision.[11]

The government's approval of the Stabilization Plan was made in the same month the Israeli army completed its withdrawal from the South of Lebanon to a security zone along the border. According to Yagil Levi, the withdrawal from Lebanon and the Stabilization Plan were linked. He argued that vacating Lebanon

> enabled Israel to increase its financial aid from the United States, which had a key interest in terminating the war in Lebanon, which threatened the

> stability of the region … from another angle, the retreat enabled the government to make a dramatic cut in military spending, in addition to downscaling the military industry.
>
> (Levi, 2003, p. 162)

Hence, by 1985, Israel had many reasons to reconsider its high level of military spending: after signing a peace treaty with its most powerful enemy and after terminating a war that had lasted for three years, it was more difficult for the military establishment to justify the huge defense budget on the basis of military needs.

The capacity of Israel to maintain a high level of military spending also depended on the willingness of the United States to finance it. Until the war of 1967, support from the United States to Israel was negligible.[12] It was only after the war, when Israel proved that it was not a transitory player in the Middle East, that the American presidents, Lyndon Johnson and Richard Nixon, saw an opportunity to deepen American influence in the region to counter the growing influence of the Soviet Union. The United States assisted Israel to build and extend its military power, but it did not push Israel to reach a territorial compromise because this could have been interpreted as a triumph for the Soviet Union's allies in the region (Shlaim, 1996; Yaqub, 2007). At that stage, the interests of Israel and that of the United States overlapped, and financial assistance grew accordingly (Bar-Siman-Tov, 1998). Following the Yom Kippur War, Israel received a one-time financial aid package of US$2.5 billion, more than half of it as a grant. Since then Israel has regularly received annual packages of between US$1 billion to US$2 billion (Lifshitz, 2000, p. 481, Table 1). By the early 1980s, Israel was receiving a quarter of its annual foreign financial aid from the United States (Razin, 1984, p. 48; Svirski, 2005, p. 95).

Whereas the United States has never attached explicit strings to its financial aid to Israel, in the second half of the 1970s and throughout the 1980s, there were changes in the US soft power approach toward Israel. During the Nixon presidency, the United States saw in its support of Israel a counterbalancing act of the Soviet Union support of Syria and Egypt. However, later presidents sought to reposition the United States in the region as a neutral arbitrator. The Yom Kippur War resulted in a restoration of the diplomatic relationship between the United States and Egypt, which was then added to the list of foreign aid benefactors. The United States assumed that in order to keep the Soviet Union out of the Middle East, it must play the role of a mediator in the region. One of the successes of the new doctrine was the peace treaty signed between Begin and Sa'adat in 1979, with the mediation of President Carter. Nevertheless, Israel continued to enjoy privileged treatment based on its "special relations" with the United States.

During Ronald Reagan's first term, the Secretary of State Alexander Haig was in agreement with Israel's decision to invade Lebanon in 1982, and Reagan embraced this position. But as the operation dragged on and George Shultz replaced Haig, the dominant view within the Reagan administration shifted (Druks, 2001). Weinberger, the Secretary of Defense, and Shultz, despite differences in tone, shared the search for a "new and more secure international system" (Schultz, 1985). As for the Middle East, Shultz saw "signs of a new realism and a new commitment on the part of key regional actors." He believed that Peres would be a reliable ally in the endeavor to reach a peace agreement between Israel and Jordan. In 1985, Schultz invested much effort in enticing Peres and Hussein to negotiate:

> We are intensively engaged this year in encouraging our Israeli and Arab friends to take further steps toward peace. We will continue to support and encourage those who seek peace against those who promote violence and try to block all progress.
>
> (Schultz, 1985)

There are no simple and straightforward causal links between Israel's security and its economic interests and policies. Nevertheless, there were two channels through which the two policy areas were connected. The first channel was the role of the United States in the two policy areas: the United States had an interest in pacifying the Middle East and therefore in scaling down Israeli military power. These interests were consistent with the assumption that the solution to Israel's economic malaise required a budget cut, including a cut in military spending. The second channel was the belief among Israeli policy-makers and technocrats that Israel's security strategy, based on a high level of military spending was simply not sustainable.

The liberalization of 1977

On the evening of May 17, 1977, the public broadcasting services announced that for the first time in 29 years, the Labor Party—*Ha'ma'arach*—did not come first in the general elections having lost almost 40 percent of its seats in the Knesset and ending up as the second largest party, having won only 32 seats. The Likud Party came first with 43 seats, four seats more than in the previous Knesset. It was on this evening of the political revolution (*Ha'ma'ha'pach*), as it was called in the media, that the story of the Stabilization Plan begins.

The Likud Party was formed on the basis of a merger of several parties, the largest of which were the Herut Party (the Freedom Party) and the Liberal Party. Herut's key policy agenda was its advocacy of a "Greater Israel" national vision, which practically implied the annexation of the occupied territories and an acceleration of settlements behind the "green line"—the borders prior to the Six-Day War. The Liberal Party promoted economic freedom, individual rights and free market practices. What brought a nationalist and a liberal party together was their common enemy: the Labor Party. Until the 1970s, both parties had been marginal players in the Israeli political system and they had to join forces in order to offer an alternative to the Labor Party (Plessner, 1994).

It was not the socio-economic issues that ended the long reign of the Labor Party, as during the 1970s, despite the low growth rate, the average citizen and the powerful interest groups had no reason to seek change. Whereas there were first signs of a political upheaval among the Mizrahi Jews in the periphery, these signs were not yet manifested in the voting patterns. The cracks in the hegemony of the Labor Party were caused by what was perceived by many as a military fiasco in the Yom Kippur War. The Israeli army eventually succeeded in pushing the Egyptian and Syrian armies back out of Israeli territory, but the toll in terms of dead and wounded was enormous. A commission of inquiry headed by Justice Shimon Agrant exonerated the political echelon from direct responsibility and put the blame on the military echelon. However, voters thought differently: in the election of 1977 almost a third of the Labor Party's voters punished the Labor Party and voted for a newly established party, *the Democratic Party for Change* (Dash), which gained 15 seats in the Knesset. The split within the center-left camp paved the way for the Likud's victory. In ensuing years the Likud Party stabilized its position by attracting voters who supported the party's Greater Israel political vision. The Likud also became a political home for Mizrachi Jews from the periphery, who had lost faith in the Labor Party (Plessner, 1994, p. 220).

One of the first initiatives of the new Likud government, which was sworn in at the president's residence on June 20, 1977, was to implement its liberal socio-economic platform. Simha Erlich, the leader of the Likud's liberal faction, was nominated as the minister of finance, and he played a leading role in the process. Two issues were particularly dear to Erlich. The first was the budget: he planned to implement a deep budget cut of 4 percent of GDP, a third of which came by cutting military spending (*Davar*, 1977a, 1977b). The second issue was the termination of the selective credit controls, a major policy instrument used by Israeli governments to allocate credit to subsidize preferential sectors and businesses (Lipkin, 1977). Erlich also sought to reduce subsidies for basic goods. He expressed his conviction that there should be "one rule for all productive sectors" (*Davar*, 1977c). "We," the Likud Party, he explained, "promote a regime based on free initiative, reduction of government intervention … and prioritization of support to private capital investment over public capital investment" (Erlich, 1977).

Erlich wanted to liberalize the Israeli economy in one stroke. The weakness of his approach was that he confronted all the major power groups in the Israeli political economy simultaneously, without having built a sufficiently powerful supportive coalition. He put himself on a collision course with exporters, manufacturers, workers and the military. The *Davar* newspaper reported that "senior officers" in the Israeli Defense Force were "surprised" by the decision to cut the defense budget and they expressed concerns that it would impact the "essential needs" of the military (*Davar*, 1977d). The former Chief of Staff and the MP, Lieutenant General Haim Barlev said to the press that the cut will "have a negative impact on equipment and training" (Eshed, 1977). General Secretary of the Histadrut Yeruham Meshel decided on a one-hour strike and emergency meetings as a protest against the minister's decision (Magen, 1977). Even the Governor of the Bank of Israel opposed the idea to cut the development budget (*Davar*, 1977e).

The intensive resistance to the plan prevented Erlich from implementing it and he tried an alternative approach: rather than starting with the "fundamentals"—the budget—he tried to liberalize the financial system, including capital control. The upside of this approach was that financial liberalization could be executed quickly and without political resistance. On October 28, the government devalued the Israeli lira by 47 percent vis-à-vis the US dollar and three days later Erlich announced in the Knesset the government's decision on "a broad liberalization of foreign exchange" (Knesset, October 31, 1977). The "economic revolution"—as the decision was portrayed in the media—consisted of three elements. First, liberalization of capital controls: any person or individual has the right to purchase, sell in Israel or outside it foreign currency. Second, a unification of the exchange rate: the government will not sell foreign currency to or purchase it from exporters at special rates to subsidize exports. There will be only one exchange rate for all. Finally, the Israeli lira was officially floated: the price of foreign currency in Israel would be determined by demand and supply.

Erlich's liberalization endeavor was an ambitious move that failed. In hindsight, economists have pointed out the flaws in Erlich's reform: he exposed a small and unstable economy to global financial markets, without fixing the "fundamentals" first. Current account liberalization, therefore, put the economy into disarray. Yakir Plessner argues that "nobody had a very clear idea as to what liberalization meant and what it was supposed to accomplish" (1994, p. 221).

However, the negative assessment of Erlich's plan must be qualified by examining it within its historical context. During the late 1970s and early 1980s, capital control liberalization was a global trend. Many countries liberalized capital control, but at the time there was not yet enough experience with the outcome of this process. The fate of Israel was not unique. The situation is explained by Eric Helleiner:

> "Vicious" circles of disequilibrium afflicted countries pursuing expansionary policies. A vicious circle began when overzealous global financial traders suddenly lost confidence in a country's economic policy, causing an exaggerated depreciation of its currency. This exchange rate "overshooting" exacerbated domestic inflation, leading to further loss of confidence and a self-reinforcing downward spiral that could be stopped only by a tough austerity program designed to restore market confidence.
>
> (1996, pp. 123–124)

Hence, the assessment of Erlich's "failure" must take into account the fact that he followed an international trend of capital control liberalization. The global trend made it increasingly difficult for any small country to sustain its export-led growth through periodic devaluations of the currency.

Moreover, it must be kept in mind that Erlich was not a technocrat, who simply tried to solve an economic problem. Rather, Erlich was driven by a genuine liberal conviction. For him, economic liberalization was not only designed to "optimize" welfare and improve efficiency. For him, liberalization had an inherent value in itself: citizens, Erlich believed, should be free to make certain economoic choices (see discussion in Schiffman *et al.*, forthcoming Chapter 4).

Most of Erlich's policy decisions were annulled within the next few years. As Yoram Ben Porat put it, "At the end of the period not much was left from the liberal economic path. We are facing an erosion and even a change of direction in the reforms that were originally congruent with the liberal platform" (1982, p. 325). But the events of 1977 had a long-lasting consequence. Erlich's "economic revolution," so to speak, "punctuated" the institutional equilibrium resulting in the crisis deepening. The institutional equilibrium was punctuated in the sense that once the government liberalized capital controls, the government was no longer capable of fully restoring the old regime. Whereas formally it tried to restore capital control, in practice, the public had lost faith in the official Israeli currency, and for many purposes the US dollar became an alternative means of payment. This was done either illegally or through dollar denominated accounts (PATAM). In that sense, Erlich's policy played a precipitating role in respect to the Stabilization Plan: its failure created the conditions and the demand for another plan that would shift the Israeli economy to a new "institutional equilibrium."

However, Erlich's plan had another long-lasting impact: it was a lesson to Israeli economists and policy-makers that the Israeli economy cannot be simply "liberalized" by lifting restrictions and regulations.

The process of liberalization—in the technocratic sense of the term—required intensifying state capacities and the creation of new forms of state intervention. This was particularly true in Israel, where the state had critical policy objectives, which it deemed of strategic importance. As we shall see below, in the following years, economists and policy-makers were more cautious in applying to Israel textbook-style economic reform proposals. The more heterodox ones were not only more effective, but they were also more consistent with the policy culture of economic control as well as with the state's preferences.

The package deals

In the first half of the 1980s, economic conditions further deteriorated. The current account deficit deepened markedly from US$481 million in 1977 to US$2.4 billion in 1983. External debt grew from 59 percent of GDP to 75 percent in 1984. Foreign reserves, after improving up to 1982 and reaching US$4.3 billion shrank again to US$3.3 billion in 1984 (Table 9.1). Inflation jumped from 137 percent annually in the third quarter of 1983 to 487 percent in the fourth quarter and then to 567 percent in the fourth quarter of 1984 (Bank of Israel, 1984, p. 46, Table Gimel-1). These numbers represent a simple fact: the economy was out of control. It was clear, therefore, that the primary task of the Labor-Likud unity government that was sworn in on September 13, 1984, was to address the economic crisis. The question was how.

Any economic plan had to satisfy two conditions: it had to be economically effective and it has to be politically viable. The Peres/Shamir unity government, with Moda'i as the minister of finance and Rabin as the minister of defense, had to come up with a plan that would satisfy the Americans and would be acceptable by the Histadrut, the manufacturers and the military establishment. Within these constraints, the government tried to reach an arrangement—a package deal—that would be accepted by all actors involved and that would be able to stabilize the economy.

The dependence of Israel on the United States deepened due to the financial crisis. By October 1984, when Peres visited Washington, he knew already that the promised American financial aid for the fiscal year 1985/6 would not suffice and therefore he handed in a request for an additional emergency grant. George Shultz, the Secretary of State, refused the request until serious economic reforms were implemented (Gwertzman, 1984a, 1984b).

Shultz requested a deep budget cut that if implemented would mean the government would have to face resistance from the military establishment, exporters, manufacturers and the workers. This was the domestic constraints within which the government operated. Peres and Moda'i had to come up with a policy solution that satisfied three criteria: it had to be effective; it had to satisfy the Americans; and it had to satisfy the Histadrut, the manufacturers and the exporters. It was not clear, though, if such a plan existed.

The first choice of the government was to put together a package deal in cooperation with the Histadrut and the Coordinating Chamber of the Economic Organizations, which represented the employers.[13] The rationale for the package deal assumed that for any given size of budget cut, the burden would have to be distributed between employers—exporters and manufacturers—and the workers: employees had to give up basic goods subsidies and had to accept real wage decrease, manufacturers and exporters would make concession concerning subsidies and prices. The government then had to decide how to distribute the budget cut within the ministries: principally, between the ministries of Defense, Health and Education.

Another actor that had to be reckoned with was the professional economists. When the first package deal was signed in November, it included a budget cut of US$500 million. The deal attracted criticism from a group of professors from Tel Aviv University, who sent the government a public letter, arguing that any budget cut lower than US$2 billion would not suffice (Zinger, 1984). The Tel Aviv professors represented a "fundamentalist" interpretation of the crisis, which assumed the key and underlying cause of the crisis was the government's high level of public spending and high budget deficit. Therefore, only a drastic spending cut would stabilize the economy.

Moda'i, on the other hand—as well as most of the policy-makers in the government—believed the key problem was Israel's external economic position: the current account deficit, the foreign reserves and the external debt. The package deal was necessary, he explained, "not because of the level of inflation, which is indeed high," but to "divert resources from private and public consumption to export." This was, he argued, "the whole economic theory of the state of Israel today" (Knesset, January 28, 1985).

However, even if Moda'i interpretation is accepted, the package deal had several major drawbacks from a political perspective. First, it consisted of voluntary agreements between the government, the Histadrut and the manufacturers, which were supposed to last—even if they were adhered to—only a few months. Therefore, they were not able to provide a long-lasting solution. Once the period of the agreement finished, the government had to go through the whole process again. Moreover, the package deals lacked a mechanism that committed the parties to the agreement. Any party could have withdrawn at any point, without any effective sanctions. For example, the second package deal signed in January 1985, was quite tough, but it was not executed because both the manufacturers and the Histadrut reneged. As early as February 1985, merely a month later, the manufacturers threatened to withdraw from the deal (*Haaretz*, 1985a). In May 1985, Eli Horowitz, the president of the Manufacturers Association declared that the Association was going to withdraw from the agreement if the government did not implement a deeper cut to its budget and increase subsidies to the productive sectors and exporters (Sherman, 1985). This implies that the package deal did not include a commitment mechanism to force the government to implement its part of the deal.

Another political drawback was that it did not satisfy the Americans. Schultz opposed the package deal approach on two grounds. First, because he sought a deeper budget cut, and, second, because he did not trust the Israeli government had the capacity to implement it. He wanted a guarantee for a long-lasting institutional change.

Shultz, Stein and Fischer

George Shultz was nominated as the US Secretary of State on July 16, 1982, after the resignation of Alexander Haig. Shultz had a more dovish perception of the situation in the Middle East than Haig and he believed that it was in the interests of the United States to push Israel into a territorial compromise with its neighbors. Moreover, Shultz believed that as long as Israel struggled with a major economic crisis, it would not be able to make a long-term political decision regarding its borders.

In early 1983, Shultz created a special advisory group, which included Israeli and American economists and policy-makers. The purpose of the group was to serve as an instrument of soft power: building trust between American and Israeli economists and policy-makers around common economic policy roadmap. On the side of Israel, the group included the Director General of the Ministry of Finance, Emanuel Sharon, Eytan Berglas from the Tel Aviv University, Nissan Liviatan from the Bank of Israel, and Eytan Sheshinski of the Hebrew University. On the American side, the group included Stanley Fischer and Herbert Stein (Fischer, 1995). After a long period of preparations, the group convened in October 1984, on the occasion of Peres' visit in Washington, and it received a formal title, the *Joint Economic Development Group* (JEDG).

The purpose of Peres' visit to Washington was to discuss Israel's request for additional financial aid, beyond the promised US$2.6 billion grant—US$1.4 billion in civil aid and US$1.2 billion in military aid—for the 1985 fiscal year (Gwertzman, 1984a). Shultz declined to make any promises as the package deal that was about to be signed did not satisfy him.

Reading American sources—in comparison to Israeli ones—one gets the impression that within the American political system the crisis was perceived as a more urgent threat to Israel than it was perceived by the Israeli policy-makers. A report of the Senate Foreign Relations Committee pointed out that "if not swiftly and effectively addressed," the economic crisis can "pose as serious a threat to the security of Israel as any hostile neighbor in the region" (*New York Times*, 1984). The Senate report made a point of emphasizing Israel's huge defense budget, which stood at 20 percent of GDP, in comparison to 6.8 percent in the United States and 1 percent in Japan, according to the report.

Shultz took advantage of the mood in the Congress and put pressure on it to postpone the approval of Israel's emergency financial aid until early April (Austin, 1985). The Chairman of the Subcommittee on Appropriations Foreign Operations, David R. Obey, supported Shultz's concerns, arguing that "I don't happen to think that increasing dependence by Israel on the United States is in their interest or ours" (ibid.). However, when Shultz realized that the Congress was likely to approve the grant in any case, he withdrew his opposition but did his best to postpone the actual transfer of the funds.

In the meantime, the economic situation in Israel was deteriorating. The publication of the April Consumer Price Index—rising at 19.4 percent monthly—indicated that the second package deal had failed. At the end of the month, the International Monetary Fund (IMF) released a highly critical report on the Israeli economy, which stated that the government debt of Israel was approaching 150 percent of GDP and that the public was losing confidence in the government's ability to stabilize the economy. The report called for doubling the budget cut to US$2 billion, to eliminate import duties, export subsidies and to execute a 20 percent devaluation of the currency (Bare'el, 1985). The IMF report was a signal to Israeli policy-makers what kind of policies they would have to implement, had the United States declined the emergency grant and if they had to apply for a loan from the IMF.

Shultz was careful not to set explicit conditions for the Israeli government, but he went a long way to make Israeli policy-makers realize that they must be the ones to take action. In March, at the end of the JEDG's visit to Israel, Herbert Stein handed in an unofficial document to his Israeli counterparts. The document, entitled "Herb's Ten Points" was leaked and was published in the news (Box 9.1). The Ten Points included a set of policy recommendations. Besides the demand for a deep budget cut and the elimination of subsidies, the Ten Points included directives designed to serve as a commitment mechanism which would force the government—and any future government—to follow the same policy direction: the Ten Points included recommendations to upgrade the independence of the central bank, which would be mandated to pursue price stability. These directives reflected the American conviction that only a legally independent central bank would be able to make a government keep its promises.

The publication of Stein's Ten Points caused uproar among the manufacturers, who were worried about abolishing subsidies to exporters, and eventually the Americans made a concession on that point. It must be noted that Stanley Fischer distanced himself from the document and he explained that the Ten Points were Stein's proposals about which he knew nothing in advance (Fischer, 1995, p. 7). This point is important because, as will be shown below, Fischer had different ideas regarding the best way to handle the crisis.

When the JEDG team arrived for another visit in early June, the economic indicators demonstrated the failure of the government to improve the situation through package deals. Of particular concern was the fact that Israel continued to lose foreign reserves and that it was on the road to a default unless an injection of foreign reserves from the United States was to be supplied. Whereas by that time the US Congress had officially approved the special grant and despite the fact that Shultz did not make any formal conditions, the combination of the deteriorating conditions and Shultz's tough love approach were sufficient to tip the balance in favor of the Stabilization Plan (Fischer, 1995; *Haaretz*, 1985d). It was therefore agreed to create a special team, consisting of Emanuel Sharon, Mordecai Frenkel, Head of the Bank of Israel's Research Department, Amnon Neubach who was Peres' Economic Advisor, Michael Bruno and Eytan Berglas to devise a plan (Fischer, 1995).

Box 9.1 The Ten Points

1. The government will adopt an inflation target as a commitment for fiscal year 1985–1986 with the agreement of the social partners.
2. The budget targets will be specified in real shekel terms for each quarter.
3. The budget law will be passed.
4. The Bank of Israel law will be passed.
5. The Bank of Israel will accept the government inflation target as its goal.
6. The Bank of Israel will conduct monetary policy in accord with the inflation target.
7. The effective real exchange rate will not be appreciated.
8. The government will express its intention to make the government debt tradeable.
9. The government will express its intention to reduce the control and subsidization of credit.
10. The government's intention to reform the PATAM system will be understood.

Source: Stein, 1985

Liviatan, Bruno and Fischer

Herb Stein's Ten Points were based on an orthodox economic rationale, which was very similar to that advocated by the Tel Aviv professors. According to this rationale, the high level of inflation in Israel was caused by irresponsible fiscal policy: high taxes, high public spending and too large a deficit. The solution, therefore, is simple: cut the budget as much as the government can, lower taxes and narrow the deficit. According to this approach, the government had to cut the budget by US$2 billion, which represented around 6 percent of GDP. In addition, this would have required the elimination of subsidies to basic consumer goods and to exporters.

For the historical context, it must be kept in mind that up until the 1980s the export subsidy was endorsed also by those economists and policy-makers, who criticized the intervention of the government in the economy for other purposes. Even the academic economists from the Hebrew University—the students of Don Patinkin—who harshly attacked the government for its intervention in the labor market, did not oppose subsidies to exporters.[14] There was a broad consensus among policy-makers and economists that exports were too strategically critical to be handled by market forces alone.

Therefore, the problem the government had with Stein's points was that they undermined two essential state strategic preferences: promoting trade and maintaining Israel military position in the Middle East. The government, therefore, needed an alternative plan that could stabilize the economy, appease Shultz, and would enable it to secure its core interests: promoting export and keeping its national security interests.

An alternative plan was eventually handed to the government by Michael Bruno, who is considered the "architect" of the Stabilization Plan. The Stabilization Plan took shape gradually by annexing ideas and policy practices from different economists and policy-makers. Bruno, however, was closer to the political establishment of the Labor Party, and therefore he enjoyed the confidence of Shimon Peres.

Bruno's plan was put together over a period of almost two years. The origin of the plan can be traced back to a lecture that Nissan Liviatan, an economist at the Bank of Israel, gave in November 1983 at the seminar of the Economics Department of the Hebrew University, entitled "Dollarization as a Monetary Reform." The lecture was later published in *The Economic Quarterly* (Liviatan, 1984). In his lecture, Liviatan made a controversial claim: "theoretically speaking, there is no simple link between the size of the government budget deficit and the inflation rate" (Liviatan, 1983, p. 4). What, then, was the cause of inflation? Liviatan offered an explanation based on "inflation inertia": Inflation inertia, he argued, was caused due to the government's periodic attempts to boost exports, the indexation of wages to the cost of living and the adjustment of public expectations to this vicious cycle. Each time the government devalued the currency to support exporters, prices rose and wages followed.

Liviatan's argument had grave political implications: if there is no direct causal link between the size of the budget and inflation, then inflation could be brought down, with a much smaller budget cut than expected by the orthodox analysis. How then would inflation be contained? This would be done by the erection of a credible monetary anchor. Liviatan suggested using the US dollar as an anchor by fixing the Israeli shekel exchange rate to it: this "will lower inflation to the level of the inflation in the United States," and it would not require the use of administrative and coercive powers which "undermine the foundation of the liberal regime" (ibid., p. 5). Liviatan, in fact, revitalized Yoram Aridor's plan for the dollarization of the Israeli economy, which was made public in October 1983 (Liviatan, 1984). Liviatan's idea was the origin of a deep split between the economists in Israel, between the "Tel Aviv professors" and the "Jerusalem camp."[15]

Michael Bruno picked up on the idea of inflation inertia, and two months later he wrote a proposal: "Stabilization without Dollarization." This plan, explained Bruno, was based on the same "philosophy" as Liviatan's dollarization proposal, but it "differs in several very central points" (Bruno, 1984). Bruno suggested fighting inflation inertia by other means: a reform of the central bank law and by introducing a new currency, the Sela (Rock, in Hebrew), which would be fixed to the dollar for one year. Bruno also suggested fixing prices and wages by administrative means and in cooperation with the Histadrut. According to his calculation, the plan required a budget cut, but not as deep as the orthodox plan demanded: a budget cut was needed, he wrote, "even if not a big one … both for the balance of payment and as an 'example' for the public" (ibid.).

In the spring of 1984, Stanley Fischer was a Visiting Professor at the Economics Department of the Hebrew University. Bruno and Fischer were invited to contribute a paper to a volume about the Israel economy edited by Yoram Ben Porath. Their article, which was published also as an NBER Working Paper, reiterated the idea of inflation inertia. The article argued that contrary to the orthodox economic view, for a similar level of public spending, there are multiple levels of inflation due to the "meta-stable equilibrium" that is caused by indexation, the financial structure, and the exchange rate system (Bruno and Fischer, 1984, p. 2). As Bruno put it elsewhere, "For a given budget deficit the economy can be in one of two equilibria: one of high inflation and one of low inflation." Therefore, "the path from high to low inflation does not go through a budget cut" (quoted in Eshet, 1986).

Bruno's Emergency Stabilization Plan was presented to the government on June 30 was based on this philosophy. The plan included a budget cut of US$500 million, far less than the US$2 billion recommended by the Tel Aviv professor and the Americans (Box 9.2). In addition, the plan did not eliminate subsides to exporters. Therefore, the plan appealed to government members and the manufacturers. Bruno's plan put most of the burden on the workers: the devaluation of the currency, while fixing nominal wages and prices to the exchange rate implied a significant reduction of real wages. The plan also included a reduction of manpower in the public sector and a reduction of subsidies for basic goods. It may be

Box 9.2 Key elements of the Emergency Stabilization Plan

Objectives:

- Rapid reduction of the inflation rate.
- Increase of foreign currency reserves.

Instruments:

Fiscal aspects

- Budget cut:
    - 462 million dollars in government spending (annual terms) (20–25 percent—in public consumption and investment; 40 percent—subsidies to industry; 8–10 percent—transfer payment; 8–10 percent—credit; 18–20 percent—tax increase).
    - 75 million dollar cut of transfer payments of the National Insurance Institute.
- Reduction of manpower in the public sector by 3 percent.

Exchange rate:

- Unify exchange rates and a devaluation of 20 percent. Fixing the exchange rate to 1500 Israeli shekels per dollar.

Export and industry:

- Canceling of directed credit in local currency.
- Canceling of exchange rate insurance and the creation of a new arrangement that guaranteed constant subsidy to exporters of 11 percent for the dollar.

Prices and wages:

- Cutting subsidies to basic goods.
- One-time rise of basic good prices by 30–100 percent and a 17 percent of all goods on average. After that, prices freeze for 3 months through emergency ordinances.
- Real wage erosion.[A]
- Fixing nominal wage to exchange rate.

Capital markets:

- Encouraging the development of market for tradeable government bonds.
- Prohibition of opening new PATAM accounts (dollars denominated saving accounts).
- Encouraging long-term saving in the local currency.

Monetary policy:

- Restricting the nominal increase in the volume of credit through interest rate policy.
- Use reserve requirements and credit ceiling to restrict the growth of credit.
- Credit by higher reserve ratios and credit ceiling.
- Intervention of the Bank of Israel in the interest rate.

Sources: Bank of Israel, 1985; Government, 1985

Note

A The Histadrut claimed the original plan was to erode real wages by 40 percent. In early July, the government and the Histadrut reached an agreement that implied around a 10 percent erosion of real wages.

argued that to avoid making a deep budget cut, to avoid making a deep cut in the military budget and to avoid eliminating export subsidies, the government sacrificed the workers.

The Tel Aviv professors

Bruno's proposal faced harsh criticism from the Tel Aviv professors. The Tel Aviv professors had started to be involved—as a group—in the public discourse around September 1984, when the unity government negotiated the first package deal. Their key argument was that the economic crisis is a simple fiscal crisis caused by "bad fundamentals," that is, by the government overspending. Therefore, any solution to the crisis would have to include a budget cut of around US$2 billion (Singer, 1984a). The different interpretations of the crisis had policy implications. The Tel Aviv professors' approach did not require the use of administrative measures—coercion—in order to implement it. Moreover, as will be argued below, the predicted distributive consequences of the Tel Aviv professors' plan were less severe compared to Bruno's plan. That is, Bruno's plan put all the burden on the workers, whereas the Tel Aviv professors' plan put more burden on the government, as it implied deeper budget cuts.

Assaf Razin, who was the most active economist in the group, published numerous Op-Eds in the daily newspaper *Yedioth Ahronoth*, in which he preached for a smaller budget and a narrower deficit. In particular, Razin pointed out the need to cut military spending, following the signing of the peace treaty with Egypt. He also called for the cancellation of the Lavie project (Lion) undertaken by Israel Aircraft Industries (Amikam, 1984; Singer, 1984b).

It is common knowledge by now that Bruno's proposal was heterodox in the sense that it was not based on a "fundamentalist" interpretation of the crisis and in the sense that it put less weight on the need to cut the budget (Shiv, 2013). It is often tacitly assumed that "heterodox" economics are more "social" than "orthodox" economics in that their policy recommendations are more favorable to workers. This is, however, not necessarily the case. In the case of Bruno's

Stabilization Plan, it was expected to put more burden on the workers than the more orthodox plan advocated by the Tel Aviv professors.

Elhanan Helpman, also a professor at Tel Aviv University, commented on Bruno's proposal, arguing that it put too much burden on the workers. The success of the plan, he explained, depends on a "deep erosion of wages in order to improve the balance of payments." This is a risky policy, he argued, because "putting the main burden on the employees is perceived as unjust and may lead to an outburst in industrial relations" (Helpman, 1985). Helpman's interpretation is supported by Emanual Sharon, the Director General at the Ministry of Finance and one of the designers of the plan, when he explained why wages must be fixed to the exchange rate: "we don't have a choice but to do that if we want to secure the profitability of the exporters" (Government, 1985, p. 37). Mandelbaum, the Governor of the Bank of Israel, also confirmed this: the plan "is based to a large extent on the erosion of wages. The erosion guarantees the profitability of exports at a time when other subsidies to exports have been cancelled" (Dish, 1985a).

This analysis shines new light on the rationale of the Stabilization Plan. The plan reflected the choice of the government to prioritize exports and maintain a relatively high level of military spending. The government was able to prioritize these two objectives by forcing sacrifice upon the workers. This prioritization explains why Bruno's plan was chosen over the more orthodox proposals, which restricted the government capacity to spend and the capacity to support exporters.

Lock-in mechanism 1: emergency ordinances

The success of Bruno's plan hinged upon the capacity of the state to control wages and prices through administrative means. "Administrative means" is a euphemism, which conceals the use of coercion means which ranged from fines in the more benign cases to incarceration in other cases.

The underlying assumption of Bruno's plan—its "philosophy" as he put it (Bruno, 1984)—was that inflation was caused by institutional inertia created by a vicious circle of prices, wages and indexed contracts. This implied that the inflation could be brought down without as deep cuts as the orthodox approach dictated. To avoid the political, economic and social costs of austerity, Bruno suggested freezing prices and wages by employing the coercive power of the state. The practical implications of these measures are obviously inconsistent with liberal principles of economic freedom and private property rights. Moreover, this approach implied that the government would have to retreat from the then common practice of negotiating with the Histadrut on wage setting, subsidies of basic goods and layoffs in the public sector.

This was the first time in Israel's history, in which the government dared to use—or to threatened to use—emergency ordinances in order to settle disputes with the workers. Government members who participated in the meeting of June 30 did not take this point lightly. The legal advisor of the government, Itzhak

Zamir, pointed out that "this is the most radical instrument in the inventory of the Jurist. In essence, this is an undemocratic instrument" (Government, 1985, p. 162).

Once the plan was announced, the Histadut fought fiercely against it. The immediate reaction was an announcement of strikes all over the country, on the grounds that the state had withdrawn from signed agreements. The Histadrut also announced that the managers of the Workers Corporations' companies—companies owned by the Histadrut which comprised one-fifth of the economy—would provide cost-of-living allowances despite the directives of the government, even if it meant breaking the law: "The managers of our firms must obey the decisions of the Trade Union," announced the Histadrut leaders (Maariv, 1985a). They also tried appealing to employers' representatives and called on them to honor existing agreements and pay cost-of-living allowances. The employers responded by pointing out that this would be illegal and that any employer who collaborated with the Histadrut could expect imprisonment (Fleisher, 1985a).

Bruno, concerned by the reaction of the Histadrut, admitted that the plan put too much burden on workers, suggested accepting part of the Histadrut demands regarding wages and layoffs, in addition to a lowering of the taxes on labor and increasing taxes on capital profit. This would entail, however, cutting the budget by an additional US$250 million (Kessler, 1985; Makel, 1985a).

However, at that point, the political situation within the government did not allow for such a decision. The Histaderut's fierce struggle resulted in an impasse within the government: Peres was more sympathetic to the Histadrut's demands, whereas Moda'i was not willing to move an inch. Peres, as the prime minister, decided not to activate the emergency ordinances and instead he tried to reach an agreement with the Histaedrut on wages and dismissals. Moda'i, on the other hand, dug his heels in and threatened to resign if the government did not implement the plan as is (Lipkin, 1985a).

By early September, it seemed like the government would not be able to implement the plan. The plan was perhaps economically effective, but at this point it seemed as if the designers of the plan had not foreseen the implications of using emergency ordinances for wage setting, layoffs and price control. The use of state coercive powers to settle industrial relation disputes in an otherwise democratic society, was one step too far. The government did not dare to use the police force to impose the plan on the Histadrut and the workers. It turned out that the weapon the government held against the workers' heads—the emergency ordinances—was not loaded: using such measures against workers and their leaders was impractical at best and a political suicide of the government at worst.

Lock-in mechanism 2: the Bank of Israel

This was when the Bank of Israel stepped in. From August 1985 until the end of the year, the Bank conducted a highly contractionary monetary policy, which put the economy into recession: unemployment rose and numerous firms were brought to the brink of collapse. The governor announced that interest rates would come down only when the government implemented the budget cuts. The Bank pursued the policy until the Knesset passed the budget bill for the 1986/1987 fiscal year, when there were first signs of the stabilization of the economy.

The Stabilization Plan was a unique opportunity for the Bank of Israel to restore its prestige after several years in which its reputation had absorbed blow after blow. During the 1970s, as the government's budget deficit widened, the Bank of Israel had to finance it, while jeopardizing its reputation as an independent policy agency. The prestige of the Bank received a severe blow with the outbreak of the commercial banks' stocks crisis in 1983. The origin of the crisis can be traced back to the mid-1970s when the major commercial banks started manipulating the prices of their shares by soliciting customers to take credit for the purpose of purchasing the banks' own stocks. So long as this circular mechanism persisted, the performance of banks' shares was exceptional. To demonstrate, the annual yield of bank stocks reached 40 percent in 1980 (Blass and Grossman, 2001). In 1983, the public started selling large and ever-growing quantities of bank stocks and the banks were required to purchase these in order to maintain their share prices. Eventually, in October, the government intervened and offered an arrangement that included a nationalization of the banks involved and a partial guarantee of the value of the shares held by the public.

The commission of inquiry headed by the Supreme Court Justice Moshe Beisky, found the Governor of the Bank of Israel, Moshe Mandelbaum, personally responsible for the crisis (Beiski, 1986). Beiski's report was only published in April 1986. However, a dark cloud hovered above Mandelbaum's head before the publication of the formal report. Therefore, by July 1985, the Bank's reputation was very low. A further blow came in the form of a decision by the Knesset in March 1985 to tighten its control over the way the central bank handled its finances. The Bank faced allegations that its employees enjoyed unjustified financial benefits (*Haaretz*, 1985b; Knesset March 27, 1985).

At this lowest point in the Bank's history, the demand by Shultz, as stipulated in Stein's Ten Points, to reform the central bank's law was an opportunity for Moshe Mandelbaum, the governor, to restore the Bank's reputation. Shultz and Stein were not the first to raise the idea of changing the mandate of the central bank. The idea is attributed to the economist Yakir Plessner, who raised it in a memorandum submitted to the minister of finance, Yoram Aridor (Gross, 2007, p. 115). Aridor included a similar idea in his dollarization plan (Finance Committee, June 17, 1985). The idea was then developed by economists at the Research Department of the Bank of Israel and was included in a memorandum prepared in December 1983.[16] In January 1984, Michael Bruno included the idea in his proposal "Stabilization without Dollarization" (Bruno, 1984) and it resurfaced in December 1984, when Mandelbaum and Moda'i made it public (Maman and Rosenhek, 2011). Two months later, a US Congress report linked the reform of the Bank of Israel law and the approval of Israel's request for an emergency grant, and in March Stein included it in his Ten Points (*Haaretz*, 1985c).

Hence, the idea of upgrading the independence of the central bank had been circulating for quite some time. However, and this is a crucial point, there were different conceptions as to what exactly a more independent central bank meant. For example, Stein had in mind an independent central bank that pursued price stability, whereas for Bruno and Liviatan, the key purpose of the independent central bank was the fixing of the shekel to the US dollar. Eventually, Amendment 15 included only the directive that the bank must not lend money to the government, the "no printing law," as it is commonly called.

The "no printing law," or formally, Amendment 15 of the Bank of Israel Law, stated that "the bank will not provide loans to the government to finance its expenses" but only in special circumstance (Bank of Israel Law, Article 45-A). The bill did not raise any significant opposition in the Knesset, but several members of the Knesset were skeptical regarding the efficacy of the law. They claimed that the new amendment would be effective only to the extent the government and the Treasury would like it to be. Meaning, the law would not suffice if the government or the Treasury wanted to circumscribe it (Finance Committee, June 17, 1985).

Around August, less than a month after the "no printing law" bill passed, in the midst of the struggle between the Histadrut and the government, Mandelbaum pulled the monetary reins. Commercial banks' reserve requirements on short-term deposits were raised from 35 percent to 50 percent and reserves on long-term deposits from 13 percent to 43 percent. Real interest rates were around 20 percent annually (Dish, 1985a).[17]

The policy of the bank raised uproar. The President of the Trade Chamber Association, Dan Gilerman, described the policy as criminal behavior: "only the mafia in the United States charges as high an interest rate as the Bank of Israel does" (Fleisher, 1985b). The minister of the economy, Gad Yakobi, demanded Peres intervene and force the bank to lower interest rates (Lipkin, 1985b), while Ariel Sharon, the minister of trade and industry, warned of "destructive interest rates" (Dish, 1985b). Even Bruno questioned the policy of the bank (Maariv, 1985b). Mandelbaum did not blink and declared that as long as the government did not implement the promised budget cuts, interest rate would stay high (Fleisher, 1985c). The governor stated very clearly: "If the government doesn't make a deep enough budget cut, interest rate will stay high and the private sector will get hurt" (Makel, 1985b). Mandelbaum did not even try to soften the wording. From his perspective, the economy would be held hostage until the government was disciplined.

The pressure imposed by the governor forced the government into implementing the budget cut it had promised. Moreover, the bank continued putting pressure on the government until December, when the budget bill for the 1986/1987 fiscal year was passed. In mid-December the Consumer Price Index of November was published and provided an early indication of returning stability: the inflation rate was lowered to 0.5 percent monthly. Moreover, monthly public spending since the announcement of the plan was lowered by up to 20 percent compared to the previous month, due to the erosion of wages and a drastic reduction in subsidies. In November, foreign reserves expanded by US$850 million. The plan was deemed as a success.

There is no disagreement that the Bank of Israel was vital to the implementation of the plan. It was the only actor that was able—so the argument goes—to force the government to keep its promises. What was its source of power? It has been argued that the single most significant factor that upgraded the Bank's power was Amendment 15 to the Bank of Israel law. Haim Barkai and Nissan Liviatan argue that Amendment 15 was "a sine qua non condition for the success of the stabilization policy." The amendment, they argue, increased the bank's power and was "a bitter pill for the incumbent government, and the political community at large to swallow" (Barkai and Liviatan, 2007, pp. 64–65). Maman and Rosenhek also assign key significance to Amendment 15, portraying it as the "declaration of independence" of the Bank of Israel. They argue that "the amendment laid one of the foundation stones for the Bank of Israel's subsequent independence and strengthening" (Maman and Rosenhek, 2011, p. 67).

However, there are certain facts that run counter to this thesis, which explains the power of the bank mainly on the basis of Amendment 15. First, the policy instruments used by the Bank of Israel during the crisis—increasing the interest rate and the reserve requirement of commercial banks—were not mentioned in Amendment 15, which only prohibited the bank from lending to the government. The fact is that *formally* all policy measures used by the Bank of Israel in the second half of 1985 could have been used without Amendment 15. Therefore, the role of the bank in the execution of the Stabilization Plan cannot be fully explained on the basis of the formal change in the Bank's mandate.

Moreover, one may even argue that in fact the Bank of Israel breached its mandate: according to the Bank of Israel law (1954), the Bank must aim for the stabilization of the currency as well as to a high level of production, employment, growth, and investment. During the last quarter of 1985, the Bank deliberately caused a recession, with the intention of forcing the government to cut public spending. By so doing, the governor overstepped its mandate and he pursued an objective, which the bank was not supposed to pursue. The confidence of Mandelbaum, therefore, cannot be explained only on the basis of the formal change of the Bank's mandate.

If not the law, what, then, was the source of Mandelbaum's legitimacy? The alternative answer is that Mandelbaum responded to the expectations of the Americans and of certain figures within the government. The Bank of Israel's policy during the second half of 1985 was surprisingly congruent with Stein's Ten Points. Stein and Shultz expected the central bank to be used to force the government to keep its commitments and this was exactly what Mandelbaum did. Moreover, it is imprecise to argue that Mandelbaum "forced the government" to keep its promises. There were elements within the government that were fully supportive of the Bank's policy: Moda'i in the Ministry of Finance. Hence, Mandelbaum's policy enjoyed the support of two key actors: the United States and the Treasury. Once Amendment 15 passed and Mandelbaum saw the Stabilization Plan teetering on the brink of failure, he took on the role of the plan's keeper. Mandelbaum knew that in the current constellation, the government would not dare dismiss him. A dismissal of a conservative governor would have had a severely negative impact on the government's relationship with the United States. Moreover, it also must be kept in mind that Mandelbaum had the full support of the Treasury.

Conclusion

In October 1985, Yitzhak Moda'i, the minister of finance, reported to the Knesset that according to key indicators the Stabilization Plan was proceeding as planned and that the economy was under control. Moda'i had just returned from the annual conference of the World Bank and the IMF, where—he told the Knesset members—people were really interested to know about Israel's success in dealing with its crisis.

What exactly did the international community wanted to learn from Israel? Was it about the new liberal spirit it had infused into its economy—the "liberal creed," as it often called (Fourcade-Gourinchas and Babb, 2002)? It seems that the global vision, as perceived by Moda'i, did not actually draw so much on liberal values but leaned to a more neo-mercantilist approach. Moda'i shared with the Knesset what he learned from the international conference:

> We learned that there is no difference between the way governments *implement economic policies and the way they implement military policies*. [As in the case of military policies], it is inconceivable that each citizen will take care of his needs by himself. I would say the following: observing the heavy competition between economic powers, developed economies as well as underdeveloped economies, we learned of the intensive struggle between them. They try to conquer markets from each other, in order to protect the domestic market from sharing it with a foreign country's factors. *The countries that can guarantee their future standard of living through economic development are those countries which have succeeded in militarizing their citizens also in the economic area*, those countries, whose economic headquarters operate perfectly, whose sectors perform in coordination, whose productivity is high and the effort—*by coercion or voluntarily*—is maximal. Contrariwise, those countries in which each person take care of its own, those countries whose economic headquarter is not coordinated, those are the beggars countries, which mainly talk on an ever growing foreign aid.
>
> (Knesset, October 1985, p. 14, emphasis added)

This phrase succinctly captures the key argument put forward in this chapter: the Stabilization Plan was not driven by a "liberal creed," neither by an attempt to normalize the Israeli economy or converge its structure to that of the advanced liberal economies. The Stabilization Plan was an attempt—a successful one—to remobilize the Israeli economy for the purpose of adjusting it to a new international political economic setting.

In the 1970s, the state overextended itself. The Israeli government sought to build and sustain the state military power as well as to expand its social welfare system, while keeping the economy more or less open to the international markets. This was done in a period when the international system was also transformed. Since the disintegration of the Bretton Woods agreement in 1971, the international economic system had gone through a gradual process of liberalization. The costs of sustaining these set of preferences were growing and this culminated in fiscal crisis.

Whereas mainstream economists portray the Stabilization Plan as an economic solution to a policy problem, in practice, the plan was an economic solution that was consistent with the state's new set of preferences. The Stabilization Plan reflected the choice of the government to prioritize its export-oriented growth strategy and maintain its military regional position. To attain these objectives, the state had to make a social sacrifice.

As previous studies on the Stabilization Plan have shown, economists were deeply involved in shaping the plan. However, this chapter has argued that it is erroneous to claim that economists made the choice for the politicians. The Stabilization Plan was the product of cooperation between politicians and economists, who together shaped Israel's path to the neoliberal era. Michael Bruno, who put together the Stabilization Plan, played a very similar role to that of David Horowitz in the 1930s and 1940s, and to that of Don Patinkin and his students in the 1960s. Bruno, Horowitz and Patinkin offered policy ideas that enabled the politicians to address policy problems in ways that were consistent with their perceptions of Israel's strategic interests.

Notes

1 Average annual GDP growth rate during the "lost decade" (1973–1984) was 3.3 percent in comparison to 13.8 percent during period from 1968 to 1973 and to 6.5 percent for the period from 1986 to 2000 (Bank of Israel Annual Report, different years).

2 Names of wars have a political significance. The terms "Six-Day War" and "Yom Kippur War" represent the narrative of Israel, whereas the respective terms "1967 War" and "1973 War" are more "neutral." Whereas this book does not aim to represent Israel's political position, it does aim to present and discuss the perceptions of Israeli policy-makers of the political economic reality. Therefore, it seemed more appropriate to use the terminology which was common in the Israeli policy discourse.

3 Ibid, as per note 2.

4 Calculated from Syrquin (1986, pp. 45, 48; Tables 2–2, 2–3).

5 Calculated from Kleiman (1986, p. 309? Table 15–1).

6 In 1966, the military-industrial sector employed 14,000 employees and in 1985, it employed 63,000. During the same period, military exports grew from US$14 million to US$1.07 billion (Lifshitz, 2000, p. 364, Table Yod-1).

7 In the United States inflation rates fluctuated between 14 percent and 6, in the United Kingdom and Spain, inflation rates peaked to above 25 percent in the mid-1970s. In Mexico, inflation rate reached 30 percent in 1977 (www.inflation.eu/).

8 The debate between the camps is further examined by Ricky Shiv (Shiv, 2013).

9 A similar argument has been presented by Michael Shalev and Maman and Rosenhek.

They argue that the crisis that led to the Stabilization Plan was a fiscal crisis caused by the state's inability to confront powerful domestic societal and market actors (Maman and Rosenhek, 2012; Shalev, 1998). It must be added, though, that Shalev and Maman and Rosenhek arrive at this explanation from a very different theoretical perspective. Whereas orthodox economists argue that the crisis required a "retreat" of the state, in the sense that it had to cut the budget, Shalev, Maman and Rosenhek argued that what the state had to do was to strengthen its autonomy.

10 Amnon Neubach, in a phone interview with the author.
11 Amnon Neubach, in a phone interview with the author.
12 It must be stated, however, that already prior to 1967, the United States was involved, indirectly, in guaranteeing financial support to Israel. The Reparation Agreement signed between Israel and West Germany was made possible by the involvement of the United States, who approved the agreement, supported it, and one may also argue that it indirectly financed it.
13 The Chamber included the Manufacturers Association, the Farmers Association, the Association of the Trade Chambers, the Association of Contractors, Hotels Association, the Israeli Diamond Industry, the Banks Association, etc.
14 See Chapter 4 for details.
15 Assaf Razin, interview with the author, May 1985.
16 The memorandum was initiated by the Research Department Head Mordechai Frenkel and prepared by Liora Meridor and Akiva Offenbacher (Gross, 2007, p. 115).
17 The actual real interest rate could not be calculated precisely given the high level and the fluctuation of the inflation.

References

Aharoni, Y., 1991. *The Israeli Economy: Dreams and Realities*. Routledge, London.

Amikam, Y., 1984. Can We Set a Price to National Security? *Maariv*. January 16.

Arnon, Y., 1984. Fools' Paradise. In: Offer, Z. and Kober, A. (Eds.), *The Price of Power*. Ministry of Defense, Tel Aviv, pp. 67–74.

Austin, J. (Ed.), 1985. Israel Gets an Aid Boost. *CQ Almanac*. Online Edition, available at: http://library.cqpress.com

Bank of Israel, 1984. *Annual Report*. Bank of Israel, Jerusalem.

Bank of Israel, 1985. *Annual Report*. Bank of Israel, Jerusalem.

Bare'el, Z., 1985. IMF Report Demand. *Haaretz*, May 28.

Barkai, H. and Liviatan, N., 2007. *The Bank of Israel: The Monetary History of Israel*. Oxford University Press, New York.

Bar-Siman-Tov, Y., 1998. The United States and Israel since 1948: A "Special Relationship"? *Diplomatic History* 22, 231–262.

Beiski, M., 1986. Beiski Commission Report. *Quarterly Banking Review* 6–8 (in Hebrew).

Ben-Basaţ, A. (Ed.), 2002. *The Israeli Economy, 1985–1998: From Government Intervention to Market Economics*. MIT Press, Cambridge, MA.

Ben Porat, G., 2005. A New Middle East? Globalization, Peace and the "Double Movement." *International Relations* 19, 39–62.

Ben-Porath, Y. (Ed.), 1986. *The Israeli Economy: Maturing Through Crises*. Harvard University Press, Cambridge, MA.

Berglas, E., 1984. The Military Burden. In: Offer, Z. and Kober, A. (Eds.), *The Price of Power*. Ministry of Defense, Tel Aviv, pp. 59–66.

Bichler, S. and Nitzan, Y., 2001. *From War Benefit to Peace Dividends*. Carmel, Jerusalem (in Hebrew).

Blass, A. and Grossman, R., 2001. Assessing Damages: The 1983 Israeli Bank Shares Crisis. *Contemporary Economic Policy* 19, 49–58.

Bruno, M., 1984. Stabilization Plan without Dollars. Israel State Archive, 4128/8-Peh.

Bruno, M., 1985b. Handwritten Notes. July 1. Israel State Archive, 4129/8-Peh.

Bruno, M., 1985a. Economic Stabilization: The Emergency Plan in its Early Phase. *The Economic Quarterly* 207–223 (in Hebrew).

Bruno, M., 1987. Israel's Stabilization: The End of the "Lost Decade"? *The Economic Quarterly* 914–925 (in Hebrew).

Bruno, M., 1997. The Inflationary Process in Israel. In: Bruno, M. (Ed.), *Growth, Inflation and Economic Stabilization*. Bank of Israel, Jerusalem, pp. 122–141 (in Hebrew).

Bruno, M. and Fischer, S., 1984. *The Inflationary Process in Israel: Shocks and Accommodation*. National Bureau of Economic Research Cambridge, MA.

Davar, 1977a. Proposal to Cut Budget. July 12: 1.

Davar, 1977b. Final Agreement: 1.4 Billion IL Cut in the Defense Budget. July 27: 1.

Davar, 1977c. The Finance Minister: One Rule for Everyone. June 30: 3.

Davar, 1977d. Senior Officers Were Surprised. July 20: 1.

Davar, 1977e. Gafni Opposes Cut. July 20: 1.

Dish, Y., 1985a. The Exchange Rate Depends on Wages. *Maariv*, November 11: 1.

Dish, Y., 1985b. Sharon Warns. *Maariv*, October 16: 1.

Druks, H., 2001. *The Uncertain Alliance: The U.S. and Israel from Kennedy to the Peace Process*. Greenwood Publishing Group, Connecticut.

Erlich, S., 1977. The Finance Minister Speech at the Annual Conference of the Israeli Center for Management. Israel State Archive, 4131/15-Peh.

Eshed, H., 1977. Defense Budget Cut. *Davar*, 29 July: 1.

Eshet, G., 1986. The Professors Go to War. *Yedioit Aharonot* June 24.

Farah-Yacoub, J., Gerling, K., Medas, P.A., Poghosyan, T. and Xu, Y., 2017. Fiscal Crises. IMF Working Paper, International Monetary Fund, Washington, DC.

Filc, D., 2006. *Populism and Hegemony in Israel*. Resling, Tel Aviv (in Hebrew).

Finance Committee. Various years. *Minutes of Finance Committee*. Knesset Archive.

Fischer, S., 1995. *Recollections of the United States Role in the Israeli Stabilization Program*. International Monetary Fund, Washington, DC.

Fleisher, A., 1985a. A Year in Prison to Any Employer Who Would Provide Cost-Of-Living Allowances. *Maariv* July 7.

Fleisher, A., 1985b. Bank of Israel Set a Mafia Interest Rate. *Maariv* September 23.

Fleisher, A., 1985c. Budget Cuts—A Condition for Interest Rate Reduction. *Maariv* September 13.

Fourcade-Gourinchas, M. and Babb, S.L., 2002. The Rebirth of the Liberal Creed: Paths to Neoliberalism in Four Countries. *The American Journal of Sociology* 108, 533–579.

Gal, J., 1994a. The Development of Unemployment Insurance in Israel. *Social Security* 3, 117–136.

Gal, J., 1994b. The Commodification of the Israeli Welfare State and its Privatization: the Case of Israel. *Society and Welfare* 15, 7–24 (in Hebrew).

Gal, J., 1997. Unemployment Insurance, Trade-Unions and the Strange Case of the Israeli Labour Movement. *International Review of Social History* 42, 357–396.

Government, 1985. Government Meeting 42, June 30. 1985, Israel State Archive.

Gross, N.T., 2007. Economic Policy in Israel as Viewed by Leading Officials of the Bank of Israel, 1954–2000. In: Barkai, H. and Liviatan, N. (Eds.), *The Bank of Israel: Selected Topics in Israel's Monetary Policy*. Oxford University Press, New York, pp. 98–129.

Grunau, R., 2012. *The Privatization of Social Services in Israel: Considerations and Concerns.* Policy Paper No. 2012.17. Tabu Center for Social Policy Studies in Israel, Jerusalem.

Gwertzman, B., 1984a. Peres Visits Washington for Warmer Ties, Increased Aid. *New York Times*, October 14: E5.

Gwertzman, B. 1984b. Israelis Say Peres will Seek Big Rise in Aid Next Year. *New York Times*, October 10.

Haaretz, 1985a. Manufacturers: A Retreat from the Deal. February 25.

Haaretz, 1985b. Bank of Israel is Concerned. March 28.

Haaretz, 1985c. The United States Demand. February 10.

Haaretz, 1985d. 400 Million Dollar. June 5.

Helleiner, E., 1996. *States and the Reemergence of Global Finance: From Bretton Woods to the 1990s.* Cornell University Press, Ithaca, New York.

Helpman, E., 1985. A Change is Needed in the Economic Plan. *Haaretz* July 14.

Keren, M., 1994. Israeli Professionals and the Peace Process. *Israel Affairs* 1, 149–163.

Kessler, G., 1985. Bruno: Concession to the Histadrut Will Bring Another Devaluation. *Maariv* July 11.

Kleiman, E., 1986. Indexation in the Labor Market. In: Ben-Porath, Y. (Ed.), *The Israeli Economy: Maturing through Crises*. Harvard University Press, Cambridge, MA, pp. 302–319.

Kleiman, E., 1997. The Waning of Israeli Etatisme. *Israel Studies* 2, 146–171.

Knesset. Various years. *Divrei Ha'knesset* [Minutes of Parliament Sessions].

Levi, Y., 2003. *The Other Army of Israel: Materialist Militarism in Israel.* Miscal-Yediot Achronot, Tel Aviv.

Lifshitz, Y., 2000. *Defense Economics: The General Theory and the Israeli Case*. The Jerusalem Institute for Israel Studies, Jerusalem (in Hebrew).

Lipkin, D., 1977. Closing the Channels of Selective Credit. *Davar* June 27: 5.

Lipkin, D., 1985a. Moda'i Made Clear to the Press. *Maariv* July 7.

Lipkin, D., 1985b. Bank of Israel Consider. *Maariv* October 11.

Liviatan, N., 1983. Dollarization as a Monetary Reform. Israeli State Archive 4128/8-Peh).

Liviatan, N., 1984. Dollarization as a Monetary Reform. *The Economic Quarterly*, 848–858.

Liviatan, N. and Piterman, S., 1986. Accelerating Inflation and Balance-of-Payments Crisis, 1973–1984. In: Ben-Porath, Y. (Ed.), *The Israeli Economy: Maturing through Crises*. Harvard University Press, Cambridge, MA, pp. 320–346.

Maariv, 1985a. The Treasury: The Allowance—an Offence. *Maariv* August 30.

Maariv, 1985b. Criticism for Delaying the Interest Rate Decrease. *Maariv* October 15.

Magen, A., 1977. Meshel Demands. *Davar* July 20.

Makel, S., 1985a. Bruno: Erosion of Net Wages Exaggerated. *Maariv* July 5.

Makel, S., 1985b. The Governor Calls for a Meticulous Implementation of the Plan. *Maariv* August 6.

Maman, D., 2002. The Emergence of Business Groups: Israel and South Korea Compared. *Organization Studies* 23, 737–758.

Maman, D. and Rosenhek, Z., 2011. *The Israeli Central Bank: Political Economy, Global Logics and Local Actors*. Taylor & Francis, London.

Maman, D. and Rosenhek, Z., 2012. The Institutional Dynamics of a Developmental State: Change and Continuity in State–Economy Relations in Israel. *Studies in Comparative International Development* 47, 342–363.

Mandelkern, R. and Shalev, M., 2010. Power and the Ascendance of New Economic Policy Ideas: Lessons from the 1980s Crisis in Israel. *World Politics* 62, 459–495.

Mintz, A., 1985. The Military-Industrial Complex: American Concepts and Israeli Realities. *The Journal of Conflict Resolution* 29, 623–639.

Ne'eman, Y., 1984. The Security Challenge: A Categorical Imperative. In: Offer, Z. and Kober, A. (Eds.), *The Price of Power*. Ministry of Defense, Tel Aviv, pp. 89–94.

Neubach, A., 1984. The Economic Burden of Security. In: Offer, Z. and Kober, A. (Eds.), *The Price of Power*. Ministry of Defense, Tel Aviv, pp. 67–74.

New York Times, 1984. Senate Report Is Pessimistic on Israel's Economic Plight, November 20, p. A4.

Peres, S., 1978. Strategy for a Transition Period. *International Security* 2, 4–12.

Peres, S., 1993. *The New Middle East*. Henry Holt, New York.

Plessner, Y., 1994. *The Political Economy of Israel: From Ideology to Stagnation*. State University of New York Press, Albany, NY.

Porat, Y.B., 1982. The Revolution that Wasn't — Ideology and Economic Policy 1977–1981. *The Economic Quarterly* 29, 325–333 (in Hebrew).

Ram, U., 2013. *The Globalization of Israel: McWorld in Tel Aviv, Jihad in Jerusalem*. Routledge, New York.

Razin, A., 1984. The Impact of the American Financial Aid. In Offer, Z. and Kober, A. (Eds.), *The Price of Power*. Ma'arachot, Tel Aviv, pp. 47–58 (in Hebrew).

Razin, A., 1985. Economic Policy in Israel 1985. *The Economic Quarterly* 323–333 (in Hebrew).

Razin, A., forthcoming. *Israel and the World Economy: The Power of Globalization*. MIT Press, Cambridge, MA.

Razin, A., Yakobi, G., Horowitz, E. and Helpman, E., 1985. Current Economic Policy: A Discussion. *The Economic Quarterly* 3–11 (in Hebrew).

Rosenhek, Z., 2002. Social Policy and Nation-Building: The Dynamics of the Israeli Welfare State. *Journal of Societal & Social Policy* 1, 15–31.

Schiffman, D., Young, W. and Zelekha, Y., forthcoming. *The Role of Economic Advisors in Israel's Economic Policy—Crises, Reform and Stabilization*. Springer, New York.

Schultz, G.P., 1985. Shaping American Foreign Policy: New Realities and New Ways of Thinking. *Foreign Affairs*. March.

Shalev, M., 1992. *Labour and the Political Economy in Israel*. Oxford: Oxford University Press.

Shalev, M., 1998. Have Globalization and Liberalization "Normalized" Israel's Political Economy? *Israel Affairs* 5, 121–155.

Sharp, J., 2016. U.S. Foreign Aid to Israel. *Congressional Research Service*, Washington, DC.

Sherman, Y., 1985. The Manufacturers Decided. *Haaretz* May 3.

Shiv, R., 2013. The Stabilization Plan 1985: "Good Practices" or Ideology? *Iyunim* 23, 315–49 (in Hebrew).

Shlaim, A., 1996. The Middle East: The Origins of Arab-Israeli Wars. In: Woods, N. (Ed.), *Explaining International Relations since 1945*. Oxford University Press, Oxford, pp. 219–240.

Singer, Z., 1984a. The Economics Professors to the Ministers. *Maariv* October 30.

Singer, Z., 1984b. The Package Deal. *Yedioit Aharonot* November 27.

Stein, H., 1985. Herb's Ten Points. *Haaretz* April 18.

Svirski, S., 2005. Political-Economic Transformation in Israel: 1967. *Iunim* 14, 91–116 (in Hebrew).

Svirski, S., 2006. Economy and Society in Times of Empire. *Iunim* 16, 592–549 (in Hebrew).

Syrquin, M., 1986. Economic Growth and Structural Change: An International Perspective. In: Ben-Porath, Y. (Ed.), *The Israeli Economy: Maturing through Crises.* Harvard University Press, Cambridge, MA, pp. 42–74.

Yaqub, S., 2007. The Politics of Stalemate The Nixon Administration and the Arab–Israeli Conflict, 1969–73. In: Ashton, N.J. (Ed.), *The Cold War in the Middle East: Regional Conflict and the Superpowers 1967–73.* Routledge, London, pp. 35–58.

Zilberfarb, B.-Z., 2005. From Socialism to Free Market—The Israeli Economy, 1948–2003. *Israel Affairs* 11, 12–22.

Zinger, Z., 1984. The Economics Professors. *Yediot Ahronot.* September 21.

10 Israel's hawkish neoliberalism

The path of the Israeli economy can be read as a success story. Three numbers summarize this success: US$10 billion, 10 percent, and US$100 billion.

In the year 2014, the current account surplus of Israel surpassed US$10 billion, demonstrating that Israel had turned from a chronic current account deficit country into a surplus country, from 2003 onwards (Table 9.1). In the terminology of Israeli policy-makers, the state has achieved *economic independence*. The aspiration to achieve economic independence goes back to the pre-state era: In the 1940s, the World Zionist Organization tried to persuade the international community that an Israeli state was a viable project. Economic viability implied that Israeli workers and businesses would produce at least as much as they consumed. After the state was established, Israel depended on foreign financial support—initially from West Germany and then from the United States. Economic independence was not deemed attainable.[1] Ironically perhaps, the dream of economic independence was realized in the age of globalization and liberalization.

The second indicator that signifies Israel's economic success is external debt: in 2013, Israel's external debt fell below 10 percent of GDP, a remarkable feat given that it stood at 80 percent in 1985 (Table 9.1). Low external debt is not only an outstanding economic achievement but also a political one, as it decreases the exposure of the state to uncontrollable global geopolitical and economic shocks, lowers the management costs of public debt, and weakens the capacity of external actors to influence domestic policy decision making.

Third, in 2017, the foreign exchange reserves held by the Bank of Israel exceeded US$100 billion (BoI, 2017). The higher the level of foreign reserves a nation holds, the higher its capacity to face external economic shocks as well as domestic political troubles. Furthermore, holding a high level of foreign exchange reserve is perceived to be a good insurance mechanism in the event of unpredicted financial crises.

What do these numbers boil down to? During the three decades since the enactment of the Stabilization Plan, Israel has built what can be depicted as an economic fortress that shelters it economically and politically. While this fortress is not made of stones and does not protect Israel against bullets, tanks or missiles, it is nevertheless a material fortress that shields it against financial crises, external political pressure and unpredictable political or military events. This sturdy bulwark has provided and continues to provide the government of Israel with more leeway to make choices in both the domestic and the international spheres.

Market nationalism

Classical liberal scholars, as well as neoliberal scholars in International Relations share the view that market practices are based on liberal governing principles domestically and internationalist and cooperative world views externally (Keohane, 2005; Smith, 1981). The internationalist vision of free markets was manifested in best-sellers such as Francis Fukuyama's *The End of History and the Last Man* (Fukuyama, 1989) and Thomas Friedman's *The Lexus and the Olive Tree* (Friedman, 1999), as well as by discourses propagated by international financial institutions, such as the International Monetary Fund and the World Bank during the 1990s.

The internationalist liberal conception of markets was opposed to practices of state intervention in the domestic economy, which was driven by national sentiments or by the power of interest groups. From a liberal perspective, this policy approach was pejoratively called *economic nationalism.* Andreas Pickel describes the conventional view of economic nationalism as characterized by four features: (1) it is defined by its economic content; (2) it refers to the same type of economic policies across time and space; (3) it is driven by interest groups rather than public interests; and (4) it has little scientific support in valid economic theories (2005, pp. 3–4).

This dichotomous vision of liberal market internationalism versus state intervention nationalism has been challenged recently by scholars who present a more complex picture of the relationship between economic policies, liberalism and nationalism. David Harvey in his seminal book on the neoliberal regime, rightfully underlines the tension between the liberal creed, based on classical liberalism, and the practices of the neoliberal state: "the neoliberal state needs nationalism of a certain sort to survive. Forced to operate as competitive agent in the world market and seeking to establish the best possible business climate, it mobilizes nationalism in its effort to succeed" (Harvey, 2005, p. 85). For example, he points out that Margaret Thatcher's union-busting endeavor was facilitated by the Falklands War: "it was only through playing the nationalism card in the Falklands/Malvinas war and, even more significantly, in the campaign against economic integration with Europe, that she could win re-election and promote further neoliberal reforms internally" (ibid., p. 77). Eric Helleiner, in his series of publications on the links between economic policies and nationalism, argues, contrary to the traditional view, that economic nationalism "can be associated with a wide range of policy projects, including the endorsement of liberal economic policies" (2002, p. 307). Along the same line of argument, Adam Harmes rightfully observes that "not only certain nationalist policies are compatible with neoliberal values, but also these values may actually be dependent on certain nationalist policies" (2012, p. 71).

The thrust of this strand of literature is that there are no simple and stable links between the economic content of policies and the ideological content it is legitimized by. Nationalism is a discourse, a sentiment and a culture. Therefore, in principle, any set of material or institutional object can be framed as "nationalist" including market-oriented policies. Market-oriented policies—liberalization policies—can therefore also be framed as "nationalist." Neo-liberalism, therefore, can be framed as an internationalist project or as a hawkish and nationalist project.

Based on this conceptualization, it makes sense to divide the neoliberal period in Israel—from 1985 to the present—into two sub-periods. During the first sub-period, from 1985 to 1995, the transition to neoliberalism was framed on the basis of an internationalist and dovish political vision. This framing of the economic policy was associated with the intensification of the peace process and with perceptions among Israeli policy-makers regarding a broader transition of the geopolitical conditions in the Middle East. The underlying assumption guiding the internationalist neoliberal vision was that the economic transition of Israel not only would make the economy more efficient, but would also pave the way to a more peaceful Middle East, based on international and regional economic cooperation and interdependence.

The link between liberalized markets and a dovish perception of security issues was embodied in the political vision of Shimon Peres, the political figure who played a key role in the realization of the internationalist neoliberal vision. Peres, one of the patrons of the Stabilization Plan,[2] regarded the Plan as a central element in his geopolitical vision, encapsulated in the notion of the *New Middle East* (Peres, 1993; see also, Ben Porat, 2005a). One cannot avoid noticing that Peres was inspired by the process of European integration, where free markets had been endorsed as a regional pacifying mechanism: "Ultimately, the Middle East will unite in a common market—after we achieve peace. And the very existence of this common market will foster vital interests in maintaining the peace over the long term" (Peres, 1993, p. 99). Guy Ben Porat describes Peres' book as a "blueprint for the future of the region based on economic rationality, peace, democracy, cooperation, mutual gain and general prosperity." The Middle East, according to Peres' vision, argues Ben Porat, needs to choose between "peace, global integration and progress" and "continuing conflicts and backwardness" (Ben Porat, 2005a, p. 39). The link between economic and national security interests was also based on the interest of the Israeli private sector, which was expected to benefit from the realization of the New Middle East vision. It was also supported by the Israeli intellectual and professional elites (Keren, 1994). Economic cooperation and economic development of the Palestinian Authority were (supposed to be) an essential element in the New Middle East policy agenda.

The internationalist neoliberal agenda was manifested in the "Paris Protocol" signed in April 1993 between Israel and the Palestinian Authority, which specified that "The two parties view the economic domain as one of the cornerstone in their mutual relations with a view to enhance their interest in the achievement of a just, lasting and comprehensive peace" (Gaza-Jericho Agreement, 1994).

The era of internationalist neoliberalism reached an end with the assassination of Prime Minister Yitzhak Rabin on November 4, 1995. Following Rabin's assassination, the Labor Party was defeated by the Likud under Netanyahu's leadership. Netanyahu served as prime minister from 1996 to 1999, was re-elected in 2009 and has been Israel's prime minister since. Between 2003 and 2005, Netanyahu served as the minister of finance. Despite his hawkish national security position, Netanyahu did not try to turn the clock back on liberalization and globalization. Rather the opposite has proven true: he pushed the process further.

Guy Ben Porat describes Netanyhau's ideology as neo-conservatism. Netanyahu, argues Ben Porat, imported the neoconservative ideology into Israel, and "therefore the linkage established earlier between peace, economic liberalization, and economic growth was, at least temporarily, suspended" (Ben Porat, 2005b, p. 239). In the United States, neo-conservatism is defined as a mixture of individualism in the form of civic virtues and a specific form of nationalism and patriotism. Whereas the neoconservatives advocate market economy, they do not legitimize market practices on the basis of individual freedom as classical liberals do. In terms of foreign policy, they advocate maintaining the hegemonic position of the United States and the active promotion of democracy in the world (Harmes, 2012, pp. 73–74).

However, Israel's hawkish neoliberal regime was not driven only by Netanyahu. In fact, Netanyahu's policies have been fully supported by the political right-wing parties in the Knesset. The strong link between neoliberal policies and the hawkish national security position is manifested in the words and deeds of Naftali Bennett, the head of the Jewish House Party (*Ha'Bait He'yehudi*), minister of the economy in 2013–2015 and previously chairman of the *Yesha Council*, a non-governmental organization representing the municipalities in the occupied territories. Bennett explicitly explains the nature of this link:

> We are in a difficult international economic situation. We are, today, under what I call political economic terror, in which nations threaten us with boycott that can harm even more the Israeli export. This is not an easy environment for doing business.... Also, the social protest did not make it easy for the industry and damaged it, usually unjustifiably. Not to mention the security situation which is not simple. Many of our manufacturers are dispersed in the periphery, sometime working under fire. As I am worried, I ask you to give them your support. Nowadays, we see more and more Israeli firms that open factories abroad. Why is that? … because the local industry is discriminated against.
>
> (Economic Committee, 2014)

For Bennett, there is an instrumental (rather than ideological) link between Israel's external foreign policy and its internal economic policy: Israel national security strategy creates external political and economic pressure. To confront this external pressure, Israel must have a sturdy industry base and the government must support domestic manufacturers.

An export-oriented growth strategy

Some economists believe that a globalized economy is a homogeneous economic space in which individual firms compete with each other. According to this perception, the best thing governments can do to promote its economic interests is not to intervene in the economy. However, more realistic trade theories reject this idealistic perception of the global economy and argue that in the real world governments do intervene in the economy to "maximize some measure of national economic welfare, rather than having their behavior determined by more fundamental individual actions such as voting or lobbying" (Brander, 1995, p. 2). Following this line of reasoning, Philip Cerny argues that, in the globalization era, "The state still has a major national role to play, but that role is increasingly to expose the domestic to the transnational, to prise open the nation-state to a globalising world" (2010, p. 6). Furthermore, argues Thomas Palley, small and open economies "need exports to keep their factories operating." These economies need to attract investment "that creates jobs, builds manufacturing capacity, and transfers technology. Moreover, foreign investors finance this capital accumulation by providing the foreign exchange to purchase the capital goods" (Palley, 2006, p. 3).

There is no doubt that since the 1980s most countries have abandoned the "traditional" policy instruments associated with protectionism and neo-mercantilism, such as formal devaluation, subsidies and tariffs. However, in the globalization era, governments have developed new means to make local businesses more competitive internationally. For instance, in a formally floating exchange rate regime, governments can devalue local currencies by either lowering interest rates or by hoarding foreign currency, even if they employ formally floating exchange rate regimes (Dooley *et al.*, 2003, 2004). Other policy instruments known to improve international competitiveness of the economy are a reduction of marginal corporate tax rates, especially for export companies. The state can also support exporters by reforming the labor protection rules and by weakening the labor organizations (Itskhoki, 2009). These policy instruments are often disguised as a "liberalization" policy, but in fact they reflect the preferences of the government to support exporters.

From the perspective of open economies, the global economy is not made of individual firms competing with one another, but of states, which use political means to promote the competitiveness of their economies. Even large economies which often employ liberal rhetoric, such as the United States, perceive the world economy as a battleground. As Michael Froman, the former US Trade Representative, put it:

> To be sure, the traditional link between economics and strategy hasn't been upended as much as extended. Beginning with the first estimates of national income, which were developed in 17th century Europe to compare the ability of states to raise and support militaries, economic power has been viewed primarily as an enabler for military power. This basic belief

> was widely adopted and held sway among most strategists through the Cold War.
>
> (Froman, 2015)

To summarize, neoliberalism has different manifestations. Here we characterized two potential manifestations: internationalist neoliberalism and nationalist or hawkish neoliberalism. Hawkish neoliberalism can be understood as a new form of neo-mercantilism. Whereas traditional neo-mercantilism restricts capital flow, imposes tariffs and provides subsidies, hawkish neoliberalism achieves similar outcomes but it employs different policy instruments.

The concept of hawkish neoliberalism can offer an explanation for the economic rationale that has shaped Israel's path to neoliberalism. Since 1985, the decisive moment when Israel entered the global economic battlefield, the country has been going through two opposing processes. On the one hand, it followed the neoliberal dogma of liberalization and privatization: the state lowered public spending and taxation, privatized government (and Histadrut) companies, abolished capital controls, canceled direct subsidies to businesses, exporters and consumers, and liberalized domestic financial markets while curtailing social services (Grunau, 2012; Maman and Rosenhek, 2012; Shalev, 1998).

At the same time, however, the state created new policy instruments designed to encourage exports. Whereas the state eliminated all manner of direct subsidies, it continued to use indirect instruments to allocate resources on a preferential basis. For example, Yaron Dishon shows that direct subsidies allocated under the Law for the Encouragement of Capital Investments fell from 3.97 percent of GDP in 1984 to 0.17 percent in 2010. However, the government partly replaced subsidies by tax exemptions: the cost of tax exemptions rose from 0.14 percent of GDP in 1989 to 0.69 percent in 2010 (Dishon, 2014, pp. 111–113, Tables 1 and 2). Although tax exemption seems more consistent with market practices, given the government's passive role, in fact it is just as discriminatory as a subsidies policy. Israeli law does not explicitly specify being an exporter as a condition for receiving tax exemptions. It does, however, require criteria of technological innovation and proven competitiveness. In practice, it is blatantly obvious that tax exemptions in Israel are preferentially allocated to the largest exporting companies.[3]

Another means of supporting export industries is by manipulating the exchange rate. Since 2008, the Bank of Israel has conducted a dollar purchasing policy. Over this period, the Bank's reserves had risen from US$28 billion to US$98 billion by the end of 2016. Avi Simhon, the head of the National Economic Council, argued that by hoarding foreign currency the Bank supports exporters, but has also led to an increase in Israel's cost of living (Hudi, 2016). This means that the Bank of Israel has in effect reduced average real wage levels in the country.

The Israeli state also promotes export through its involvement in the arms industry. According to Israeli officials, military exports rose in 2016 by US$800 million and reached US$6.5 billion, more than 12 percent of Israel's total exports (Ahronheim, 2017). Israel is the 10th largest arms exporter globally (2010–2014), accounting for 2 percent of the world arms export (Wezeman and Wezemans, 2014) and three Israeli companies—Elbit Systems, Israel Aerospace Industries and Raphael—were listed among the top 100 arms-producing and military service companies in the world in 2010 (SIPRIs, 2010).

The fact that Israeli governments have put so much effort into boosting Israel's exports is in no way unique or surprising. The quest for economic independence—as this book has demonstrated—has been a long-standing ambition of Israeli governments from both right and left. However, since the perceived failure of the Oslo Agreement, the assassination of Rabin and the failure of the Camp David talks in 2000, the political right had to build an economic fortification in order to limit the capacity of external actors—primarily the United States—to influence Israel's policy in the national security field, through the economic leverage of foreign financial aid.

Israel's independence and the United States

The question of Israeli governments' economic independence was directed to minimize the capacity of two key international actors to affect its national security policies: the United States, its political ally, and the European Union, its key trade partners. In respect to both actors, Israel has tried to minimize its political dependence, while at the same time maximize the economic benefit it can extract.

The United States was considered by Israel a political ally. However, hawkish Israeli governments sought to minimize the capacity of the United States to restrict Israel national security choices. Immediately following his election in 1996, Benjamin Netanyahu announced in a speech at the US Congress that his objective was to bring Israel closer to economic independence: "We are deeply grateful for all we have received from the United States," he said, "but," he continued:

> I believe there can be no greater tribute to America's long-standing economic aid to Israel than for us to be able to say: We are going to achieve economic independence. We are going to do it. In the next four years, we will begin the long-term process of gradually reducing the level of your generous economic assistance to Israel. I am convinced that our economic policies will lay the foundation for total self-reliance and great economic strength.
>
> (Netanyahu, 2017)

What were the motives that made Netanyahu make such a commitment to the United States? Israel, a small economy which perceives itself as a "villa in the jungle," is constantly concerned by its capacity to shape its own behavior without external constraints.[4] Therefore, it seeks to minimize its economic reliance on external actors. At the same time, however, Israel cannot sustain its current level of public expenses and standard of living without external financial aid. These two seemingly contradicting preferences have shaped Israel's relationship with the United States for decades. Therefore, Netanyahu's declaration in the US Congress signaled to the United States that his government was determined to maintain Israel autonomy.

Israel, as a state, kept Netanyahu's promise in two senses. First of all, since 2003, Israel has turned from a trade deficit to a trade surplus country, thus achieving economic independence. Since then, the current account surplus of Israel has been rising. Second, the size of Israel's economic aid from the United States has since 2003 gradually reduced, terminating altogether in 2008. However, Israel has been compensated for this through increased military financial aid. Nominally, except for periodic fluctuations, the net sum of American aid to Israel since 1998 has not changed (Sharp, 2016). In September 2016 Netanyahu and Obama agreed on a 20 percent increase in annual military aid for the next 10 years, with an annual amount of US$3.8 billion. As a result, American military aid has now reached levels of around 1 percent of Israeli GDP and represents approximately 18 percent of its defense budget.

Recently, Naftali Bennett called for minimizing Israel's dependence on American military aid:

> U.S. military aid is roughly 1 percent of Israel's economy … I think, generally, we need to free ourselves from it. We have to do it responsibly, since I'm not aware of all the aspects of the budget, I don't want to say "let's just give it up," but our situation today is very different from what it was 20 and 30 years ago. Israel is much stronger, much wealthier, and we need to be independent.
>
> (Yanover, 2013)

Bennett made the point that Israel is *capable* of giving up foreign aid. The political question is whether it is to Israel's advantage to actually give up the foreign aid. In any case, the fact that Israel became a potentially self-sustained economy, weakens the capacity of the United States to twist the government's arm when it comes to Israel foreign and security policy. Whereas the sum of the US foreign military aid to Israel is still considerable, reaching a quarter of the defense budget, hypothetically it is clear that Israel would have been able to finance it by itself, had the United States cut the foreign aid. In other words, Israel has a good default strategy, a fact that contributes to its negotiation power.

Barack Obama admitted that Israel's economic success increases its negotiation power vis-à-vis the United States in regard to the Israeli/Palestinian conflict: "In some ways because Israeli society has been so successful economically, it has, I think, from a position of strength been less willing to make concessions" (Obama, 2016).

Israel and the EU

A different situation prevails in regard to Israel's relations with the European Union, which has traditionally been Israel's largest trade partner. In 1960, 56 percent of Israeli exports were destined for the European Common Market. During the same year, 48 percent of Israel imports arrived from the European Community. In recent years, Israel has diversified its exports and in 2015 the European Union was the third largest export destination (25 percent of total exports), after North America (30 percent) and Asian countries (28 percent). In terms of imports, Europe is still the largest trade partner, accounting for 36 percent of Israel's total imports. Asia comes next with a 25 percent of total imports.[5]

The falling share of Israeli exports to Europe has probably been driven by the twin factors of the growth of the Asian economies and a deliberate policy choice arising from the tension between Israel and the EU regarding Israel's policy in the West Bank. Contrary to the United States, the EU established a connection between Israeli national security policy and the economic relationship between the two political entities.

The first significant trade agreement between Israel and the European Community was signed in 1975. Two decades later, Israel and the EU signed an Association Agreement, which granted Israel a "special status" in the context of the Barcelona process and the Euro-Mediterranean Partnership. The Association Agreement, which was ratified and came into force in 2000, was not simply a free trade agreement. It included also political clauses, related to the commitment of Israel to peace, security, democracy and human rights (EC, 2000). As a report of the United Nations points out, EU Association Agreements serve "as the European Union's principal instrument for promoting democratic change." The Mediterranean partners were obliged to "endorse the human right clause, which stipulates a commitment to democratic reform" (Yacoubian, 2004, p. 4). Hence, from the perspective of the European Union, a formal link between Israel's national security policy in the West Bank and trade relations with the EU was enacted (Plessix, 2011).

Since 1995, the peace process between Israel and the Palestinian Authority has largely stalled and the policy of Israeli governments in the West Bank has been deemed as inconsistent with EU human right standards, democratization and the rule of law. In July 2013, the EU issued a directive on the exclusion of any entity residing in the "territories occupied by Israel since June 1967" from eligibility for grants, prizes or other funding instruments (EU, 2013). In November 2015, after several years of discussions, the European Commission issued an "interpretative notice on indication of origin of goods from the territories occupied by Israel since June 1967." The notice stipulated that

> The European Union, in line with international law, does not recognise Israel's sovereignty over the territories occupied by Israel since June 1967, namely the Golan Heights, the Gaza Strip and the West Bank, including East Jerusalem, and does not consider them to be part of Israel's territory,

> irrespective of their legal status under domestic Israeli law. The Union has made it clear that it will not recognise any changes to pre-1967 borders, other than those agreed by the parties to the Middle East Peace Process.
>
> (EC, 2015)

The European Union's sanctions were perceived by the right-wing MP and the minister of the economy, Naftali Bennett as an act of "economic terrorism" and politicians threatened to withdraw any type of cooperation with the European Union (Ravid, 2013). In response, Bennett put much effort to promote Israeli exports to East Asia and East Europe.

It must be kept in mind that the European Union is not a unitary actor, and therefore when it comes to decisions on foreign policy, it depends on the interests and positions of all the member states. Therefore, it is unlikely that the European Union would declare actual sanctions against Israel, especially given the special relationship between Israel and Germany. However, in Israel, the explanatory statements have already been perceived as interfering with its internal matters.

To conclude, this précis of Israel's economic relationship with the United States and the European Union demonstrates the link between Israeli national security strategy and its domestic socio-economic choices: the more hawkish its national security strategy is, the more efforts the leadership has to make to sustain Israel's external economic position, an approach that deepens the gap between the preferences of the state and the welfare of the citizens.

The costs of economic fortification

It is thus understandable why the hawkish governments in Israel had a very strong incentive to fortify the Israel economy and to shield it against political or economic pressure. A highly stable economy has been perceived by the Israeli political right as a precondition for pursuing foreign and security policies, inconsistent with global norms and with the interests of Israel major ally and trade partners. The question, which can be only partly answered in the context of this book, regards the expected cost of this policy.

An immediate outcome of Israel's export-oriented strategy is its high and growing level of export concentration. In 2007, the 10 largest exporting companies in Israel accounted for 36 percent of total exports. By 2014, that share had risen to 50 percent (CBS, 2009; IEICI, 2014). In 2010, the four largest Israeli pharma and Hi-Tech companies—Teva, ICL (Israel Chemicals), Intel and Check Point—which comprise half of the companies in the upper percentile in terms of turnover—received tax exemptions worth US$4 billion, which amounted to half of the current account surplus and 70 percent of all tax exemptions that year. Around one quarter of the companies in the upper decile received 90 percent of total tax exemptions (Koren, 2013; MoF, 2015). The lion's share of exported goods and services—65 percent—is produced by the high-value-added industries, principally Hi-Tech and pharmaceutical companies as well as the chemical industry (Milard, 2015).

Export concentration also affects the structure of the labor market. Gilad Brand and Eitan Regev argue that the division between low-value-added sectors and high-valued-added sectors creates a social division between two groups of workers. Workers in the high value-added sector are characterized by high productivity and high real wages, whereas workers in low-value-added sectors are characterized by low productivity and low wages. This disparity creates a social problem because of the proportion of the two sectors: most of Israel's labor force—82 percent in 2011—are employed in low productivity and low wages sectors. The socio-economic gap between the two groups of workers has only grown with time: between 1995 and 2010 low-productivity-job wages increased by only 0.5 percent, whereas high-productivity-job wages rose by 1.5 percent. These differences perpetuate and increase income inequality which has been a social issue since the 1990s. Brand and Regev conclude that:

> Over the past two decades, two very different sectors have formed in the Israeli labor market. The first includes High-Tech, finances and advanced industries, characterized by high-productivity and high wages, which increase rapidly as well. The other sector is the commerce and non-tradable service industries in which productivity is low, wages are low and growth is marginal.
>
> (2015, p. 36)

The division of the labor market into those who have benefited from the export-oriented growth strategy and those who carry the burden is a well-known phenomenon. The opening-up of small economies increases wage inequality due to the fact that global trade benefits the most productive economic agents (Itskhoki, 2009). Helpman and others show that "the opening of trade raises wage inequality for any inequality measure" (Helpman, *et al.*, 2010). Therefore, "trade disproportionately benefits the most productive agents within sectors and occupations, leading to greater income inequality in a trading equilibrium than in autarky" (Itskhoki, 2009).

Export concentration and the divided labor market are definitely not the only reasons for the increase of social inequality in Israel since 1985, but they most probably are contributing factors. Prior to 1985, market income inequality measured by the Gini coefficient, after taxes and transfer payments, was below 0.35. It rose to a maximum of 0.3892 in 2009 and dropped slightly to 0.37 in 2014 (Ben-David and Bleikh, 2013, p. 3, Figure 1; SII, 2015, p. 32, Table 12). By 2013, according to OECD data, Israel suffered from the second highest income inequality of any OECD country, after the United States. Moreover, since 1985 the percentage of citizens below the poverty line has been remarkably increasing. In 1985, this percentage, after taxes and welfare payments, was less than 15. Since 2005 it has stabilized around 20 percent and has proven remarkably resilient to attempts to lower it (Ben-David and Bleikh, 2013, p. 6, Figure 2).[6] According to the OECD definition, in 2014, Israel had the second highest level of poverty after Mexico among OECD countries (SII, 2015, p. 27, Figure 5).

State preferences versus public interest

The neoliberal regime in Israel is highly successful so long as its success is measured by the aggregated economic variables of the National Accounts. However, this success is not translated into the social welfare of the median citizen. As many observers of the Israeli political economy have pointed out, Israel became a rich country with poor citizens.[7] Whereas most observers explain this situation as the product of corruption and crony capitalism, this chapter argues that this situation is the result of a gap between the preferences of the state and the public interest.

How are state preferences formed? Liberal theories assume that state preferences are shaped by a weighted aggregation of the interests of societal and market actors. Andrew Moravcsik, for example, argues that states "represent some subset of domestic society, on the basis of whose interests state officials define state preferences" (1997, p. 518). Representation, he argues:

> is not simply a formal attribute of state institutions but includes other stable characteristics of the political process, formal or informal, that privilege particular societal interests. Clientelistic authoritarian regimes may distinguish those with familial, bureaucratic, or economic ties to the governing elite from those without. Even where government institutions are formally fair and open, a relatively inegalitarian distribution of property, risk, information, or organizational capabilities may create social or economic monopolies able to dominate policy. Similarly, the way in which a state recognizes individual rights may shape opportunities for voice.
>
> (Ibid., p. 518)

State-centered—or realist—theories assume that states are endowed with partially autonomous apparatuses that shape and define state preferences, which do not necessarily respond to the interests of the public, the voters and interest groups. Eric Nordlinger explains:

> The preferences of the state are at least as important as those of civil society in accounting for what the democratic state does and does not do; the democratic state is not only frequently autonomous insofar as it regularly acts upon its preferences, but also markedly autonomous in doing so even when its preferences diverge from the demands of the most powerful groups in civil society.
>
> (1981, p. 1)

Moravcsik and Nordlinger's models of state preference formation are not mutually exclusive and they can easily be combined. State preferences are shaped by a weighted aggregation of the interests of societal actors, while the state itself is considered an actor, whose preferences are weighted in, just like the interests of any other "interest group."

For our purposes, the essential point is that both the liberal and the realist models of preference formation acknowledge that it may be the case that state preference does not represent the public interest, as it is shaped through the democratic political system. This chapter argues that, in Israel, the security interest of the state, as perceived and shaped by recent hawkish governments, dictates an extreme form of neoliberal policy designed to fortify the Israeli economy, a political choice which has high social costs. The question that comes to mind, is why the democratic political system is unable to translate the public socio-economic interests into state preferences and policy-making choices.

Socio-economic issues and national security issues

To understand why the Israeli political system is unable to translate the public socio-economic interests into policy choices, it is necessary to understand the security/socio-economic conundrum in the Israeli policy discourse. Whereas the majority of the Israeli public is not satisfied with the hawkish neoliberal policy strategy, the prioritization of national security policy issues prevents it from expressing its dissatisfaction in the polls. A survey conducted in 2014 by the Israeli Democratic Institute (IDI) demonstrates this point.

The survey found that a majority of the Israeli society, 65 percent, believes that that the socio-economic conditions in Israel justify a social protest (Herman, 2014, p. 227, Table 49). When the respondents were asked to prioritize specific policy objectives they considered most pressing, most of them voted for minimizing socio-economic gaps (19.6 percent). The second top objective was also associated with socio-economic issues: financial assistance for young citizens to purchase an apartment. Only a minority voted for the prioritization of national security objectives. Response rates on strengthening Israel's military power and eliminating Iran's nuclear project were much lower than the above socio-economic issues (5.2 percent and 5.4 percent respectively) (ibid., p. 210, Table 13). Moreover, when asked which of the two policy issues—socio-economic or national security—should the government prioritize, 37.1 percent of the respondents selected the former while only 26.3 percent voted for the latter (ibid., p. 211, Table 14).

These findings reflect the high level of public socio-economic discontent. Why, then, is the discontent not translated into political change? Digging deeper into the survey, one finds an explanation to the puzzling situation. When respondents were asked to specify how they believe the government should handle its national security issues, one-fifth of the respondents, 20.4 percent, voted for strengthening Israeli military capacity. Another fifth, 18.3 percent, selected improving Israel's international image and position. Almost 14 percent voted for the elimination of Iran's nuclear plan, and 6.7 percent for minimizing Israel's dependence on the United States (ibid., p. 209, Table 12). That is, when respondents are asked about socio-economic issues versus national security issues, they prioritize the former. However, at the same time, almost two-thirds of the respondents support a hawkish national security policy, which, it is argued here, is inconsistent with a socio-economic strategy with a more benign distributive outcome.

Here is where the crux of the matter lies: there is a policy linkage between a hawkish national security policy and the prevailing form of neoliberal policy. Once the government has made the national security choice to embrace a hawkish position, it narrows down its economic policy space. This is in contrast to the internationalist neoliberal regime, which provides governments with a broader economic policy space.

To put this claim in historical context: until 1967, the national security strategy of Israeli governments was consistent with the trend of lowering socio-economic disparities. Policy-makers perceived the creation of jobs and the expansion of production as a strategic national objective. During the 1970s, the government was able to finance higher and ever rising standards of living as well as a generous welfare system, coupled with a high level of military spending on the basis of extensive foreign aid from the United States. This situation was unsustainable and it resulted in a rolling crisis, which culminated in the critical events of 1985 that led to greater dependence on the United States.[8] Between 1985 and 1996, policy-makers—particularly Peres and Rabin—followed a neo-liberal internationalist and dovish political economic vision, according to which economic liberalization, coupled with the promotion of a peace process, would bring Israel into a sustainable growth model, based on lower levels of military spending (in comparison to the 1970s), economic openness and higher but still mild levels of inequality. However, this vision crumbled in the 1990s. Since the Second Intifada, which broke out during the implementation of the Oslo Accords, the perception entrenched both in the public mind and among policy-makers was that Israel is doomed to a constant struggle in order to survive in an unstable and hostile region. In such conditions, a hawkish national security is not a political choice but a necessity. Hence, despite the fact that the majority of the public is unhappy with the socio-economic situation, the latter's stability is guaranteed by public support of a hawkish approach, prioritizing national security over socio-economic issues.

The Social Protest

The story of the Social Protest Movement in the summer of 2011 supports this analysis. The Social Protest was an exceptional event in the economic history of Israel, both in terms of the issues it raised and in regards to its scale and mixture of social groups that took part in it. Previously, social protest in Israel revolved around ethnic and religious issues or questions concerning the peace process and the future of the occupied territories. The Social Protest Movement of 2011 was unique in the sense that it emerged on the basis of socio-economic discontent rather than on the basis of national security issues, and because it brought together groups from both the upper and lower middle class, from urban centers and the periphery (Rosenhek and Shalev, 2013). It was also the largest protest revolving around socio-economic issues that had taken place in Israel since its establishment. The protest culminated in a cluster of public rallies that took place simultaneously across the country and included more than 400,000 citizens (Schechter, 2012; Sherwood, 2011).

The Social Protest Movement originated in a Facebook "event" posted on July 14, 2011, by a Tel Aviv student, Daphni Leef, addressing the high cost of housing in Tel Aviv and in Israel in general. Within days, Rothschild Boulevard, a main street in Tel Aviv's center, was filled with protester tents. This core of protesters spread rapidly and similar tent camps sprung up in all the main cities. The peak of the protest was a nationwide demonstration which took place on September 6, 2011 (Schechter, 2012; Sherwood, 2011).

The atmosphere was explosive and at that time many believed the government would be toppled, unless it responded to the protesters' demands. After an initial desperate attempt by the government to downplay the significance of the protest, Prime Minister Netanyahu agreed to appoint a committee, headed by economist Manuel Trajtenberg, mandated to contemplate "changing priorities in order to ease the economic burden on the citizens of Israel." To attain this aim, the committee was asked to study taxation, social service provision, competition policies, housing and fiscal policy (Trajtenberg, 2011).

The recommendations of the Trajtenberg Committee were based on a rather orthodox economic philosophy, postulating the government should maintain the current budget framework. Whereas it recommended stopping the recent trend of tax cuts, it did not opt for a radical change in the size of the budget and suggested covering the costs of its recommendations in areas of education, health, housing and social services by cutting the defense budget by ILS 5–6 billion per year over the following five years.

Trajtenberg believed cuts in the defense budget to be essential for the feasibility of the Committee's recommendation. According to the testimony of Trajtenberg and of Eyal Gabay, the Director-General of the Prime Minister Office at the time and a member of the committee, they demanded Netanyahu sign a written commitment to bring about a cut in the defense budget, prior to publishing the recommendations, but Netanyahu refused.[9] At the end of the process, the recommendation to cut the defense budget was not implemented at all.[10]

Trajtenberg explains that only in hindsight he "understood what prevented the budget cut [in military spending] and what prevented an historical change in priorities. In one word: Iran." Trajtenberg accused the Defense Ministry of spreading "apocalyptic threats in the air." What are we supposed to learn, he asked, "That we have to choose between military collapse and an economic collapse?" (Kaneh, 2012).

Eyal Gabai believed that the defense cut was avoided due to the resistance of the Defense Ministry and the army:

> Contrary to fairy tales, the prime minister is not omnipotent. When the Chief of Staff arrives … and says to the prime minister, listen, with this budget one cannot defend the state of Israel … the prime minister is dead.

The high military officers, he continues, "excel in slideshows … [they make you believe] that if you don't shift all the state's budget to the defense, then a day later the state of Israel will be effaced from the face of the earth."[11]

Support for the interpretation of Trajtenberg and Gabai was supplied by the testimony of the retired Mossad-Chief, Meir Dagan, who revealed that since 2010 Netanyahu and Ehud Barak, the defense minister, had been planning a military intervention against Iran (Cohen, 2012). This implies that in the summer of 2011, while hundreds of thousands of protesting citizens filled the streets, the prime minister and the defense minister were preoccupied with what seemed to them the critical issues for the physical survival of Israel. In September 2012, Netanyahu held one of his famous speeches in the General Assembly in the United Nations, in which he called on the international community to set a "clear, red line" to stop Iran from producing a nuclear weapon (Borger, 2012).

The Social Protest Movement did have, however, some long-lasting effects. Primarily, it raised awareness of the centrality of socio-economic issues in the public discourse, which had been dominated for decades by national security issues centered on the "conflict" and the "peace process." Nevertheless, the impact of the Social Protest on policy and the national priorities was very limited, to say the least. It is hard to judge whether national security issues are used as a smokescreen to distract the attention of the public from their socio-economic woes or whether there is a real trade-off between Israel's ability to defend itself and its capacity to create a more equal and fair society. In either case, the link between the two issues is undeniable and must be taken into account.

The Social Protest Movement is an event which provides a closure to this book. It is the first significant event that in hindsight can be considered a milestone in a process, in which the Israeli market economy is turning away from the its state-centered and nationalist characteristics, to become a more civil and liberal market economy.

Where from here?

This book has traced how policy-makers in Israel have perceived, defined and shaped state preferences, and how these preferences have shaped Israeli socio-economic policies over the nation's economic history from the 1930s to the 2000s. Over this period, the rhetoric which policy-makers used and their mobilizing ideologies changed markedly. However, there was one element that remained constant: the primacy of state preferences as a factor that shaped its socio-economic strategy.

There were times when Israeli governments and technocrats used socialist ideologies to justify the use of policy instruments designed to industrialize the economy and absorb immigration. There were other times in which policy-makers adopted a more liberal rhetoric to justify the use of policy instruments, which were designed to boost export and improve the Israeli external economic position. The use of socialist or liberal rhetoric, however, masked the fundamental drivers of the government, which were shaped on the basis of its national security interest. Whereas in the Knesset, in public rallies and interviews, politicians talked highly of socio-economic issues, such as equality or private initiative, within the closed fora in which policy-making decisions were made, economic rationality prevailed over economic values and ideologies. The economic rationality of policy-making, however, was not based on textbook mainstream economic ideas. Whenever professional economists had a say in shaping state preferences and policies, they served the political cause and not vice versa.

From an early stage in the economic history of the Israeli state and of Zionism—to be precise, since the late 1930s—politicians and technocrats realized that assigning a significant role to markets was consistent with the state preferences (or the quasi-state institutions in the pre-state era). However, the adoption of market practices in Israel was not accompanied by the adoption of liberal governing principles, such as economic freedom, equality before the law and private entrepreneurship. These principles were used to legitimize certain privileges to certain firms, when state preferences justified it, but they were not recognized as having their inherent value. Markets, the Israeli economic history shows, are policy instruments, and they can be used for different purposes. They can be shaped on the basis of liberal governing principles, but they can also be used to serve the state interests.

The internal tension between the dominance of the state and the neoliberal regime has intensified in recent decades, with right-wing Israeli governments promoting a more hawkish foreign policy and at the same time embracing a radical neoliberal rhetoric. This internal tension, as is argued here, is a feature of a quasi-neo-mercantilist regime designed to safeguard the autonomy of the Israeli state, vis-à-vis external pressures. Policy-makers in Israel believe that such autonomy is a prerequisite for the continuation of the hawkish national security of recent Israeli governments.

An implication of this analysis is that the socio-economic malaise in Israeli society is not only the product of "liberalization" or of "free markets" as such, but it is rather the result of the re-nationalization and the mobilization of the Israeli economy. The Israeli society is carrying a significant social burden, the price of maintaining the hawkish foreign policy approach conducted by recent governments.

The book should end here. However, one questions must be at least put forward, even if it is left without a full answer: is the social burden of the Israeli neoliberal regime justified? The answer to this question depends on the convictions of the reader. If one believes that Israel's hawkish foreign policy approach is legitimately derived from a sober and cautious reading of the geopolitical conditions in the Middle East, and if one believes that the existence of Jewish state is a justified cause in itself, then the social burden is the price that must be paid. "It is not Europe here," as a popular Israeli hit says: this is the Middle East and it has its own political economic rules. However, if one believes that the Israel hawkish national security strategy is based on wrong political choices and ideology, the necessary conclusion is that the extreme form of hawkish neoliberal regime in Israel is also a mistaken policy choice.

Notes

1 See Chapter 4 for details.
2 See Chapter 9 for details.
3 According to a policy paper prepared by Assaf Zimring and Omer Moav the Encouragement of Capital Investments Law was designed to promote export (Zimring and Moav, 2016). Zimring and Moav question the rationale of the export-oriented growth strategy and they argue that "the idea that export, in itself, is desirable, sounds strange to any modern economist" (ibid., p. 9). Zimring and Moav, however, assume that the primary aim of economic policy is efficiency and they do not take into account—as I do here—that state preferences are not—and should not be—derivatives of economic theories that take into account only part of the considerations a real policy-maker actually takes.
4 The term "a villa in the jungle" is often used by Israeli policy-makers to portray the situation in the Middle East from the perspective of Israel. For example, Barak (defense minister at the time) argued: "We are not residing in West Europe or North America. This is a truly difficult environment, this is really a 'villa in the jungle' and we are surrounded by hostile forces" (Haski, 2012).
5 Data calculated from Annual Abstracts of the Central Bureau of Statistics.
6 The poverty line is defined as half of the median income. The information presented here is for disposable income, after taxes and welfare payments.
7 This claim has made in several occasions by Yaron Zelekha, a former accountant general in the Ministry of Finance.
8 See Chapter 9 of this book.
9 Trajtenberg and Gabay presented their testimony in the documentary film on the Social Protest, *Who Killed Rothschild?,* made by the *Calcalist* journalists, Naama Sikuler and Shaul Amstradamski (Sikuler *et al.*, 2016).
10 The recommendation of the Trajtenberg Report was only partially implemented. According to a report prepared by Amit Ben-Zur and Amnon Portugali of the Van Leer Institute, the government implemented most of the recommendations that did not have fiscal costs. The government did not embrace the key recommendation, to increase civil spending and cut military spending (Ben-Zur and Portugali, 2014).
11 Author's own translation of interviews presented in the documentary made by Naama Sikuler and Shaul Amsterdamski on the social protest (Sikuler *et al.*, 2016).

References

Ahronheim, A., 2017. Israeli Military Exports Rise to $6.5 Billion. *The Jerusalem Post* JPost.com, March 30. Available at:www.jpost.com/Israel-News/Politics-And-Diplomacy/Military-exports-rise-to-65-billion-485574.

Ben-David, D. and Bleikh, H., 2013. "Poverty and Inequality over Time: In Israel and the OECD." Policy Paper No. 2013.03. Taub Center for Social Policy Studies in Israel.

Ben Porat, Guy. 2005a. A New Middle East? Globalization, Peace and the "Double Movement." *International Relations* 19 (1): 39–62.

Ben Porat, Guy. 2005b. Netanyahu's Second Coming: A Neoconservative Policy Paradigm? *Israel Studies* 10 (3): 225–245.

Ben-Zur, A., and Portugali, A., 2014. *Implementation of Trajtenberg Report.* Jerusalem: Van Leer Institute (in Hebrew).

BoI. 2017. Bank of Israel Foreign Reserves: April 2014. Bank of Israel Web Site. (accessed May 17).

Borger, J., 2012. Binyamin Netanyahu Demands "Red Line" to Stop Iran Nuclear Programme. *Guardian*, September 28.

Brand, G., and Regev, E., 2015. The Dual Labor Market: Trends in Productivity, Wages and Human Capital in the Economy. *State of the Nation Report 2015*. Taub Center, Jerusalem.

Brander, J.A., 1995. Strategic Trade Policy. Working Paper 5020. National Bureau of Economic Research, Cambridge, MA.

CBS. 2009. *Export Concentration in Israel, 2006–2008*. Central Bureau of Statistics Jerusalem (in Hebrew).

Cerny, P.G., 2010. The Competition State Today: From Raison d'État to Raison Du Monde. *Policy Studies* 31 (1): 5–21.

Cohen, G., 2012. Netanyahu and Barak Ordered to Prepare for Attacking Iran in 2010. *Haaretz*, November 4.

Dishon, Y., 2014. Capital in (Ex)Change: State Agencies and Institutional Changes in the Law for the Encouragement of Capital Investments, 1959–2013. Thesis, Master of Arts.

Dooley, M.P., Folkerts-Landau, D. and Garber, P., 2003. An Essay on the Revived Bretton Woods System. NBER Working Paper 9971. National Bureau of Economic Research, Inc., Cambridge, MA.

Dooley, M.P., Folkerts-Landau, D., and Garber, P., 2004. The US Current Account Deficit and Economic Development: Collateral for a Total Return Swap. National Bureau of Economic Research, Cambridge, MA.

EC. 2000. Euro-Mediterranean Agreement. European Communities.

EC. 2015. Interpretative Notice on Indication of Origin of Goods from the Territories Occupied by Israel since June 1967 [C(2015) 7834 Final]. European Commission, Brussels.

Economic Committee. 2014. Economic Committee of the Knesset. Protocol 207. February 11.

EU. 2013. Guidelines on the Eligibility of Israeli Entities and Their Activities in the Territories Occupied by Israel since June 1967 for Grants, Prizes and Financial Instruments Funded by the EU from 2014 Onwards. *Official Journal of the European Union* 2013/C 205/05 (July).

Friedman, T.L., 1999. *The Lexus and the Olive Tree*. Farrar, Straus, Giroux, New York.

Froman, M., 2015. The Geopolitical Stakes of America's Trade Policy. *Foreign Policy*, February.

Fukuyama, F., 1989. The End of History? *The National Interest* 1–18.

Gaza-Jericho Agreement. 1994. Gaza–Jericho Agreement Annex IV-Economic Protocol (Paris Protocol). Paris, April 29.

Grunau, R., 2012. The Privatization of Social Services in Israel: Considerations and Concerns. Policy Paper No. 2012.17. Taub Center for Social Policy Studies in Israel, Jerusalem (in Hebrew).

Harmes, A., 2012. The Rise of Neoliberal Nationalism. *Review of International Political Economy* 19 (1): 59–86.

Harvey, D., 2005. *A Brief History of Neoliberalism*. Oxford University Press, Oxford.

Haski, B., 2012. Minister of Defense: We Are A "villa in the Jungle." *Channel 7*. September 10.

Helleiner, E., 2002. Economic Nationalism as a Challenge to Economic Liberalism? Lessons from the 19th Century. *International Studies Quarterly* 46 (September): 307–329.

Helpman, E., Itskhoki, O. and Redding, S., 2010. Inequality and Unemployment in a Global Economy. *Econometrica* 78 (4): 1239–1283.

Herman, T., 2014. *The Israeli Democracy Index 2014.* Israel Democratic Institute, Jerusalem (in Hebrew).

Hudi, U., 2016. Prof. Simhon: Foreign Exchange Intervention and the Cost of Living. *Globes*, June 6.

IEICI. 2014. Export Concentration Report. Israel Export & International Cooperation Institute, Research Division, Jerusalem (in Hebrew).

Itskhoki, O., 2009. Optimal Redistribution in an Open Economy. Meeting Paper 967. Society for Economic Dynamics.

Kaneh, H., 2012. Trajtenbert: "Defense Budget Should Not Be Higher than NIS60 Billion." *Calcalist*, August 20.

Keohane, R.O., 2005. *After Hegemony: Cooperation and Discord in the World Political Economy.* Princeton University Press, Princeton, NJ.

Koren, O., 2013. Teva, Khil, Intel and Checkpoint. *The Marker.* May 5.

Maman, D. and Rosenhek, Z., 2012. The Institutional Dynamics of a Developmental State: Change and Continuity in State–Economy Relations in Israel. *Studies in Comparative International Development* 47 (3): 342–363.

Milard, I., 2015. *Changes in Export of Goods and Services.* Center for Information and Research, The Knesset, Jerusalem.

MoF. 2015. *Report on the Benefits Under the Law for the Encouragement of Capital Investments.* Ministry of Finance, Jerusalem.

Moravcsik, A., 1997. Taking Preferences Seriously: A Liberal Theory of International Politics. *International Organization* 51 (04): 513–553.

Netanyahu, B., 2017. PM Netanyahu- Speech to US Congress July 10, 1996. Israel Ministry of Foreign Affairs, Jerusalem.

Nordlinger, E.A., 1981. *On the Autonomy of the Democratic State.* Harvard University Press. Cambridge, MA.

Obama, B., 2016. President Obama Town Hall in Buenos Aires, Argentina at Usina Del Arte, Weds. Mar. 23, 2016. *Shallow Nation.* March 23.

Palley, T.I., 2006. The Fallacy of the Revised Bretton Woods Hypothesis: Why Today's System Is Unsustainable and Suggestions for a Replacement. PERI Working Paper Series 114. Political Economy Research Institute, Amherst, MA.

Peres, S., 1993. *The New Middle East.* Henry Holt, New York.

Pickel, A., 2005. Introduction: False Oppositions: Reconceptualizing Economic Nationalism in Globalizing World. In: Helleiner, E. and Pickel, A. (Eds.), *Economic Nationalism in a Globalizing World.* Cornell University Press, Ithaca, NY.

Plessix, C. du., 2011. The European Union and Israel. Trans. J. Grumbach. *Bulletin du Centre de Recherche Français à Jérusalem*, no. 22 (December).

Ravid, B., 2013. This is How Israel Was Surprised. *Haaretz* July 17.

Rosenhek, Z., and Shalev, M., 2013. The Political Economy of the Social Protest. *Theory and Criticism* 41: 45–68 (in Hebrew).

Schechter, A., 2012. A Short Guide to Israel's Social Protest. *Haaretz* July 11.

Shalev, M., 1998. Have Globalization and Liberalization "normalized" Israel's Political Economy? *Israel Affairs* 5 (2–3): 121–155.

Sharp, J., 2016. *U.S. Foreign Aid to Israel.* Congressional Research Service. Washington, DC.

Sherwood, H., 2011. Israeli Protests: 430,000 Take to Streets to Demand Social Justice. *Guardian*, September 4.

SII. 2015. *Poverty and Social Gaps: 2014. Annual Report.* Social Insurance Institute. Jerusalem (in Hebrew).

Sikuler, N., Amsterdamski, S. and Suisa, M.S. 2016. *Who Killed Rothschild?* Documentary. Available at: http://newmedia.calcalist.co.il/j14/.

SIPRI. 2010. *The SIPRI Top 100 Arms-Producing and Military Services Companies in the World Excluding China*. Stockholm International Peace Research Institute, Stockholm.

Smith, A., 1981. *An Inquiry into the Nature and Causes of the Wealth of Nations*. The Glasgow Edition of the Works and Correspondence of Adam Smith 2. Liberty Classics, Indianapolis.

Trajtenberg, M., 2011. *Socio-Economic Change Commission Report-Trajtenbrerg Committee*. The Committee on Socio-Economic Change, Jerusalem (Hebrew).

Wezeman, P.D., and Wezeman, S.T., 2014. *Trends in International Arms Transfers. 2014*. SIPRI Fact Sheet. Stockholm International Peace Research Institute, Stockholm.

Yacoubian, M., 2004. *Promoting Middle East Democracy*. Special Report. United States Institute for Peace, Washington, DC.

Yanover, Y., 2013. Naftali Bennett: Stop US Aid, Slash Israel's Military Budget. January 8, 2013, JewishPress.com.

Zimring, A. and Moav, O., 2016. Does the Law for the Encouragement of Capital Investments Contribute to the Economy and Society and Achieve Its Objectives? Policy Paper: 2016.01. Aaron Institute for Economic Policy, Herzliya.

Index

Page numbers in *italics* denote tables, those in **bold** denote figures.

For Product Safety Concerns and Information please contact our EU representative GPSR@taylorandfrancis.com
Taylor & Francis Verlag GmbH, Kaufingerstraße 24, 80331 München, Germany

www.ingramcontent.com/pod-product-compliance
Ingram Content Group UK Ltd.
Pitfield, Milton Keynes, MK11 3LW, UK
UKHW021005180425
457613UK00019B/812

* 9 7 8 0 3 6 7 5 9 3 3 3 9 *